Welcome to the *EVERYTHING*® series!

These handy, accessible books give you all you need to tackle a difficult project, gain a new hobby, comprehend a fascinating topic, prepare for an exam, or even brush up on something you learned back in school but have since forgotten.

You can read an *EVERYTHING*® book from cover-to-cover or just pick out the information you want from our four useful boxes: e-facts, e-ssentials, e-alerts, and e-questions. We literally give you everything you need to know on the subject, but throw in a lot of fun stuff along the way, too.

We now have well over 100 *EVERYTHING*® books in print, spanning such wide-ranging topics as weddings, pregnancy, wine, learning guitar, one-pot cooking, managing people, and so much more. When you're done reading them all, you can finally say you know *EVERYTHING*®!

E FACTS
Important sound bytes of information

ESSENTIALS
Quick handy tips

E ALERT
Urgent warnings

QUESTIONS?
Solutions to common problems

THE EVERYTHING Series

Dear Reader,

There is nothing more exciting than bringing home a puppy for the first time. Filled with curiosity and vitality, puppies bring out the best part of ourselves. They are so innocent, mischievous, playful, cuddly, warm, and friendly that even the hardest heart is instantly melted by their trusting and open gaze. Like living stuffed animals, they climb into places too small, attempt to surmount obstacles too big, and yet curl up in a ball on your lap with happy contentment.

Like owning your puppy, reading this book shouldn't be a chore—it should be fun! It is filled with information, with inside stuff, and the tricks of the trade, so that in the end, you'll know just what the professionals do. So much so, that you'll be able to train and live with your puppy with confidence and understanding.

What makes this book so different from others? First, it is every person's puppy book. Second, we write for people like you—because we are people just like you. We're not writing for the dog professional (be it breeder, trainer, walker, etc.). This is a book for everyday people who want to have a puppy and need answers and information made as simple and clear as possible. You need the important directions, and tips and hints outlined for easy access and quick instruction, because you and your family want to spend time with your puppy, not the manual!

So sit back, read, laugh, and learn . . . and most of all, have fun with your new little friend!

Sincerely,

Carlo DeVito   and   Amy Ammen

THE EVERYTHING PUPPY BOOK

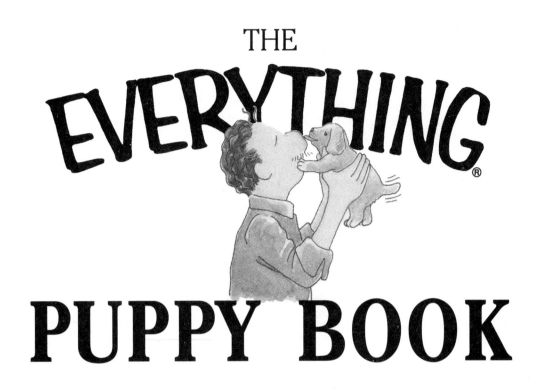

Choosing, raising, and training
your littlest best friend

Carlo DeVito and
Amy Ammen

Adams Media Corporation
Avon, Massachusetts

EDITORIAL

Publishing Director: Gary M. Krebs
Managing Editor: Kate McBride
Copy Chief: Laura MacLaughlin
Acquisitions Editor: Bethany Brown
Development Editor: Michael Paydos

PRODUCTION

Production Director: Susan Beale
Production Manager: Michelle Roy Kelly
Series Designer: Daria Perreault
Layout and Graphics: Arlene Apone,
Paul Beatrice, Brooke Camfield,
Colleen Cunningham, Daria Perreault,
Frank Rivera

An Everything® Series Book.
Everything® and everything.com® are registered trademarks of F+W Publications, Inc.

Published by Adams Media, an F+W Publications Company
57 Littlefield Street, Avon, MA 02322. U.S.A.
www.adamsmedia.com

ISBN: 1-58062-576-2

Printed in the United States of America.

J I H G F E

Library of Congress Cataloging-in-Publication Data
is available from the publisher

This publication is designed to provide accurate and authoritative information with regard to the subject matter covered. It is sold with the understanding that the publisher is not engaged in rendering legal, accounting, or other professional advice. If legal advice or other expert assistance is required, the services of a competent professional person should be sought.
 —From a *Declaration of Principles* jointly adopted by a Committee of the American Bar Association and a Committee of Publishers and Associations

Illustrations by Barry Littmann.

*This book is available at quantity discounts for bulk purchases.
For information, call 1-800-872-5627.*

Visit the entire Everything® series at everything.com

Contents

Introduction

I have been privileged to have lived with and owned a great many dogs in my life. At one time or another I've had two Poodles, a Maltese, an Irish Setter, two German Shorthair Pointers, a Dalmatian, a German Shepherd, and several very lovable mixed breeds. Each dog had a distinct personality and specific needs. Grooming, eating habits, exercise needs, and trainability varied greatly. There was no one way to deal with them all.

So what does this have to do with a book on puppies? First, do you know what we mean when we say the word "puppy"? What is a puppy? The best way to demonstrate what we mean is to provide two examples. The first is my very first puppy, a Dalmatian named Bentley. The other came along many years later in the guise of a German Shorthair Pointer named Exley.

As I have previously written in *The Everything® Dog Book,* Bentley was the answer to a sixth grader's dreams. He was a confidant, a play pal, someone to talk to late at night. He was never judgmental, always loyal, someone who would definitely sneak downstairs with you for a late-night snack and one who would fight for space on the bed with you—covers and all. Bentley was a Godsend who arrived at my door at what just happened to be three days before my twelfth birthday.

He had an extremely square head for a Dalmatian, and a deep, broad chest. And of course he had a tremendous number of spots. He had one large circle around his eye. My grandmother used to say to him, "Bentley, you smudged your mascara, again." With his red collar and wonderful, bouncy gait, he was what every child envisioned a Dalmatian to be. He loved attention, food, sleeping, and running.

He was a typical puppy. He got into a lot of trouble. He ruined floors and rugs. He ran off. He jumped out of a moving car. He chewed anything within his grasp, including furniture.

My mother did not want the dog to sleep upstairs, but I implored her. On countless nights, after discussing the day's events, I would explain to Bentley in earnest that he could not nibble on my bedroom furniture again that evening, lest he should be banished to the washroom. However, it was a full bureau before he caught on to this.

There were other transgressions typical of puppyhood. There was the Saturday when the entire family went food shopping, and left him alone in one room. I can proudly say that he did not go to the bathroom while we were gone at all. Instead, he rewarded us by tearing up the entire kitchen floor. Or, there was the time we came home and the kitchen table looked like the Titanic going down to its watery grave after he had wholly gnawed off one of the legs.

Bentley had his positive attributes, however. He was great fun. He loved to cuddle. He loved to play. He was a great companion.

Puppyhood is a difficult time for all involved. Bentley had to learn that he was not allowed on the living room furniture, a rule he fought his entire life. He had to be taught not to beg at the table. He had to be taught that jumping on guests would not be tolerated. He had to learn that he was allowed on my bed, and no one else's (okay, so maybe I spoiled him).

We had to learn a lot too. We began making regular visits to the veterinarian's office, sometimes for check-ups, and sometimes through necessity, i.e. cut paws, sprained leg, etc. And of course, training was necessary. Not only would proper training prevent him from running off every time we opened the door, but it would ensure his health and safety as well as our mental health. Looking back, we weren't perfect. Bentley was never a well-trained dog. You couldn't walk him on lead. He wouldn't heel (and neither were we up to snuff on how to train him). He would not always come when called. But he was well behaved. He would behave himself once inside the house.

Of course, his better manners and abilities shone as he got older and wiser to the desires of the household. He eventually did wise up on some things. He would always run off before my mother found out that he had been sleeping on the good living room sofa, as soon as he heard her car pull into the driveway.

The other puppy in my life has been Exley. I adopted Exley from the German Shorthair Rescue organization. He had been picked up from the animal control folks in Trenton, where he had been suffering from Lyme disease. He had run off from a horrible situation, and had finally been picked up after wandering the streets for weeks. The rescue volunteers, especially Judy Madsen and Nancy Campbell, both successful German Shorthair breeders, nursed him back to health. It was then that I found and adopted Exley. He was gray and brown and spotted, almost like a Dalmatian. He was thirteen months old.

Now, you are probably sitting there saying to yourself that thirteen months old is an adult dog. Physically, that's close to the truth. However, dogs and humans have a few similarities in their development. Firstly, even though your dog may be one year old, it's probably true that your dog will still take some time to fill out. It's the same with people. We don't all stop developing at the age when we go through puberty. Maturity is another issue. Again, humans are not mature just because they finished growing to full size. My wife and parents have told me a million times to grow up. The same goes for a dog.

Exley was wonderful. He was bright, energetic to a fault, playful, affectionate, and incredibly stubborn. He could perform extremely well in obedience training, and then turn around two minutes later and run off after squirrels, birds, etc. There were more than a few people who enjoyed a good laugh at the park when Exley would take off in some direction.

The ability to achieve a long stay (indoors or out), sitting on command, automatically sitting at a street corner, and lying down and leaving us alone during our dinner were tasks that were eventually achieved through long hours of training. Frustration? It was my middle name in those days. More than one time I had to race off red-faced after my beloved puppy. Of course, my frustration would quickly dissipate with a lick of the face, or a happy greeting on my finding him, scouring the brush, looking for ducks, squirrels, or whatever else was there that had drawn his attention. Exley, at heart, was still a puppy, despite what I am sure was his belief that he was a full-grown dog.

In the end, he had to be occasionally reminded not to nibble on your hands, not to get on the furniture, to go lie down when we were eating, not to jump on guests when they arrived. In short, much of the training that most puppies had already gone through still had to be reinforced with Exley. I knew that he had been housebroken and minimally trained. However, education continued long after he had reached bodily maturity.

Every family who has had a dog has these same types of stories. While dogs come in a variety of physical packages, they are all big where it counts—personality. In their character they are all colossal. People who are lucky enough to open up their lives and let in a friend as true and loving as a dog find a bond that transcends the verbal. It does not have the intimacy of a human relationship, nor does it have its deceits and disappointments. Dogs do not know how to lie. There is no exchange of ideas—unless that idea is the inherent goodness of cookies or treats. There is something special in the expressive eyes of a dog that is difficult to explain to someone who does not understand. However, if you are lucky enough to let one of these animals into your life, you already know what I mean.

This is all a long-winded but effective way of saying that puppyhood, happily enough, lasts a long time. Yes, it can be tiring, frustrating, and mad cap, but it can also be fun, exciting, and rewarding. All those hours of training and teaching those two dogs were rewarded with two loving animal companions who have turned out to be some of the best friends I and my family have ever had.

It would be nice if dogs didn't require instruction booklets, but they do. There are lots of things that you need to know: grooming, body language, training, health, food, and medicines, as well as breed histories and the understanding that some dogs aren't right for some people.

Dogs don't know how to speak, and better yet, they don't understand language. However, in the world of communication, I believe that they have made more progress in understanding us than we have in understanding them. I have been lucky. I have met many breeders, show people, trainers, veterinarians, walkers, sitters, and groomers. Some of these professionals helped me to understand better and hopefully make me a better pet owner, leader, and friend. I believe that reading this book will help you better understand your dog too.

Youth is not wasted on the young. And when you see a puppy at play or curled up in a ball asleep or romping outside, you know that they are a special thing in the world. And at that time, YOU are a special thing in their world too. If you take the time in these early stages, you can mold these small balls of wonder and joy into the dog you have always wanted. With kindness and forbearance, with love, determination, and knowledge, you and your new friend will have a happy and wonderful relationship for years to come.

CHAPTER 1
The World of Dogs

Puppies are cute! They love to play with toys, boxes, bones—pretty much everything. And since they are so cuddly, we invite them on the couch or in the bed with us. You just want to squeeze them and let them know how wonderful they are. Puppies are also fun! Everything is a new adventure for them. They look adorable rooting through the laundry or playing in the yard. It's fun to watch them running in giant circles or just chasing their tail. You simply cannot keep up with a puppy. Oh, the joy. This may get you wondering about how it all started.

The Beginning of the Human/Canine Bond

The history of dogs is closely woven with that of humankind. Historians and archaeologists cannot agree on when or how we were introduced. Some experts contend that people learned how to hunt following packs of dogs, learning the fundamentals of hunting in coordination with groups of others. Others contend that people stole the dogs' kills, or vice versa.

Prehistoric people found many good uses for dogs in their lives. Once domesticated, they proved to be excellent early warning detection systems against intruders, both human and animal. Of course, one of the greatest uses early civilizations had for their canine companions was hunting.

Different geographical areas demanded different survival skills of the people who occupied them. Those who kept livestock found the dogs in their lives to be excellent protection for their flocks, and were further assisted by some breeds' herding instincts. Ancient canines also assisted our forebears in fishing and living on the coast. Dogs became loyal and loving companions—unlike almost any other species, they were welcomed in the home.

ESSENTIALS

The dingo, an Australian species of dog that evolved over 130,000 years ago, has also been theorized as being the first domesticated dog. Aboriginal rock engravings dating back thousands of years depict dogs in domestic postures. However, the earliest carbon dating of a dingo fossil dates back to only around 3,500 years ago.

Why We Got Together

What was in it for dogs? According to experts there were mainly three things—food, fire (for heat in winter), and community. They thrived on the same things we did!

Lloyd M. Wendt, a noted historian of the human/dog connection, states in his book *Dogs: A Historical Journey* (Howell Book House) that domesticated dogs can first be traced back 100,000 years to northern Africa and the Middle East. The human and canine remains found there suggest a communal burial. Historians believe the working aspect of the human and dog relationship began approximately 80,000 years ago, with the advent of the spear. The spear gave humankind a weapon to fend off aggressive animals as well as something to kill them with. It was probably about this time that man and dog began hunting together.

Great Dane

Photo by Mary Bloom©

It is important to note that the image of a human walking with his or her dog would look nothing like we might picture it today. During the first stages of this relationship, man was a Neanderthal, and then Cro-Magnon. Back then, while a dog would have been a mutt of sorts, it was more closely related to a type of fox or jackal than the dog we know today. Much like man, domesticated dog has changed so much in some instances that it is classed separately from those dogs today that remain wild. The pet dogs we have today are classed by experts as *Canis familiaris*.

The Domesticated Dog

The first domesticated dogs bred in captivity appear to have come from nomadic Berber tribes. While the Egyptians used their dogs for hunting and guarding livestock, the warlords of the Middle East had different uses for theirs. The Egyptians were relatively safe from other warring neighbors with the sea on one side and a desert on the other, whereas the kingdoms and fiefdoms of the Middle East, with no physical boundaries, were in constant conflict. The Persians, Assyrians, Hittites, Sumerians, and Babylonians all favored large fighting dogs.

As humans became more adept at navigating the seas and expanding their horizons, they also began to seek dogs that were optimal for specific tasks in new or different environments. Large, powerful dogs were bred for hunting wolves, bears, and lions in Abyssinia and Persia. The best of the herding dogs came from Tibet. And the swiftest hunting Greyhounds came from Egypt.

The Egyptians

The dog achieved its first great fame among modern man in Egypt. There, dogs played an important part in everyday life; so much so that they were celebrated by the Egyptians' religion. The god Anubis was portrayed as a being with a human's body and a dog's head. It was not uncommon to have the form of a dog sculpted to rest on the sarcophagus of a deceased king to deter grave robbers, and to symbolize a faithful guide for the entombed through the afterlife.

The Egyptians so loved their dogs that theirs was the first civilization that had a law to punish humans who were cruel to dogs.

ESSENTIALS In addition to dogs, the Ancient Egyptians domesticated cats, cheetahs, ferrets, ducks, and geese as pets. They also raised horses, sheep, goats, cattle, oxen, pigs, and various fowl for farming, hunting, and religious uses.

The Greeks and Romans

Alexander the Great and later the great Roman emperors were also fond of dogs. However, unlike the Egyptians who prospered in semi-isolation, the Greeks and the Romans were products of the very heavily populated and mercantile-minded Mediterranean and Middle Eastern cultures. Life was competitive and land came at great cost. The Greeks used dogs for a variety of tasks, a practice continued by the Romans.

Greece Develops Specialized Breeds

Learning from the Persians and their other warlike neighbors, the Greeks began to favor two types of dogs. One, the Molossian, was massive in build, with a large, broad face. The other was also large, but had a more pointed snout. This type was faster and sleeker, and was known as the Laconian Hound. Aristotle was a fan of both dogs, saying that the Laconian female was gentler and smarter, but by no means fit for war, and that the Molossian was the dog of choice for such activities.

The Molossian was named for the tribe for which it became known, a tribe from northern Greece. The Molossian of Alexander the Great's time is the ancestor of today's Mastiff. For centuries, the Molossian was considered the ultimate dog of war. Large, strong, fearless, and smart, these beasts were used in war the way later armies would use a cavalry charge.

It is believed the Laconian Hound was developed in Sparta. The Laconian was also used as a warrior. Its narrower frame and swifter carriage made it particularly effective in skirmishes.

The Mother of Rome

Dogs were instrumental in Rome's rise. It was the Romans who first outfitted their war dogs with thick leather collars, studded with sharp metal blades to keep other attacking dogs off of them. As its famous roads were built and expanded, guard posts all along the way were manned by small militia and hosts of guard dogs. The roads were kept safe for Romans to use.

The Romans also used their large dogs as beasts of burden. It was not unusual to see dogs, along with cattle, oxen, horses, and ponies, pulling carts of all sizes from all different parts of the Empire.

The Middles Ages and Renaissance

After the fall of the Roman Empire, the Middle Ages came to be defined by the outbreak of the bubonic plague, or Black Death. It was during this time that the dog came to be known not as a human's best friend, but as potentially his or her greatest enemy. Fleas carried the bubonic plague, and dogs have always been a flea's favorite feasting ground. Historian Mary Elizabeth Thurston points out in her book *The Lost History of the Canine Race,* that the dog, "with its inborn resistance to the plague bacillus," was now on its own. Most livestock was killed by the disease, and people were killing each other for food. Survival was tough enough; few kept any kind of animal as a pet. Ownerless, dogs ran wild, usually in packs.

During feudal times, the aristocracy assumed ownership of many fertile lands, especially the great forests where many wild animals, as well as many natural resources, were still abundant. Thurston points to this as the great "Cult of the Hunt." The hunt, during these times, became very ritualized and many different dogs were used to bring down various types of game. Lords and barons had different dogs to hunt deer, bears, bulls, wolves, large fowl, and foxes; other dogs hunted small game, mostly vermin and fowl. Still others were bred for specific duties, like tracking, coursing, and retrieving on land and in water.

ALERT

The bubonic plague still lingers in several pockets around the world, including the United States. Outbreaks in the American Southwest still occur, often spread from prairie dogs and other wild rodents. Dogs that become infected from one of these animals generally only experience minor symptoms, but in humans this disease is over 50 percent fatal if left untreated. Human symptoms include swollen lymph nodes, fever, chills, headache, and abdominal pain. The disease is easily treated if caught early, but is often misdiagnosed.

Thurston notes that Henry I of England had a kennel of 200 dogs, and employed the huntsmen to train, care for, and deploy them. As the aristocracy grew, so did their land claims. And unless you were someone of rank, you could not claim game from a claimed preserve.

It wasn't until about this same time in the western world that still another kind of dog grew in popularity: the lap dog. While the male aristocracy had its hunting dogs, their spouses had small house dogs upon whom they doted. There are many portraits of women from this period that include their smaller companions.

Weimaraner

Photo by Mary Bloom®

It was not until after the fall of the French royalty in the late 1700s, during the French Revolution, that more people were allowed to hunt in the largest and most heavily stocked game forests. In the early 1800s many lands across Europe were opened up in an attempt to dissuade the masses from overthrowing different monarchies. While land use and regulation were still part of a larger political agenda across Europe, all of which worked to varying degrees, one huge success came of it: the popular love of hunting.

The different dog breeds we are so familiar with today are the result of everyone's continuing quest to find the perfect dog during this time. Never before had people had the time or the luxury to invest in breeding dogs for such a specific and wide range of purposes. Consequently, this period became the golden age of the dog.

Fortunately for all of us, the relationship between dogs and humans has continued to grow and flourish. Dogs are not just our companions or helpers; they are our friends, our families, our heroes, our healers. For centuries, the dog has been more popular than any other pet. From *The Call of the Wild* to the newest version of *101 Dalmatians,* man's love of his canine companion has been celebrated in literature, song, art, folklore, and popular culture.

Today's World of Dogs

For as many different lifestyles that people lead, there are different kinds of dogs. And there are many organizations that are helpful in understanding what dogs are all about and are willing to help you.

Different dog clubs have different aims, but they all share several things in common. Firstly, they are very much into promoting dogs, and shining the best possible light on the breeds they favor or the agenda they promote. The second thing many of them have in common is that they are intended to help people understand dogs better.

FACTS

The *New York Times* recently reported that there were approximately 300 deaths due to dog attacks between 1979 and 1997. Give or take, that's approximately sixteen deaths per year. Among reported attacks on children up to nine years of age, 73 percent were made by a Rottweiler, Pit Bull, or German Shepherd. The profile of the child most likely to get bitten is a boy, five to nine years old. This group accounts for more than 60 percent of all emergency room visits.

Many of these clubs offer pamphlets on choosing, training, pet health care, and many other things that go along with responsible pet ownership. They offer many valuable tools, some of which are free, to make you a good fit with your dog. They are also doing everything they can to encourage pet owners to be more considerate of their non-pet-owning neighbors. While you might think your "puppy" is the best, cutest, cuddliest, friendliest little animal ever to grace the face of the earth, there is always someone out there that sees your dog for the slobbering, dirty, ill-mannered beast he or she really is.

All of these different kinds of organizations are broken up into two categories: breed registries and animal advocacy groups. Breed registries are more concerned with breed standards and quality, while animal advocacy groups are aimed more at the prevention of cruelty.

Breed Registries

As interest in purebred dogs grew in the late 1800s, organizing bodies were formed to govern and set rules for breeding and maintaining purebred species. Registries are primarily involved in sponsoring events aimed at setting the bar for a purebred's most desirable qualities. Breed registries are usually comprised of member breed clubs, rather than individual dog owners. In the United States the American Kennel Club (AKC) is the foremost breed registry. For dog owners with pets not a part of a major breed registry there are numerous smaller registries. The American Rare Breed Association (ARBA) and the American Mixed Breed Obedience Registry (AMBOR) allow members to join with their dogs and compete in various sponsored events.

The American Kennel Club

The most famous organization that represents purebred dogs in the United States (and arguably the world) is the American Kennel Club. Established in 1884 to advance interest in purebred dogs, today the American Kennel Club recognizes over 140 breeds in seven groups (Sporting, Non-Sporting, Working, Herding, Terrier, Hound, and Toy). It is a nonprofit organization whose members are not individual dog owners, but breed clubs. Each member club elects a delegate to represent the club at AKC meetings. The delegates vote on the rules of the sport of dogs, and elect the AKC's twelve-member Board of Directors, who are responsible for the overall and daily management of the organization.

Most people are familiar with the Westminster Kennel Club show that's televised from Madison Square Garden every February. Westminster is one of the member clubs of the AKC. Besides the hundreds of member clubs, there are nearly 5,000 affiliated clubs that conduct AKC events following AKC rules of conduct. Purebred dog fanciers participate in over 3,000 dog shows a year, as well as over 5,000 performance events.

The AKC oversees the establishment of recognized breeds in the United States, and also enforces the standards by which breeds are judged. To carry out its many functions, the AKC maintains offices in New York City (where it was founded) and Raleigh, North Carolina. The AKC maintains a reference library of over 15,000 books, including editions of some of the earliest books ever published on dogs.

FACTS

The American Kennel Club publishes a monthly magazine and many public education materials to inform the public. To learn even more about the AKC, you can contact Customer Service Department, AKC, 5580 Centerview Drive, Raleigh, NC 27606-3394; (919) 233-9767. You can also visit the AKC on the World Wide Web at *www.akc.org*.

The United Kennel Club

The United Kennel Club was founded in 1898 by Chauncey Z. Bennett. The UKC registers more than a quarter-million dogs each year. Their largest number of registrations are for American Pit Bull Terriers. Those two important facts make the UKC "the second oldest and second largest all-breed dog registry in the United States." The UKC "has always supported the idea of the 'total dog', meaning a dog that looks and performs equally well." They are located in Kalamazoo, Michigan.

The UKC, like the AKC, sponsors events of many kinds, from dog shows to a host of performance events. The UKC is made up of 1,200 different clubs that oversee 10,000 licensed dog events. The UKC claims that many of their events are very easy to enter and compete in, promoting owners to show and compete with their dogs, as opposed to hiring professional trainers or handlers.

UKC offers something called the P.A.D. (Pups And Degrees) performance pedigree. This is basically a tracking system that records all the puppies a registered dog has produced and follows those puppies and their performance in the ring. The UKC also sponsors a program for DNA profiling of your puppy, in association with PE Zoogen, a DNA testing firm.

The Canadian Kennel Club

Much like the AKC, the CKC is the primary registrant and overseer of the sport of purebred dogs in Canada. Many Canadians who want to compete in the United States register their dogs in both clubs. Much like the AKC, the Canadian Kennel Club "is devoted to encouraging, guiding and advancing the interests of purebred dogs and their responsible owners and breeders in Canada."

The Kennel Club

The first dog show was held in England on June 28 and 29, 1859, in the Town Hall, at Newcastle-on-Tyne. More than sixty pointers and setters were entered. The winner of the show was not recorded. This began a series of shows and events in England which it was soon decided needed to be legislated and overseen.

In 1870 Mr. S. E. Shirley called together what was then called the National Dog Club Committee. It was later agreed that twelve gentlemen meet at No. 2 Albert Mansions, Victoria Street, London, on 4th April 1873 to further discuss canine regulation. This meeting marked the founding of The Kennel Club.

There are 188 breeds currently eligible for registration with The Kennel Club. The breeds are identified by groups according to their origins; the six groups are Hound, Gundog, Terrier, Utility, Working, and Toy.

One of the earliest undertakings of the newly formed Kennel Club was the compilation of a Stud Book, containing the records of shows from 1859 to 1873. The Committee formulated a code of ten rules relating to dog shows. It was announced that societies that adopted this code of rules for their shows would be eligible for the Stud Book. In 1875 the Committee decided to disqualify dogs that were exhibited at unrecognized shows, but this rule was not enforced for some years.

The FCI

The Federation Cynologique Internationale is very much like the AKC of Europe. The FCI is not so much a club as it is a governing body that oversees many different clubs. Many of the clubs that belong are the national dog clubs of Western Europe, including Italy, Germany, France, and Spain, among others. This club sponsors two of the world's largest dog shows: The European Dog Show and the World Dog Show.

Pet Advocacy Groups

Since Egyptian times, there have been people who set in motion laws to protect dogs. As ownership became more widespread, and dog breeding more profitable, activist groups formed to protect our furry friends. There are literally hundreds of pet advocacy groups throughout the world. The primary objectives of these groups are to lobby for laws and policies to ensure the welfare of animals, and to provide information and resources to people in an effort to improve animal rights awareness.

The American Society for the Prevention of Cruelty to Animals

The American Society for the Prevention of Cruelty to Animals is one of the most active pro-pet groups in the world. A nonprofit company, the ASPCA sponsors countless numbers of groups and events to protect animals' and pet-owners' rights. ASPCA has attempted to reduce pain, fear, and suffering in animals through humane law enforcement, legislative advocacy, education, and hands-on animal care.

The ASPCA was founded in 1866 by a diplomat named Henry Bergh, who served in the U.S. delegation to Russia. Bergh modeled the ASPCA on England's Royal SPCA.

The ASPCA managed to get the nation's first anti-cruelty laws passed in the state of New York in its first year. The ASPCA provided ambulance service to horses in NYC two years before the first hospital provided them for humans. Immediately following these successes, a number of other humane organizations began modeling their operations after the ASPCA.

Border Collie

Photo by Mary Bloom©

Today, the ASPCA supplies a number of different services to pet and animal lovers all across the country. They are perhaps best known for helping shelter strays and foster adoptions. Their foster care program encourages sympathetic homes to help animals who are "too young, sick, or aggressive to be offered for adoption right away a chance to have a long and healthy life by placing them in temporary homes."

People often confuse the New York–based ASPCA with other SPCAs around the country. There are Societies for the Prevention of Cruelty to Animals (SPCAs) in many states. The Massachusetts and San Francisco SPCAs are particularly active in promoting animal welfare through adoption and public education.

The Humane Society of the United States

The Humane Society of the United States (HSUS) is another of the nation's animal-protection organizations. While the ASPCA is more focused on pets, especially dogs and cats, the Humane Society has a much wider scope. HSUS's mission is to promote the "humane treatment of animals and to foster respect, understanding, and compassion for all creatures." The HSUS uses such venues as the legal system, education, and legislation to ensure the protection of animals of all kinds.

The HSUS was founded in 1954, and currently has nine major offices in the United States. Unlike the ASPCA, the HSUS does not have any affiliate shelters. The HSUS mainly concerns itself with wildlife protection, companion animals, and animal research violations. However, they do sponsor many events for pet owners and do encourage pet rescue (adoption). Some of the events they sponsor include free spaying clinics for those pet owners of insufficient means.

The American Humane Association

Based in Englewood, Colorado, and founded in 1877, the American Humane Association (AHA) is a welfare organization involved in assisting both animals and children. These days the AHA oversees the treatment of animals on movie and television sets and is working to establish standards for dog trainers, among many other things.

CHAPTER 2
Dog Breeds

Even if your puppy is a mixed breed, you can learn a lot about his behavior by reading this chapter. The way your puppy acts has a lot to do with how he looks. That is, if he looks like a hound, he's going to act a lot like a hound. By learning how hounds act, you're going to understand his behavior. This section is intended to help you better understand your dog, and to help you figure out what type of dog would best suit your lifestyle. That's why it's important to learn as much as you can about your dog's breed. But remember, every dog is an individual.

Where to Begin

There are several hundred breeds of dogs from around the world—and many encyclopedias that show pictures of them. In this book, we're going to base our discussions on the classification system established by the American Kennel Club (AKC). Kennel clubs around the world use similar systems of breed classifications; in fact, the American Kennel Club's is based on one developed by The Kennel Club in the United Kingdom.

Basically, the AKC categorizes the different breeds by groups to make understanding the big picture a little easier. Each breed group has distinguishing characteristics that are shared by all the breeds in it. Currently, there are seven breed groups recognized by the American Kennel Club. They are as follows:

- Sporting
- Working
- Herding
- Hound
- Terrier
- Non-sporting
- Toy

E

FACTS

The American Kennel Club also has a Miscellaneous Class, a sort of "holding" group for breeds that have not met all the criteria for full registration, of which there are many.

The Sporting Group

The Sporting Group is made up of some of the oldest and most popular breeds registered by the AKC. Many of the dogs in this category were bred for hunting. Specifically, they were bred for either one or two of the following purposes: to point, retrieve, or flush game birds. That is why the Sporting Group is composed of pointers, retrievers, and setters.

While many people who own sporting breeds will never need them to do anything but be the family pet, they will get to see their dogs using their hunting instincts around the house. These traits can be some of the most enjoyable aspects of owning a sporting dog. For example, it's wonderful to see your Weimaraner go on point while running along a hedgerow; it's fun to have your Lab or Golden tirelessly retrieve a tennis ball from a lake or the ocean; it's reassuring to have your English Springer Spaniel go back and forth in front of you on a walk (this is called quartering in the hunt field). But be forewarned: your dog is a dog, and one day he may come back with not just a ball or toy, but with the real thing: a dead animal.

Another characteristic of the sporting breeds is an outgoing personality. As dogs who worked singly or in pairs with their masters, the sporting dogs needed to be enthusiastic, responsive partners. Sporting dogs had to be able to do this all day, if necessary; strength and stamina were highly desired. The better and longer the dog worked, the more prized it was.

Golden Retriever

The Golden was bred to be tough and strong. Don't let the happy, silly face fool you. While any Golden will delight in lazing around the house, mooching for leftovers, or wrestling on the floor with your family, the breed is also adept in the field.

Golden Retriever

Photo by Mary Bloom©

As puppies, Goldens are full of energy and can be especially mouthy. Make sure you direct your puppy's need to chew to appropriate chew toys. Remember, puppies aren't fussy and don't discriminate. A chair leg works as well for them as a sterilized bone. Goldens are very trainable, athletic, and good-natured. They have a keen desire to please. You can find them performing with tails wagging and eyes shining in the obedience, agility, and flyball arenas. They are also excellent with children.

The Golden Retriever is generally light yellow to deep golden honey in color. The coat tends to get a little deeper in color after the first year. They tend to be about twenty-four inches tall at the withers (shoulders), with females being slightly shorter. Their coat should be long and either flat or wavy. They'll need to be brushed properly or their coat will form thick mats that are difficult to brush out.

QUESTIONS?

What are the withers?
The withers refers to the height of an animal at the highest point of its back, right at the shoulder blades. Besides dogs, the term is also often used to measure the height of horses and several other domestic animals.

Labrador Retriever

The Labrador Retriever has been the most popular breed in the United States for over ten years, and with good reason. They are excellent family dogs that love the water and love to work. Sportsmen, especially water fowl hunters, have prized these dogs for a great part of this century for their patience and ability to swim in icy autumn and winter waters to retrieve fowl from rivers, lakes, and ponds. But the Lab is as at home living with a family as he is in an icy marsh. Like Goldens, Labs live for mutual affection. They are enthusiastic and easily trained companions, sturdy enough for a day's sport, always ready for a game of fetch, happy to stroll the neighborhood and make new friends, a reliably friendly playmate for children of all ages, and the first in the family to crash on the couch after dinner.

Your Lab puppy will spend equal amounts of time rambunctiously exploring his world and soundly snoozing. His easygoing and curious nature make him a fearless investigator, and you'll need to be diligent about puppyproofing unless you want to come home to your puppy's idea of decorating, which is a mess (and can be dangerous for your puppy). Everyone will want to love your Lab, and while your puppy will be happy to smile and sniff everyone equally, it's important not to wear him out with too many visitors.

Labs are not tall dogs, averaging less than twenty-three inches at the withers, and tend to weigh around sixty to eighty pounds. They come in three solid colors—yellow, black, and brown. The brown Labrador is known as a chocolate Lab.

Cocker Spaniel

The Cocker Spaniel is one of the nine spaniels currently in the Sporting Group. While the spaniel family can trace its roots back to the fourteenth century, it has become ever delineated over the last five centuries. The original Spanyell was more or less a Spanish dog that, over the years, was bred for different purposes. There are even spaniels in the Toy Group.

FACTS

In the United States, the American Cocker is simply called the Cocker Spaniel; in England, the English refer to what we call the English Cocker Spaniel as the Cocker Spaniel.

With its boxy head, heavy brow, short, up-turned nose, and merry disposition, the Cocker Spaniel has, in the last twenty years, become one of the most popular dogs the AKC has registered. This is because the dog is also an excellent show competitor and a great family pet. Because he is the smallest of all the sporting breeds, he is also considered by many a lap dog. Great all-around pets, Cockers love attention and are very trainable.

Because Cockers were hugely popular in the 1980s, they did suffer some results of overbreeding, including nervousness and health problems. Breeders have worked hard to restore the merry, reliable temperaments of these dogs, and owners will say there's nothing like the loving gaze of a sound Cocker, one you can trust with family and strangers alike.

Cocker Spaniels come in four varieties of colors: solid black, any other solid color other than black (ASCOB), Parti-Color, and Tan Points. They should be no taller than about fifteen inches in height, and weigh no more than twenty-eight pounds. While they are not speed demons, Cockers should have no problem keeping up a pretty good average speed regardless of the terrain. They are small, lean dogs, with a forward chest and lines that narrow toward the powerful hindquarters. Their coat is long and luxurious when properly groomed.

English Springer Spaniel

Where the Cocker tends to be more a pet these days, the English Springer is still a popular hunter. Back in the 1880s, the Cockers and Springers were taken from the same litters. The larger dogs from a litter were grouped together with like-sized dogs and called springers. An English Springer Spaniel weighed more than twenty-eight pounds.

Springers can be liver (brown) and white or black and white in their markings. They have a longer muzzle than a Cocker and are taller. They should not be more than twenty inches in height, and have a fine, wavy coat with feathering on the chest, legs, and stomach.

They are high-energy dogs, and are fond of working or any kind of activity. They need attention and are best suited for families that don't mind going for extra walks. Springers are very affectionate and make good house pets. As a watchdog or companion, they are smart and alert.

Springers have the most adorable puppies. Remember your eager friend is a baby, and he'll need his naps. Keep him occupied when he's up and feisty by providing plenty of appropriate play and exercise. This is a dog who doesn't like to be bored!

German Shorthaired Pointer

The German Shorthair was bred to have the energy to hunt all day, be able to swim strongly to retrieve water fowl, and have an excellent nose to find game. There are bits of Spanish Pointer, Bloodhound, and Foxhound in his make-up.

The Shorthair is usually either solid liver colored, or white and liver, or liver with flecking. In the United States and Australia the dogs have docked tails, while that is no longer practiced in the United Kingdom. The tails were originally docked because they were long and skinny and were prone to break easily, thus keeping the dog from working. He is lean with a broad chest and lines that narrow perceptibly at the powerful hindquarters.

Shorthairs are fast dogs. Many hunters like to work these dogs on horseback so they can cover as much ground as possible. If you want this dog as a pet and don't intend to hunt him, be prepared to take up jogging, hiking, or some other outdoor activity. From puppyhood, these are high-energy dogs which, while responsive and trainable, are energetic to the point of distraction. It takes a lot to tire them out, and they want to go with you and be with you all the time.

The Hound Group

The Hound Group has in it some of the dogs whose ancestors were man's earliest companions and assistants. Alexander the Great hunted with hounds. This group also offers the widest range in size of any group. The smallest hound is the Dachshund, which is the only dog in this group that is neither a sight- nor a scenthound, but rather a dog that was bred to hunt smaller game "to ground," going gamely into burrows and dens for small mammals like a terrier. The largest dog in the group is the giant Irish Wolfhound, a giant bred to pursue and bring down wolves.

ALERT

Hounds don't just bark, they bay. Baying is like a loud, prolonged bark combined with a howl. This trait proves very useful to hunters who need to follow their dogs which have gone off, but might not be very useful to you while you (and your neighbors) are trying to sleep.

Hounds are generally categorized into two groups. The first are the scent hounds. These are the trackers who hunt with their noses. The best known of these are Beagles, Bassets, Bloodhounds, and Foxhounds. The other group is sighthounds. These are the hounds bred to pursue swift game by keeping their eyes on it. Popular breeds of sighthounds include the Greyhound, Afghan Hound, and Basenji.

All hounds were bred for very specific purposes, and many date back either to the feudal hunts or back to ancient Egypt. The Irish Wolfhound hunted wolves; the Beagle hunted rabbit; the Otterhound hunted otter; the Scottish Deerhound hunted deer; and the Rhodesian Ridgeback hunted lions.

The most popular hounds (by AKC registrations) are the Beagle, Dachshund, Basset Hound, Bloodhound, and Rhodesian Ridgeback. Most scenthounds have loud voices—and they like to use them! The sighthounds are more catlike and aloof. All hounds share the characteristic of being independent thinkers, even though many hunt in packs. In a pack, each hound's duty is to nose up the game and keep on the trail, or, as a sighthound, to outsmart the prey by not just matching it swift turn by swift turn, but to close in for the kill at the same time.

Bloodhound

Photo by Mary Bloom©

Scenthounds tend to be social and easygoing, though their noses so dominate their lives that it can be hard for them to pay attention to anything but what's around to be sniffed. And since a dog's sense of smell is infinitely better than ours, your scenthound may become distracted by something you didn't know was there. He will seem to spend his every waking moment engaged in sniffing the floor, sidewalk, yard, kitchen—his whole environment. When you feel like your scenthound puppy is being inordinately stubborn, remember that he's from the same family as the Bloodhound, a dog whose whole reason for being is to find a trace of scent that could be months old and find its source. You've got to have one amazing nose to do that!

Sighthounds seem particularly aloof to strangers, but those who live with them know that like all hounds, they are motivated by good food and soft beds. For breeds that can achieve some of the fastest speeds of all land animals, sighthounds can be the biggest slugs around. The fact is, their top speeds and intense pursuits only come in bursts. The rest of the time they're happy to sit in your lap. Hounds may not demand the most from you in terms of exercise requirements, but their independent natures can occasionally try your patience.

Beagle

The AKC splits Beagles into two competition classes: Beagles under thirteen inches in height at the withers and Beagles between thirteen inches and fifteen inches in height at the withers. The Beagle is still one of the most popular breeds around the world. They are sturdy, lovable dogs. While they are very friendly and can warm even the coldest of hearts with their sad eyes, they can be hearty, courageous, and steadfast. Your Beagle puppy will need daily outdoor exercise to keep him physically and mentally fit and sound. Beagles are notorious for freely expressing themselves any time of the day or night. Remember, it's your job to keep your Beagle in the good graces of your neighbors.

FACTS

The first Beagle was officially registered with the AKC in 1885. More recently, the Beagle has enjoyed notoriety by being the model for the world's best-known pet dog, Charlie Brown's Snoopy.

Beagles shouldn't be taller than fifteen inches and should have a smooth coat of mixed colors. They should have warm, brown, expressive eyes. They are very sturdily built and have energy to spare.

Dachshund

The Dachshund is one of the most recognizable breeds. Best known for its length and shortness, the Dachshund has always been a dog that lends itself to musings from cartoonists. This deft little hunter was originally bred to hunt badgers and rabbits. Mostly, because of its unique size and shape, it was used to hunt burrowing animals, actually forcing its way into the ground and bringing back the killed animal.

Dachshund

Photo by Mary Bloom©

The Dachshund comes in three different varieties and two sizes: smooth coat, wirehaired, and longhaired, and standard or miniature. They should always have a long body, short legs, and dark brown eyes. Standards generally weigh sixteen to thirty-two pounds, miniatures eleven pounds and under.

Basset Hound

The Basset Hound's long, low body, droopy ears and jowls, and sad eyes compare to no other. After all, his name literally means "low to the ground." There are still many actively hunting Basset packs around the country. In a pack, the Basset is a slower hunter than the Beagle. He is the epitome of patience and perseverance on a scent, plodding tirelessly and dutifully toward what he is confident will be a happy ending for him.

The Basset is a friendly, ambling dog. Speed is not his game. He shouldn't be taller than fourteen inches at the withers, but make no mistake, Bassets are sizable dogs and are quite powerful. Your Basset puppy will soon be growing into his soft folds of skin, and eventually his ears won't drag on the ground as much. But he will always be perpetually curious, especially when it comes to the refrigerator or pantry. Bassets look good carrying a little weight, but you'll want to watch out as your puppy grows that you keep him in good shape. A breed that doesn't need a whole lot of exercise, loves to eat, and is built low to the ground is one that needs the human companion to take special care of their physical needs. The Basset is a smooth-coated dog that loves being outdoors, but is just as happy in the house with family and friends.

Bloodhound

Like the Basset Hound, the Bloodhound is a well-known dog because of his characteristically sad-looking, jowly face. But don't let that face fool you. The Bloodhound is as solid a dog as there is. One of the oldest dogs known to man, the Bloodhound has the most acute sense of smell known to canines, which has always made him a valuable friend.

The Bloodhound isn't just an invaluable resource for law enforcement officials. He is also considered the most tried and true of friends for many pet owners, some of whom train their special hounds for search and rescue work or tracking to take full advantage of their canine's special abilities. Bloodhounds are smart dogs who are quick to learn, but who may be obstinate. They are very loving and good-natured. They are big dogs, and very strong, and they are persistent when on a scent. They can weigh up to 110 pounds, and inspire loyalty from their owners that's as big and intense as they are.

Rhodesian Ridgeback

The Rhodesian Ridgeback is so named because it has a ridge of hair growing against the grain along the spine of its back. In the late 1800s, the Rhodesian Ridgeback was introduced to the top big game hunters of the day. The Ridgeback found instant fame with them, as they used the dogs to hunt lion from horseback. The dog came to be known after that time as the African Lion Hound. Once they became popular and made their way to different parts of the world, people found that this great lion hunter also made an excellent pet and family companion. Ridgebacks
are very intelligent and trainable if you can work with their essential "houndness" of doing what pleases them most despite what you may be asking of them. Because of their short coat, they are easy to maintain; they have friendly and lovable personalities. They are devoted to their families and are good watchdogs. They should be twenty-five to twenty-seven inches in height at the withers and weigh approximately seventy-five pounds.

The Working Group

Most of the dogs in the Working Group were bred for specific jobs other than hunting. Many of the breeds date back to Roman times, where guarding valuables, like property and family, was often a daily necessity. However, there were other jobs to be done. The Portuguese Water Dog was the fisherman's dog, used to retrieve items, or people, that had fallen overboard or to carry messages from one boat to another. The Newfoundland was bred for hauling in huge fishing nets laden with fresh fish. Saint Bernards were rescue dogs, saving lives throughout the Alps. And of course the Alaskan Malamute and the Siberian Husky were sled dogs, pulling men and their families back and forth across frozen tundra.

There are many popular dogs in this group, most notably the Rottweiler, Doberman Pinscher, Akita, and Mastiff, which were bred primarily as guard dogs. They are powerful dogs, and when properly trained and socialized, make invaluable friends. These dogs will risk life and limb to protect their families, and are a great source of pride and love. However, there are many people who have given these dogs a bad name. Because they are powerful, large dogs, if they are not trained and socialized with other dogs properly, they can become a menace. It is not in their nature to be—it is in the nature of people who buy these dogs and then train them to be that way.

Siberian Husky

Photo by Mary Bloom©

The Rottweiler is the best example of this kind of training. Rottweilers, by nature, are very sociable dogs. They are even cuddly and fun-loving, like big teddy bears. But they need to be socialized at a young age and given proper training. Take that same dog, don't socialize him, encourage his aggressive behavior, and give him the kind of training that uninformed people perceive is right for guard dogs, and you have a dog that is a danger not only to himself, but to his own master as well. These dogs desire love and affection. If you discourage their aggressive behavior at a young age, you will have an excellent pet who is great with children and a wonderful, safe guard dog.

Owners of breeds like Bernese Mountain Dogs, Siberian Huskies, and Giant Schnauzers now delight in training their dogs to pull sleds or wagons laden with people and things. Samoyeds make great hiking companions, able to nimbly carry packs with supplies along steep mountain trails. The athletic and noble Boxer excels in almost all canine performance events. Your now-wee Working pup will soon grow into his feet, and he'll be happiest if he can put them to use assisting in the daily enjoyment of his family unit.

Rottweiler

Admitted to the AKC Stud Book in 1931, today the Rottweiler has become quite popular; his playfulness and his deep desire to guard home and hearth have made him invaluable to families around the world. For many years in the 1990s he was the second most popular dog in America, behind the Labrador Retriever. Breeders are glad his popularity is waning and that he is no longer the "guard dog du jour."

Many Rottweilers are very calm, and their eyes should show a certain sense of calm and happiness. They are very much family dogs, and revel in attention and play. If trained properly from birth, they are excellent with children, and their guard dog instincts are still very strong.

Rottweilers are relatively big dogs with wide heads and stout bodies. They can grow as high as twenty-seven inches at the shoulder and weigh up to 120 pounds. Being shorthaired dogs with a flat coat, they should appear compactly built, with wide chests and lean lines. While they might like to sleep for long periods of the day, and don't run as much as you might expect, they are capable of great bursts of speed, and have tremendously powerful jaws.

Siberian Husky

Siberian Huskies are strong, independent-minded dogs who were bred for pack life and are full of energy. They require regular exercise and grooming. Huskies all want to lead the pack, and know their place in their own very complex society. You need to be loving, but firm.

The fact that they are bred from local Siberian dogs comes as no surprise, as the Siberian Husky looks like a tamed wolf. They have a thick, double layer of fur, which requires lots of attention in the summer, unless you want to burn out a vacuum cleaner every other year. During the molting season, you'll be able to pull the fur out in little clumps. But don't. Use a very good brush, or better yet a shedding blade. With their whitish coat, they should stand no higher than approximately twenty-four inches and weigh approximately sixty pounds. The coat can range from pure white to a mix of other colors. The most common is a grayish black and white. They can have either brown or blue eyes; some have one of each.

Doberman Pinscher

The Doberman Pinscher was first developed in Thueringen, Germany, by a local town watchman named Herr Karl Friedrich Louis Dobermann. Dobermann wanted a nimble, quick-thinking dog of action to accompany him on his rounds during the 1870s. The breed was a combination of all the qualities that Dobermann was looking for in the ultimate police dog. He had the strength and musculature of the Rottweiler, the Pinscher for compactness, and several other local breeds including the Black and Tan Terrier.

Expect your Doberman puppy to be a handful from the very beginning. The breed is super-intelligent and will thrive on your fair direction. Make sure your whole family understands the training protocol; your Dobe will be so fun to work with that it won't be hard for everyone to want to be involved. You'll watch your gangly puppy blossom into a sleek, responsive, adoring friend.

Great Dane

Standing around thirty-two inches at the shoulder, the Great Dane is one of the largest dogs known to man. Coming in a variety of colors, this dog is among the most fascinating of domesticated animals. He was originally developed to hunt wild boar in the late Middle Ages. There are fanciers who believe that early descriptions from around the world make this dog much older than it might actually seem. The fact that it is from the Mastiff family might confuse the issue somewhat. Regardless, nobility used this dog for some of the most dangerous and ferocious hunting of the time, and the dog made a name for itself in accomplishing this feat with power, speed, and deftness.

Today, few, if any, Great Danes are used for hunting boar. These magnificent beasts are now family pets. They are somewhat active dogs that do need a lot of space. These dogs need room because they are so big. Room to run around outside would be nice, too, since a dog this big needs an equally big space to stretch out in. It's also important to have plenty of food on hand; these dogs require more than most!

Great Danes are large, tapered dogs, with heads held high and eyes alert. They have a bouncy, elegant gait to them. While they are indeed imposing physical specimens, they are in fact quite friendly, and love attention. One of the most famous Great Danes is, of course, Marmaduke, the classic cartoon character.

You need to train these dogs when they are young. It is important to remember that these are big, powerful dogs, and they were bred to do some very difficult tasks. An untrained Great Dane has the strength to pull even a big man a city block or two if he wants. It is important to make sure you have your Dane under control before he grows too large and strong. Like some of the other relatives in the Working Group, the Great Dane's ears can be cropped or left natural.

If you have a Great Dane puppy now, take lots of photos! Once he's matured, you will look back and laugh that your furry friend was ever so small. And remember that while he's a big guy, your Dane is a gentle giant. Don't bully him!

Boxer

The Boxer is currently winning a lot of popularity contests in the United States, and it's not hard to understand why. Here's a dog with a rich history who is compact, muscular, easy to care for, athletic, and truly handsome. He is playful, charming, and smart. His coat is smooth and is mostly rich tones of mahogany or brindle with white patches. He has large, round, expressive eyes, a flat but not over-exaggerated nose, and cropped or natural ears.

The Boxer was developed in Germany by breeding together the Mastiff and the Great Dane. Since its early days the Boxer has become a refined and substantive dog unto itself. He is called the Boxer because of the way he "boxes" with his paws when he plays. The Boxer's steady temperament

Boxer

Photo by Mary Bloom©

and joie de vivre earned him a trusted place alongside policemen and soldiers for many decades. He is smart, athletic, and reliable. It was in 1904 that the first Boxer was registered with the American Kennel Club.

Your Boxer puppy will attract the affection of everyone who sees him. This is a great thing for your puppy. Teach him to sit before he gets cuddled and petted, and he'll have that request down in no time. You'll find that as you and your puppy grow together, there will be nothing the two of you can't do as a team.

St. Bernard

It is important to note right from the start that all the stories about St. Bernards saving people in desolate winter landscapes are absolutely, undeniably true! The dogs were originally known as Alpine Mastiffs, and were short-haired dogs until about a century ago. Their story begins in a small passage between the Swiss and Italian Alps, where a group of monks had a monastery that was used by erstwhile alpine travelers.

ESSENTIALS

One St. Bernard, Barry, was known to have saved forty people in a ten-year period beginning in 1800. Thereafter, for a while, the dogs were called Barryhunds. They were also called Hospice Dogs. It was not until 1865 that the dog was officially recognized by the name they go by today.

In the late 1800s, the St. Bernard line almost died, and the monks so famous for breeding them went outside for the first time to try and strengthen the breed. An early cross of the original St. Bernard was with the Newfoundland. It was then that the longhaired version of the dog appeared. While it was initially thought that the longhaired dogs would be an improvement (it was hoped that they would be able to better weather the bad winters), it was soon proven that the shorthaired dogs fared better in the harsh climate, as their fur didn't mat with snow and ice.

The St. Bernard is usually between twenty-eight and thirty-four inches tall and can weigh well upwards of 200 pounds. They are very large dogs, who, while they don't require great amounts of exercise, do necessitate large amounts of space just to turn around. They come in longhair and shorthair versions. They are massive, extremely friendly, and are excellent family pets—just keep the paper towels handy to avoid being slobbered all over in the breed's excitement to be with you.

The Terrier Group

The dogs in this group are by turns tenacious, lovable, energetic, and downright funny. Terriers are basically a group that is mostly made up of a number of wire-haired, smaller dogs that were originally bred to help landowners and gamekeepers keep undesirables off their properties—namely raccoons, foxes, rats, weasels, and badgers.

Terriers were bred to start digging to either kill or chase out animals that went to ground for cover or safety. They would bark and dig simultaneously, driving away vermin, or fighting their adversaries right there in the den's entrance. Indeed, many dogs in the Terrier Group have short, strong tails that many a gamekeeper or huntsman used to pull the little fighter out when it seemed he might be getting the worse of the scrap.

For the most part, terriers are well suited to urban, suburban, or rural life. However, they are determined little dogs, and require kind and consistent training to keep them on the straight and narrow. Like some of their larger brethren, these dogs need obedience and love; they need a real leader to keep them from ruining the house or backyard.

There is another thing that must be stated here: Don't be fooled by the package. Just because some of the terriers are small doesn't mean they make good apartment dogs. Terriers are opinionated, scrappy, feisty, fun-loving, high-energy animals that require extensive exercise, attention, and time. Their wiry coats also need special grooming. Many of them don't shed, and left to grow, your should-be-sleek terrier could look like a poor bedraggled orphan of a dog.

Norfolk Terrier

Photo by Mary Bloom©

Jack Russell Terrier

Few dogs are so well liked and so misunderstood as the Jack Russell Terrier. The trendy, adorable, feisty little dogs have long been popular. Their popularity soared even higher with the success of Eddie, the canine character on the popular television show *Fraiser*. However, while this sturdy, squat warrior is as huggable as can be, he is in reality a very strong-willed, incredibly energetic animal whose number-one aim is to dig into the earth and find something—preferably something living. He has his group's most famous attributes—ferocity, tenacity, willfulness, independence, and indefatigability, times two. He is an apartment dog only if his owner takes him out regularly and often.

He is short, and strong, with a personality that is second to none. He is sometimes less tolerant of other dogs, especially his own kind. Left alone all day, especially in an apartment or small house, the Jack Russell may get into trouble. He is mischievous when not employed doing something, or outside, left to his own devices.

Jack Russell Terrier

Photo by Mary Bloom©

Jack Russells need lots of attention, and an owner with an active lifestyle. If you like to exercise, then the Jack Russell is for you. Boredom is the Jack Russell's worst enemy. Loneliness is his second worst enemy. While they do like love and attention, they do not want to be smothered. If you have children, you will have to work hard to make sure that the Jack Russell knows his place in the pack.

If properly trained and exercised, this breed is a wonderful, if rambunctious, companion animal, whose high energy and bright disposition will keep you smiling and exhausted for a long time.

American Staffordshire Terrier

Few people who own these dogs even know their real name, let alone their real history. The Staffordshire Terrier originated in England in the 1800s. The dogs were a combination of the Bulldog and a terrier of unknown distinction. It is important to know, claims the American Staffordshire Terrier Club of America, that the Bulldogs of the 1800s were leaner and more agile than those we know today. The Bulldog of 100 and 200 years ago was actually used to bait bulls, and was an aggressive, strong, and courageous dog.

Because the dogs in England were originally a mix of two breeds and were used for fighting, they were known by many names. They were alternately known as Bull-and-Terrier Dogs, Pit Dogs, and Bull Terriers. The American Staffordshire was even known as the Yankee Terrier. Eventually the name that became prevalent was Pit Bull Terriers, and even that was finally shortened to just Pit Bulls.

It is important to state this unequivocally: The Pit Bull is a generic term applied to all the dogs of this category. However, the American Staffordshire Terrier is a specific breed, with specific characteristics. He is not the American Pit Bull Terrier, which is a close, but distinct, relative. Many Pit Bulls that are bought in the United States are not AmStaffs. Many have other dogs bred into them, and therefore vary in characteristics.

The American Stafforshire Terrier is a better dog than what he was bred for. Many were used by the U.S. Army, especially in the First World War. As pets they are relatively docile and do not require great amounts of exercise. They do need lots of obedience and socializing to help them become more accepting of others. They love family life, and revel in its benefits. They are also exceptional guardians, who are very alert, quick, and muscular, and good at detecting strangers or intruders.

West Highland White Terrier

Westies, as they are affectionately known, come from the large family of terriers that emanated from Scotland. Many believe that they were originally part of a breed that also included Scotties, Cairns, and Dandie Dinmonts.

The Westie has a double coat that consists of soft, thick fur underneath, and coarse hair on top. For the average pet owner, the Westie requires visits to the groomer to be seasonally clipped and properly groomed. To keep the coat clean, more often than not, the dog needs to be combed or brushed regularly. They are hardly little dogs, with great spunk and vitality. They are very trainable. Like many smaller breeds, while they are courageous and loving, they make better watchdogs than guard dogs, and will always be first to alarm the rest of the house of approaching strangers. They are good in houses or apartments, but like many terriers may dig in yards and gardens.

Scottish Terrier

Like other terriers, the Scottie was born to hunt foxes, vermin, and other small animals. He dug into lairs and dens, ready to confront those he had chased down. It is contended that the Scottie is one of the oldest among the Terrier Group. Scotties are immediately recognizable by their short, squat stature, their long muzzle, and their very bushy eyebrows. Their faces are very malleable, and capable of great expression.

Active, spry, and tenacious, the Scottie is an excellent apartment or house pet. They need regular exercise, but not too much. Their coat is dense and requires proper grooming by a professional. Also, regular brushing and combing will keep the coat shiny and clean for long periods of time. A Scottie should weigh no more than twenty-two pounds.

Cairn Terrier

During the late 1800s, in both England and America, Cairns and Westies were interbred. That stopped when they began to be registered. The first Cairn Terrier was registered with the AKC in 1913. It is felt by many fanciers that the dog has not really changed its appearance in more than 150 years.

The most enduring image of a Cairn, without a doubt, is Toto. Dorothy's peppy little accomplice was the ultimate Cairn. Agile, inquisitive, tenacious, and loyal, this friendly little dog was the epitome of what every Cairn represents to his or her owner. Both a good house and outdoor dog, the Cairn loves to cover untamed ground as well as curl up near his owner.

Miniature Schnauzer

How did this relative of the Schnauzers from the Working Group come to be a member of the Terrier Group? The reason is because this smallest schnauzer has all the characteristics of his terrier brethren. He is scrappy, saucy, smart, tenacious, and a farmer's best friend when it comes to keeping his property clear of vermin. Bred from a combination of Standard Schnauzer and Affenpinscher, and possibly Poodle, the Miniature Schnauzer is a spirited but trainable companion. He can't be missed when he's just come from the groomer—his distinct eyebrows, handsome gray body, and self-assured gait instantly draw attention to him.

As a puppy, you may not think your bundle of blue-gray fur is going to grow up to be the distinguished-looking gentleman he is known as. But just you wait. Your ragamuffin is going to transform in front of your eyes. Don't be fooled by his irresistible puppy charms, either. Your Mini Schnauzer will need the same kind of patient and persistent training as any headstrong dog, and you'll delight in learning with him.

The Toy Group

The Toy Group is comprised exclusively of some of the smallest dogs in the canine world—and also some of the cutest! Many of these cuddly little rascals have been bred purely for companionship, and were never intended for anything other than being a pet. Some of them come from very obscure backgrounds, but make no mistake—these are dogs. The most amazing thing about little dogs is that they think just like big dogs. They mark territory; they are loving; they are protective; they are great watchdogs; and they will bite if they feel threatened.

ALERT

If you are a parent, it is important that you consider the following before you undertake buying a Toy breed. They are delicate little animals that will be easily injured if handled roughly, and may also bite if cornered or mistreated. All dogs love attention and hugs, but be sure your child understands the difference between gentleness and play that is too rough.

Some of these dogs are so small, that many centuries ago in Europe they were called sleeve dogs, because ladies of means hid the dogs in their sleeves! Many of these breeds have stories about them regarding royalty.

Toy dogs tend to be smart and feisty. They can be trained easily for the most part and many do not require too much exercise. These are all good house and apartment dogs. They love attention and they expect to get it. They also require grooming, and they love that, too.

Chihuahua

Photo by Mary Bloom©

If Toy dogs are small, imagine how small Toy puppies are! This is why many breeders discourage households with small children from getting a Toy breed puppy. Even well-meaning and well-behaved children can cause serious damage to a tiny Toy breed puppy. But because Toy breeds don't necessarily think of themselves as "toys," many of them can handle the youngest members of a family just fine. If a Toy breed is for you and you have very young children in the house, talk to other owners and breeders before bringing a puppy home.

Yorkshire Terrier

These are spirited little dogs. While they are considered little darlings by many because of their size, long luxurious coat, and spunkiness, make no mistake, these animals consider themselves dogs—and even worse, they consider themselves terriers. They are tenacious and, while they love affection, you need to dole out love and obedience in equal measure, or else they will be more than happy to run your house for you. They love to investigate everything

These dogs became popular in Victorian England, but had a job at one time, too. They were the favorite dogs of weaving and clothing factories, where they chased rats and mice. Being terriers added to their ability—and desire—to perform this role.

The Yorkie, as he is known, travels easily and likes to be taken everywhere. It likes the outdoors, but like all Toy breeds, should have a warm coat or sweater if you're out on a chilly morning.

These are excellent, alert family dogs that love to be part of the family and part of the fun. Their long coats require maintenance at least twice a week.

Pomeranian

These furry little fireballs are aggressive and tenacious watchdogs and excellent companions. They sometimes can be wary of strangers or other animals and will not hesitate to act. They respond well to training and are very affectionate.

Like other spitz breeds, they have pointy ears and an appearance of foxiness, which also comes from the reddish color coat. The fur is a double layer of soft, dense undercoat and long, glistening overcoat, and grooms easily with regular brushing.

FACTS

The most famous story about a Pomeranian comes from Queen Victoria, who was a great dog lover. She had been to Germany on a visit when she saw her first Pom and brought one back with her to England. When she was dying, she asked that her favorite dog, a Pom known as "Turi," be set beside her. She died with him at her side.

Miniature Pinscher

The Miniature Pinscher Club of America was founded in 1929, and interest in the breed blossomed from then on. The Min Pin has consistently been one of the most popular of the Toy breeds. His nickname is the King of Toys because of his regal bearing and outgoing personality.

The Miniature Pinscher resembles the Doberman Pinscher in almost every way, keeping the same proportions, though he is not bred down from that dog. The Min Pin's flat, short, shiny coat makes him an easy dog to take care of. He also requires that you hand out obedience and love in equal measures. This dog has a distrust for strangers and other animals, of which his high-pitched bark will frequently remind you.

Pug

Photo by Mary Bloom©

The Pug first became well known in China before the advent of the modern calendar. The Buddist monks of Tibet kept them and carried these dogs with them for companionship. They were first brought to Europe by the Dutch East India Company.

In the most famous story about Pugs, they saved the life of William, Prince of Orange, in 1572, as they woke up his camp before the Battle of Hermingny. The Pug became the official dog of the House of Orange, and his likeness was carved into William's tomb. Later, the breed was the favorite of Josephine, wife of Napoleon. It was alleged that one of her dogs bit him as he entered her bedroom on the night of their wedding.

The Pug became especially popular after the English stormed the Chinese Imperial Palace in 1860, and brought back to England with them a large number of the small toy dogs. They are very playful and very loyal. They love affection and need little grooming, as they have a thick, short coat. They are the largest of the Toy breeds, weighing up to eighteen pounds.

Maltese

The Maltese are best known for their white, flowing coat, which must remain well cared for if the Maltese is being shown. They should have a good gait and look like a little mop without a handle happily bouncing around the floor. They are active, but can get most of the exercise they need running around the apartment, house, or backyard. They love the outdoors, but this can pose a problem to those in show coat; most owners of pet Maltese keep their dogs clipped to make their life and their dog's a bit easier. Maltese are excellent watchdogs. They love being at the center of the family's attention and are very loving and playful in return.

Chihuahua

Today's Chihuahua is even smaller than his ancestor, which is the result of American breeders' efforts. The average Chihuahua weighs around four pounds. He is the tiniest dog in dogdom. He is very perky and has many big dog characteristics, but truth be known, he is a house dog, and can be very fragile.

He is not recommended for a family with young children because of his size and fragility. Generally speaking, Chihuahuas are not outdoor dogs. They can find plenty of exercise in the house and do not require great amounts of obedience training. You may, however, want to make sure house training is strictly enforced. Other than that, they are large-hearted Toy dogs whose faces are made for television. With their small, apple-shaped heads and their big, watery dark eyes, they can easily wiggle their way into even the hardest heart.

Chihuahuas come in two different varieties—smooth coat and long coat. The smooth coats look even tinier than the long-coated Chihuahuas, because the fur isn't there to puff them out a little bit. These dogs should be spry and alert, and tapered toward the hindquarters. As with most shorthaired dogs, the smooth coats require little grooming. The long-coated dog should have a smooth feel to it, regardless of whether the coat is flat or wavy. Both varieties love family, but need to be socialized to accept strangers. Alternately, they are very affectionate, loving, and loyal.

The Non-sporting Group

These dogs have one thing in common—none of them fits neatly into any of the breed groups. While some of them were working or sporting dogs in previous lives, their jobs have been so long outmoded that they have primarily been companion dogs for almost a century, in some cases longer.

Other than that, let's be honest, this is a miscellaneous crowd as far as the AKC and other breeders are concerned. But in here you have some very popular, if disparate, dogs. You have the Poodle (originally one of Europe's finest hunting dogs); the Dalmatian (the ubiquitous coach dog); the Bulldog (used to bait bulls centuries ago); the Bichon Frisé (a companion dog too big for the Toy group); and many, many others.

Deciding on a breed from this group is even tougher than the others because you won't have those common traits you can refer back to when you're trying to explain your breed's behavior. Discovering the pros and cons of these dogs is even more fun! The histories on these breeds are usually fairly extensive, so you can be assured you're getting a dog with characteristics that have been mulled over for a long, long time.

Poodle (Standard and Miniature)

Photo by Karen Taylor©

There are few dogs more world-renowned than the Poodle. Who doesn't know what one looks like—with their foppish clipping and their poofy heads. Clipped in some extreme pattern or simply shaved down, beneath all that curly coat is a talented, intelligent, and sporty dog.

The Poodle comes in three sizes—Standard (the largest, at fifteen inches at the shoulders and taller), Miniature (between ten and fifteen inches in height at the shoulders), and Toy (ten inches in height or less). Only the Standard and Miniature are in the Non-sporting Group; the Toy Poodle is in the Toy Group. Other than that, all Poodles are essentially the same. They should have a curly, wiry topcoat and a slightly thicker undercoat.

The Poodles are known for their coiffures. These originated during their time as prime hunters. The head, chest, and forefront were left shaggy, to provide warmth to the dog, especially in seasons when it was cold and he was called upon to retrieve game in frigid waters. Today, Poodles are generally groomed in one of three clippings: the Sporting clip, the English Saddle clip, and the Continental clip. Generally considered more desirable for showing are the English Saddle clip and the Continental clip. The Continental is the most severe, with seven pom poms decorating what is essentially a half-shaven body. The Saddle clip leaves more fur on the body, but it has different sculpted rings, especially around the hindquarters.

Today, the Poodle isn't generally considered a hunter, and few use him for this sport. The Miniature and the Toy are both excellent house pets that need some exercise. However, the Standards should get a little more; while the two smaller Poodles could live in an apartment with proper exercise, the Standard Poodle might feel confined. All Poodles need lots of exercise and love to run. Playful, energetic, and loving, the Poodle, regardless of size, has a big heart and a sound disposition.

Dalmatian

Certainly, the Dalmatian is one of the most affable dogs around. He is also one of the most easily recognizable. While the Dalmatian may have obtained its greatest fame in Walt Dinsey's two classic renditions of *101 Dalmatians,* he was popular even before that. He was used to herd stray livestock, or was used as a warning for humans and other animals to beware of the oncoming coach. In other lands and times he has performed admirably as a retriever, and as a ratter.

Due to their birth, breeding, and training, the Dalmatian is tireless, and is not the most suitable dog for all people. He is smart, gregarious, and loving, but he has an insatiable desire for activity and exercise. Owing to his former life, the Dalmatian can run at a medium pace for long, long periods. This makes him an undesirable apartment dog, where he might go crazy with boredom. Some can become destructive as a result of inactivity. The Dalmatian needs plenty of exercise, so if you have the desire to exercise and the room to keep him comfortable, he is an excellent companion who loves the activity of family life and being on good terms with its members, and who is an excellent watchdog. With their short, smooth coat, they require little upkeep.

Boston Terrier

There are three classes of Boston Terrier: twenty to twenty-five pounds; fifteen to twenty pounds; and under fifteen pounds. The Boston Terrier has a shorthaired, smooth coat, which is white and either black or brindle. They are squat dogs, like the Bulldog, but lean like a terrier. Their rather large, round, dark eyes are set widely apart. These dogs are very even-tempered, very congenial, and make excellent watchdogs. They are as fearless as they are loving.

They make excellent companions and are adaptable for life in an apartment or country home. While they are of a generally very amiable disposition, they have the heart of a Bulldog and terrier, and will fight furiously to defend themselves. They would rather spend a Saturday sleeping with you on the couch than do just about anything else.

Bulldog

The Bulldog of today is somewhat different than his ancestors. Bulldogs were originally bred for fighting. Their original work came in the form of "bull baiting," which involved packs of these small dogs surrounding and taking down a maddened bull. It was wild, mean, and grotesque, and was outlawed in 1778. In bullbaiting, the Bulldog would eventually pin the bull by the nose.

The Bulldog also gained fame in a time when, in England, dog fighting was legal and popular. Among the most accomplished dogs in this field were the Bulldogs. They were somewhat leaner than the dog we know today, and much more vicious, known to be able to sustain incredible injuries and continue to fight. To this day, the Bulldog's tenacious legend lives on, as he is the mascot of many school athletic programs as well as that of the United States Marine Corps.

After dog fighting was outlawed, there were a number of dog fanciers who decided to save the breed they had come to admire. Many years were spent breeding out the violence that had long been bred into them.

Today, the Bulldog is one of the friendliest of all canine companions. With his distinctive waddle and trademark folds of skin, this stout little fellow will tug with great determination—at your heart. He is good natured, excellent with children, and friendly with other dogs. While his coat is shorthaired and requires little maintenance, he needs his face to be cleaned several times a week, in order to avoid infections. He is goodin an apartment or a country house. He requires only light exercise. The dog should weigh between forty and fifty pounds.

Bichon Frisé

Photo by Mary Bloom©

Pronounced "BEE-shon Free-ZAY," this is an exotic little breed whose history has been somewhat obscured by time. We do know that he is a descendant of the Barbet Water Spaniel. Bichon Frisés are known to have come from the Mediterranean, though no one is sure of exactly where. Over the centuries, the Bichon Frisé has been known by four different names, but in all, it has been known for some time. It has been the choice dog of fashionable society in many European countries at one time or another, including Italy, Spain, and France. Bichons became endangered after the French Revolution, as they were very much associated with the aristocracy. They did not come back into vogue until the 1930s on the continent, and were not recognized by the AKC until 1972.

These small dogs are quick, alert, and energetic. They are famous for the way they are groomed, which makes them look like a living powder puff. They are loving and playful, and a good family dog. They require more grooming than exercise, in order to avoid matting, but they don't shed much and are considered good pets for people with allergies.

The Herding Group

The Herding Group is a relatively new group, having been established in 1983. Herding breeds were originally part of the Working Group, but when it became so large as to be unmanageable, the Herding Group was established independently. Some of the oldest dogs we know are in this group because their early jobs were guarding and managing the livestock of our early nomadic ancestors.

Among dogs, these are some of the smartest, most trainable, and energetic of dogs. It is important to remember that these dogs have been bred to do a job, and it is in their genes to perform it. They herd. While you are walking down the street they will want to circle you—especially if you are with a friend, loved one, or family. The bigger the crowd, the more they want to shape you into a nice group.

These are dogs whose natural instincts are to communicate with one another and with man. Having been used through the centuries to generally guard sheep and cattle, it is not above them to nip and snarl to get their charges to move where they want them to. They are generally happiest in homes with large yards, and should be given plenty to do. These dogs really, really want to work; they have the bodies and minds to do jobs and do them well. That's why you find so many herding breeds in obedience, agility, herding, and flyball competitions.

They usually make excellent guard dogs. Herding dogs were meant to guard the sheep and cattle as well as herd them. They were an especially important part of keeping away other predators. Herding breeds have long been employed as police dogs, as well. Some have even been trained as guide dogs for the blind. Not all of these dogs are for the novice owner. Indeed, many of these dogs were developed to think on their own, or do the bidding of their human counterpart. With some of them, when you are unsure, you will either fill them with confusion or they will fill the breach, and make decisions for themselves. Many dogs in this breed will respond quickly and easily to obedience. In fact, they excel at it.

German Shepherd Dog

The German Shepherd Dog is the most versatile in the world. He serves as a police dog, guard dog, a guide dog, and excels at rescue as well. Shepherds also make excellent pets. They are sometimes slow in accepting children, but once they bond with a child, that child has a protector and friend for life.

Shepherds are intelligent, active, and above all, they are herding dogs. They have very strong personalities, and expect a strong leader. Obedience goes a long way in establishing pack leader status. Because of their herding instincts, they will always want to assert their position in the pack, especially with other dogs. They can get along well with other dogs, but they must be socialized at a young age. They are generally suspicious of strangers.

The key to owning a German Shepherd Dog is knowing that they live to please their owners. They require lots of exercise and do not tire easily. They have tremendous stamina and require someone who will provide them with a number of tasks to confront them and keep them busy. They are powerful and quick, with an ability to concentrate. The dog is twenty-four to twenty-six inches at the shoulder, and can weigh quite a bit. This dog should always be confident and fearless.

Shetland Sheepdog

Shelties look like miniature Collies, and Collie breeders did a lot to curtail confusion about the breeds by requesting that they not be recognized by the Kennel Club as Shetland Collies, but as Shetland Sheepdogs instead. Shelties were first recognized by the AKC in 1911.

The breed is highly trainable and has long been a big winner in the obedience ring. It is also a gregarious animal whose good looks have earned it much praise in the breed ring. And its resemblance to Lassie, but in a small package, has made it popular with families who love the dogs as pets. Shelties still retain their herding instincts, and are watchful of the children in their care.

The Sheltie's colors can include black, blue, marble, and sable, ranging from golden through mahogany, marked with varying amounts of white and/or tan. Shelties need exercise, but not an excessive amount.

Collie

Photo by Mary Bloom©

The Collie of today is the one that has been used in the Scottish Highlands to guard and herd sheep for more than 100 years. He was made popular because of the Lassie stories, movies, and television shows. Today he is more a house pet than a herder of sheep.

There are two kinds of Collie: the Rough Collie and the Smooth Collie. Lassie is an example of a Rough Collie. The Smooth Coated Collie is the same dog, but with a hard, dense, flat coat with abundant undercoat. Both are very affectionate dogs with very good personalities. They get along well with other dogs and love to be part of the family.

FACTS

Recently, the Border Collie has found employment in the Eastern United States. A number of golf course groundskeepers came up with the idea of using the dogs to chase away migrating geese that marred the courses with their droppings.

Not a very good apartment dog, the Collie loves exercise and companionship. Loving, devoted, but smart and independent, the Collie wants obedience. This is a somewhat laid back dog, compared to the rest of the Herding Group. They can weigh between fifty and eighty pounds.

Pembroke Welsh Corgi

The difference between the Pembroke Welsh Corgi and the Cardigan Welsh Corgi is that the former has no tail while the latter has a full tail. Also, Pembrokes are usually red or sable colored, while Cardigans are typically black. The Pembroke also has a slightly different build, seen most easily in the higher, more pointed ears.

Corgis stand about ten to twelve inches at the shoulder, but were bred for herding cattle. They did it well. Corgis were called "heelers," as they would scamper behind the bulls and nip at their legs to get them moving. Because they were so low to the ground, and built somewhat like a pointy-eared Basset, they could easily get underfoot, and could easily avoid getting kicked by angry cattle.

The Pembroke is an excellent watchdog and a great family dog. He requires only moderate exercise, and can survive in a large apartment or a spacious house. He is a gentle dog who gets along well with others, and can enjoy the rigors of both the country or city life. He is a gregarious pet, who gets along well with children. He has a short, heavy coat that comes in a variety of colors.

Australian Shepherd

The Australian Shepherd as we know it is not registered in Australia, probably because this breed was really bred and developed by sheep farmers in the Western United States; thus, the Australian Shepherd is really an American breed. These dogs have been used for various jobs all around the country.

Much like the Collie, the Australian Shepherd has a luxurious coat of many colors. They have thick, dense undercoats, and coarse, long hairs on top. This dog requires lots of exercise and obedience training, though he makes a wonderful family pet. He is as smart and loving as they come, and will work tirelessly, intelligently, and faithfully. That's why he's becoming more and more popular as an obedience and agility star.

Other Non-AKC Breeds

Most certainly there are other breeds. We have only skimmed the surface here of the most popular breeds in the seven AKC-recognized groups. There are a great many dogs in the world that are not recognized by the AKC. This isn't because they're not good enough; it's because they don't have a large enough representation in the United States, or a well-organized breed club, or a proven breeding record. The AKC does maintain a Miscellaneous Class, in which you'll find the Polish Lowland Sheepdog, the Plott Hound, the German Pinscher, and the Toy Fox Terrier. These breeds are up-and-coming breeds, or breeds that want to participate in some AKC programs without gaining full recognition.

Argentine Dogo

The Argentine Dogo is a rare breed coming out of Argentina. Also called the Argentinian Mastiff, this breed is a solid and strong dog weighing up to 100 pounds. This all-around working breed was originally developed in the 1920s for hunting large wildcats. The breed is also used extensively for protecting cattle, as a security dog, and for police work.

American Pit Bull Terrier

The American Pit Bull Terrier is a very close relation of the AKC-recognized American Staffordshire Terrier. The APBT is registered by the United Kennel Club, and is a popular animal (whether registered or not). Unfortunately, the Pit Bull has gotten a bum rap as a vicious breed by people who want to use him as a guard dog.

Pit Bulls have large heads, strong jaws, and short, smooth coats with some brindle coloring. They are sinewy and tough, and may weigh as much as fifty pounds. Improperly trained, they can become dangerous to their owners, their family, friends, or unknowing strangers.

If you are dead set on getting a Pit Bull, make sure you do some asking around about the person that is breeding and selling them to you. Be very careful. These dogs are very popular, and many people are being irresponsible in their breeding and are turning out unsound animals. In many instances, you should talk to your local licensing bureau, as they are banned or outlawed in certain areas.

Mixed Breeds, Mutts, and Hybrids

There is a lot of information written about purebreds because, as you've hopefully learned here, they've been selectively bred to look and act in particular ways. This should make choosing a dog to join your family simpler. But it can also make it seem quite complicated! There are so many choices, so many things to think about. After investigating all the breeds, you may find that none especially does it for you.

Mutts

If you're worn out on the purebred route, or it simply doesn't matter that much to you how much you know about your dog's genetic makeup, you may want to adopt a mixed breed dog. Yes, a mutt! While these dogs are sometimes not the most beautiful dogs you have ever seen, they can make superlative pets.

Mixed breed dogs often marry the best traits of the dogs they're descended from. It is fun to try to guess what breeds went into making your dog. In some cases you'll know, like if your Lab bred the Australian Cattle Dog next door by mistake, but in many cases you won't know at all. The British magazine Dogs Today runs a monthly contest for its readership to try to guess the parentage of a mixed breed dog.

In the end, neither a purebred nor a mixed breed is going to be a better dog than the other. Both are dogs. The important considerations are, again, how well your lifestyle accommodates your dog's basic needs. Whether you choose purebred or mixed, you have to realistically assess the amount of time and energy you have to take care of your dog the way he deserves (and needs) to be taken care of. Remember, while quality breeding is important to keep the various breeds alive, dogs, unlike humans, don't differentiate between breed and non-breed. Dogs only care that you are their primary caregiver and leader.

Wolf Hybrids

Wolf hybrids are dog/wolf crosses that are bred and kept as domesticated companion animals. In many cases, however, the concept doesn't work, because wolves have always resisted domestication, and the instinct in the wolf hybrid to return to a wild state is often very strong and can break an owner's heart (and get him into serious legal trouble if the wolf/dog damages property or people).

Dog-wolf hybrids are quick, powerful, and incredibly resourceful. They are also very independent-minded, usually being a mix of wolf and spitz or herding breeds. What none of our backyard Frankensteins have figured out though, is how to blend the best of the wolf with the best of the dog. What they want is the strength and tenacity of the wolf with the obedience and domestication of the dog. Usually it's the strongest characteristics of the wolf that result. While they are incredibly cute puppies, they usually grow up to be more than most folks can handle. They tend to revert, rather than progress.

Many wolf dog stories end very badly. There are three typical scenarios:

1. The wolf dog escapes and runs off into the wild. Chances are very good he will not be accepted in any wild packs, and may be considered game himself.
2. The wolf dog attacks a family member or a stranger for no apparent reason. Sometimes it is a child. He is put down.
3. The wolf dog escapes and hangs around the suburbs. He picks off other small, domesticated animals or small livestock. Eventually he is subdued by animal control and brought into an animal shelter. He is then usually put down, because few, if any, animal shelters will let any potential pet owners own one of these animals.

Are they bad animals? No, but they are not really pets. The best case scenarios include being chained or penned up in a kennel, far from the family, which results in a never-ending life of loneliness for an animal that very much wants to be part of the pack.

ALERT

In many areas, wolf hybrids are banned or outlawed. If you are caught with one, your pet may be confiscated and you may be fined.

These animals are usually very wily, but are not good at obedience. They are very difficult to house train, and are sometimes dangerous with children. In short, these are not good pets.

CHAPTER 3
Before Getting a Puppy

You've decided that you want a puppy. Remember, puppies are very cute and cuddly, but in the end, they will grow up to be adult dogs. You want to have the responsibility of caring for and loving and training an animal. You can't wait to groom him and walk him and take him to the veterinarian and pay the bills. You can't wait to find friends to watch him for that weekend when you have to go away.

Are You Ready for a Puppy?

Of course, you can't wait for that cute little devil to turn your best pair of shoes into the most expensive doggy toy ever created. You can't wait for an accident that permanently scars your off-white rug in the living room. And you can't wait to go home at night instead of hanging out a little later at your favorite nightclub or restaurant with your friends. And of course, most of all, you can't wait for fuzzy-wuzzy to someday slip his leash and make a mad dash across the road, in heavy traffic, so he can finally catch that tasty, tantalizing squirrel.

One of the toughest things about puppies is that it's really hard not to forgive them. One look at that little, furry mug, and you know your heart is absolutely going to melt.

Okay. Okay. You're still reading, you must really want a dog.

Let's be honest, there is nothing better than coming home from a hard day's work and finding that tail-wagging, sloppy-tongued mop of a dog who can't wait to greet you when you arrive home. Dogs are so bouncy and loving and wonderful; there's no getting around it, dogs are wonderful companions. They are fun, friendly, love attention. They love to play, go for long walks, and be mischievous.

Dachshund

Photo by Mary Bloom©

But know going in that dogs are a tremendous amount of responsibility. While they are fun to cuddle up with while watching television, and they are fun to go hiking and running with; while they are great fun at the beach or in a park, or in the snow, they also require forethought and attention, even on days when we would rather think only of ourselves.

There are thousands of dogs that are left homeless each year and are sheltered in dog pounds and rescue homes all across the country. Often this is no fault of the dog's. When the cute puppy turned eight months old and started showing an ornery streak, that was the last straw. When an over-obliging owner suddenly finds himself with a dog who growls when he's told to get off the bed, well, the dog may become a casualty. People give up their dogs because they didn't fully understand doggy behavior, and all the things that need to be done to keep a dog healthy and well-behaved. They find out that Dalmatians require too much exercise; they didn't know St. Bernards grew THAT big; those tiny Maltese are mischievous balls of fire. Suddenly old Rover finds himself at the shelter with a haunted look on his face, cowering at the back of his pen, as countless strangers pass by and he remains alone. In a day when razors, pens, diapers, and even spouses are disposable, dogs are not untouchables. Unfortunately, dogs pay for being disposable with their lives. In fact, every year, thousands of dogs are put down because of neglect or homelessness.

This speaks volumes about how many people don't think through the addition of a dog in their lives. Don't let this happen to you! Ask yourself some important questions before you go running out to get the dog your kids are screaming for or that you think will fill the gap in your life: What kind of life do you lead? How much room do you have, and what kind of house do you live in? What kind of attention do you think you can offer the animal? Will someone be home all day to housetrain and socialize a puppy? Do you have a fenced yard? How old are your children? Does everyone in the family want a dog, or are you caving in to a demanding child? Do you want an active dog, a laid-back dog, a big dog, a small dog, a hairy dog, a hairless dog, a slobbery dog, a neat dog? Take this time to think about what you and your family want. Be responsible, and enjoy the comfort, love, and happiness that owning a dog can bring for a long time to come.

ALERT

Puppies are little bundles of joy. But just remember, junior will grow up. A ten-week old puppy will probably weigh less than 5 to 10 percent of its final body weight. For example, a Labrador Retriever puppy will weigh approximately five to ten pounds. A full-grown Lab might weigh anywhere from sixty-five to 100 pounds.

New Puppy, Older Puppy, or Adult—Which Is Best for You?

This is a question most people don't stop to think about, but should. Most of the time when people think of getting a dog, they think about getting a puppy. They think of the cute ball of fluff running around the house making the family laugh. They want to nurture and raise the dog from a pup.

Do You Really Want a Puppy?

But think about it: Do you really want a puppy? Is a puppy the best fit with your family's lifestyle? Having a puppy is like having a two-year-old in the house. Puppies want to get into everything, and they use their mouths to explore. They need to chew, and if you don't supply a variety of toys, they'll chew what's available. Puppies need to be kept on very strict schedules in order to be housetrained. That means taking the puppy out first thing in the morning, several times during the day, and last thing at night. It means monitoring the puppy during the day to try to prevent accidents from happening. It means making a real commitment to training and socializing, because when your puppy gets big and he doesn't know what's expected of him, he'll make the rules. It may be cute to have your puppy curl up on the couch with you or sleep in your bed or jump up on you to greet you, but then don't be surprised if you meet with resistance when your pup's grown up and you don't want him doing those things anymore.

**SSENTIALS**

Bringing home a puppy is very exciting. There's nothing like a little fur ball. But remember, a dog doesn't have to be eight to ten weeks old to be a puppy. Animal shelters are filled with dogs under the age of one year that are perfectly wonderful dogs. They are not "used" dogs. Saving the life of a dog available for adoption is a wonderful feeling, and can add special resonance to your relationship with your companion for years to some.

What Older Dogs Have to Offer

When you get a six-month-old dog you obviously miss those early days of playfulness and cuteness. But let's be honest, a six- to twelve-month old puppy is still pretty darn cool. These slightly older puppies are generally slightly calmer, they're usually housetrained, they're more set in their ways, and people report that they seem grateful to be in a new home in which they're loved and appreciated.

FACTS

You should always remember that you really don't want a puppy before it is eight to ten weeks old. It hasn't had time to be properly weaned. Dogs that are taken from their mother early often do not develop well. They need the nutrition of their mother's milk and the socialization that comes with being a part of the litter. Many puppies that have been torn away from their mothers too early often display signs of being skittish later on in life, as well as a host of other problems.

There's also the feel-good part of getting a slightly older puppy, because whether you adopt one from a shelter or a purebred rescue group or just take one in from a neighbor, you are essentially saving that dog's life. Yes, you are inheriting behaviors that the dog has learned from its previous owners or circumstances, but contrary to the old saying, you can teach an old puppy new tricks.

Adopting an older puppy doesn't mean going to the dog pound and rescuing a mangy mutt on death row (though those who do are blessed). There are many older puppies available, both purebred (through breed supported rescue groups as well as the local shelters) and mixed-breed, that are physically and mentally sound. The obvious thing about taking in an older puppy is that you are making a difference in a dog's life. But the thing you need to consider is: Is an older puppy going to make a difference in your life?

My German Shorthair Exley was such a dog. I had wanted a puppy. And of course I had come into the market at a time when none of the East Coast breeders were expecting a litter any time soon. I was crestfallen. I was determined to find a puppy. Then I spoke to Nancy Campbell of the German Shorthair Pointer Rescue group. She wasn't sure I should have a dog at all at the time, but I convinced her of my sincerity in understanding the responsibilities of owning a dog, especially as one as active as a GSP. The more I pressed her for any information on puppies, she kept telling me about several older dogs. I resisted, and put her off several times. Finally, I gave in and decided to listen to her suggestion about taking an older puppy or an older dog.

German Shorthaired Pointer

Photo by Mary Bloom©

When I got Exley he was twelve to thirteen months old. He had had a difficult path. But still he had many of the characteristics of a puppy, and in a very real sense was in fact still a puppy, despite his appearance. Exley was as fast as the wind and stronger than an ox and dumber than a post. And I loved him to death. I have to admit that the more I grew attached to him the more I resented having missed his youngest stage, but I was truly grateful that the universe had somehow conspired to ensure our collision.

As with any other puppy, there were days of anger, rage, disappointment, and frustration, but there were also days of excitement, pride, joy, and absolute happiness. We have been lifelong pals. And I think back in horror as I try to imagine life without Exley the last ten years, as he has been a friend, companion, and joy. As in any relationship we've had our ups and downs, but it has been marvelous on the whole.

Puppies vs. Older Puppies: Pros and Cons

	Puppies	Older Puppies
Pro	Cute Playful Cuddly Bonding between you and your dog establishes pack position early	Easily (if not already) housetrained Doesn't usually require lots of training Playful Active
Con	Needs to be housetrained, socialized, and obedience trained Has to work through chewing and adolescent stages	Miss the cute early puppy stage May inherit someone else's problems

Looking and Learning

The only way to get a good grasp of what a specific dog is like is to actually see the dog in action. From veterinarians to breeders to trainers, there are numerous professionals who are usually more than willing to share their wisdom about questions you might have. Asking people who are well aware of dogs and specific breeds also will lead you to information you may not have considered, which could help you avoid getting yourself into a bad situation.

Going to Dog Shows

The best way to find out about the idiosyncrasies of various breeds, and to really get a good look at them, is to go to dog shows. You'll find representatives of just about all the AKC breeds at a dog show, and best of all you'll find their breeders, the people who understand them best. Not only that, because you'll get to look around and talk to so many people, you may leave with a completely different idea about what kind of dog you want than you had before you went to the show.

Seeing is believing, and being able to talk to breeders is invaluable. Breeders are used to dealing with people in the same situation as you. Also, they are concerned that the dogs they breed find the right homes for them. A Husky breeder would not recommend that one of her pups go to a home in which the primary caretaker was wheelchair-bound. That wouldn't be fair to the person, and it wouldn't be fair to the dog.

FACTS

Most dog shows, in each breed, sponsor puppy sweepstakes, which are showing competitions for puppies from six to eighteen months of age. The dogs aren't always fully trained, but you'd be surprised how well they behave. It's a lot of fun, and of course, they're all puppies!

How do you find dog shows to attend? Call the veterinary offices in or near your town. They should know the names of breeders who can tell you if shows are coming up in the area. You can call the American Kennel Club and ask for show information. The AKC's customer service number is (919) 233-9767. You can also find show information on the AKC's Web page, *www.akc.org*. Good luck and have fun!

Many dog shows will feature puppy sweepstakes. No, you won't win a puppy. These are competitions for breeders to show some of their younger dogs. The puppies will be six months to eighteen months old. This is an excellent opportunity for prospective dog buyers to see their breed of choice up close. It's also an excellent way to see what these dogs are like as puppies.

Talking to Breeders

Breeders are your best source of information about a specific dog you are interested in. After all, these folks are passionate about the breed!

Plus they've lived with the breed, some for several decades, and can tell you the breed's positive and negative qualities.

Good breeders will want to interview you, too, which will help you decide if the breed is truly right for you. A breeder may ask you how often you like to go hiking, say, or how often you travel. You may realize you're not the sportsperson you thought you were, or that your schedule is tighter than you thought. Then again, you may be relieved to hear that a breed you thought was too active actually doesn't need as much exercise as you thought, and the breeder has helped you figure out how to fit in a good workout for the dog without compromising your daily habits.

Better breeders will ask if you have the time, energy, and disposition to take care of a young puppy. They will bring up to you many of the things we will discuss here, and maybe some that aren't. Some points may be very specific to their breed.

QUESTIONS?

Are all breeders the same?
In general, most breeders are reputable and helpful. However, there are some in the business only for the money. You should try to check as many references as you can about the breeder you are dealing with. Ask for several references, and see what types of responses you get.

Another great thing about talking to breeders is that you will get a good sense of who you want to get your puppy from. The person who's especially helpful, or with whom you "click," or whose dogs seem the most well-behaved and mellow of the lot you've spoken with—this is the person from whom you want to acquire your new family member. You should feel comfortable calling your breeder at any time during your dog's life to ask him or her about any kind of problems you're having. If your pup's chewing is getting out of control, or if housetraining isn't working, or if your adult dog suddenly goes lame, it's nice to know there's someone you can call who not only knows the breed, but knows your dog personally.

Golden Retriever

Photo by Mary Bloom©

A responsible breeder will tell you all about your potential puppy's past—what the parents and siblings are like, whether there's working stock in the bloodlines, what kind of traits he's been breeding away from (or for), particular health problems to look out for, and much more. In fact, a breeder who doesn't want to inform you of all these things, particularly health records for breeds prone to hip dysphasia or other genetic conditions, is one to stay away from—he's probably got something to hide.

Responsible breeders want their puppies to find homes in which they'll be loved and cared for as real family members for the duration of their lives. Many of them will put in writing that if for any reason you can't keep the dog any longer, that you contact them first before surrendering the dog to a shelter. Doesn't this sound like the kind of grandma or grandpa you want for your dog?

Veterinarians

Studies prove that veterinarians are the first ones most pet owners turn to for help with a variety of problems, from health to behavior. And because they're on the "front lines" of dealing with various breeds and their owners, they can give you some solid advice about general traits of some breeds.

The veterinarians at the clinic nearest you may know that Labrador Retrievers are being over-bred in the area and they're seeing a lot of chewing, digging, and nervous behavior problems. They may be able to tell you that 70 percent of all German Shepherds they see develop hip dysphasia. They may also tell you that Bichon Frisés make ideal family pets. It's important to remember that even though they see a lot of different dogs, they are not experts on all breeds.

What is important is that once you've chosen your puppy, you need to establish a relationship with a veterinarian you can trust completely. If a veterinarian makes you feel silly about asking a basic question, or doesn't seem to want to spend much time examining your animal, keep shopping until you find someone with whom you can discuss anything. It's the same scenario as shopping for a breeder—this is someone you'll trust your dog's life with.

FACTS

Veterinarians can be a great help to those people who want to buy a puppy. Many veterinarians will allow local breeders and other folks who have litters to announce them on bulletin boards in their offices. Other puppies might be up for adoption. Many times the veterinarian will know these people and be able to tell you about the puppies' history.

Friends

You may spend months reading books, going to dog shows, and exploring the wide world of dogs to find just the one for you, and suddenly a friend will tell you they know someone whose dog just had a litter and she needs good homes for the puppies. You ignore all your instincts, go see the litter, fall in love, and come home with a puppy whose genetic background is a mystery to you, that will grow to look like something you've never seen before, and that's three times bigger than you ever imagined. Does that mean you're going to suffer with the wrong dog for the rest of your life? Maybe. But then again, maybe not. Animals are adaptable, and luckily, people are too. It may not have been the smartest move on your part, but if you vow to be a responsible dog owner and walk, feed, exercise, groom, and look after your dog's health, the two of you will do just fine.

This is not as unlikely as it sounds. It happens very often. If this is your case, here are some things to think about. Do you know these people? If not, do you know anyone who does? Do they have a reputation for treating their dog well? What kind of medical history does it have? What kind of disposition does the mother have? The father? Are they active dogs or couch potatoes? The questions really don't change. You just have to be a little better at ferreting out the answers.

ESSENTIALS

There is nothing more homey than getting a free puppy from a neighbor or friend. You go into the house and see the box with the nursing mother and fluffy little litter. You just can't help yourself. Whenever you are getting a puppy, remember to ask a lot of questions. Just because you're taking home a local puppy doesn't absolve you from asking questions or taking responsibility once you've taken possession.

Your Lifestyle and Schedule

I'm not talking about Martha Stewart or *Better Homes & Gardens* style. You can't pick out a dog because you think he'll look good with your sofa, or he'll go well with your English garden. You don't pick out a dog that matches your Ralph Lauren outfit or goes with your rugged Levi's and Timberlands. A dog is not a designer emblem. It's a crazy little animal, with a mind of its own, and a sense of humor all its own. It's like having another person in the house.

Puppies can be one of the most difficult things you can add to your life. While they are absolutely adorable, they can also be fur-covered wrecking balls. Plants, throw pillows, carpets, oriental rugs, furniture—absolutely anything is open season. They are seen by the puppy as toys and objects of affection. So, whatever dog you choose, you should make sure it fits into your version of what life is like.

When I am talking about lifestyle, I'm talking about what you do every day. What is your idea of fun? Rollerblading? Riding your bike? Watching a movie or sports on television? Going hiking? Going on little day trips in the car? Going to the park or beach and lying out in the sun? Do you work? Part-time? Full-time? Are you a career sociopath who puts in seventy hours a week? Do you like to come home, shower, and go back out to dinner and the movies or to your favorite bar? Are you obsessively neat? Are you allergic to pets? You have to ask yourself these kinds of questions when you are choosing a dog so that you can pick the dog that's best for you. Believe me, you probably already know what dog you want, but couldn't answer the questions I just asked honestly. Try!

You're Cramping My Style

It's important to think about your life before you buy your dog, so that six months later poor Fido isn't back out on the street looking for a new job. You don't want to be coming home and cursing your happy little pooch, just because he's at home drawing breath, keeping you from meeting your soul mate at tonight's hottest party. Many times people who don't think about what kind of dog they really want are at cross purposes with their dog. You don't want a pet that's going to cramp your style. And of course, you don't want to pick a dog whose life you're going to make miserable.

Dalmatian

Photo by Karen Taylor©

If you're a rollerblader, you want to know that when you come home, you can suit up, put a leash on Rover, and bring him along. Obviously, you can't do this with a puppy. However, you want to choose a dog that will want to share in that fun. You need an athletic dog who has the stamina and explosive energy to keep up with you. You don't want some sedentary hound who's panting after the first half-mile. Likewise, if you like going for an evening stroll, you don't want some drooling half-lunatic pulling you around the block like a crazed demon. You want a good dog who shares your pace and enjoyment of the evening air.

Lester is a Scottie. When Lester was a puppy, his owner Justin had just bought an inflatable chair and several inflatable pillows. The pieces were fun, bright, and comfortable. While Justin was gone one day, Lester discovered that these items could also deflate. Each piece proved to be very susceptible to punctures. Justin decided that however cool inflatable furniture was, it was not the right fashion choice for Lester and him.

Maybe you need a dog who can keep up with your children and who you can trust to watch over them. You need your dog not to be a substitute parent or some kind of living, unbreakable toy, but a companion and playmate for your kids to share in their well-behaved fun.

Evaluate Your Lifestyle

If you are a career person, working tons of hours per week, you should probably put your dog-owning desires on hold until your life settles down. If you have roommates or family living with you that are willing to give a dog its needed attention then you probably could get a dog. However, a dog will perceive those who show it the most attention as its closest "pack members." Would you really like to own a dog that perceives you as a semi-stranger?

A young married couple who both work and have no children should determine how much time at least one person is home. A dog cannot be left alone for long periods of time, especially as a way of life. Children can often be an asset in caring for a dog. However, if the child is not old enough to help out with caring for the dog, a young couple might find themselves raising two babies!

The main thing to consider is how often your home is empty. If you can afford a dog walker who can get your dog in the middle of its "home alone" period, that can be a help. Remember, your home is not empty only when you are at work. How often do you like to go out at night? How many weekends do you spend out of town? Does your job send you on a lot of business trips? The less time you can spend at home, the less likely you are ready for a dog.

ESSENTIALS Many puppies find themselves out in the cold each year because the buyer didn't bother to understand the characteristics of the breed. In years past, television, movies, and other entertainment outlets have led to surges in dog buying. In the last decade Dalmatians, Jack Russell Terriers, Chihuahuas, and St. Bernards rose sharply in popularity due to popular media. However, these dogs are not for everyone. As a result, dog shelters around the country filled up with completely innocent, six-month-old abandoned puppies.

Your Activity Level

There is a dog for every activity level. But it is extremely important that you match your activity level with the dog you choose. It is all well and good to think: "I should get a dog that will force me to walk more often to get more exercise." In practice, however, most people will revert to their old habits and create an unfair environment for a dog that has been bred for a specific energy level that you knew about well in advance.

On the flip side, if you are a very active person who enjoys outdoor activities, you should make sure to get a dog that can keep up with you. A breeder is usually a good person to ask if his or her specific breed of dog is a good match for you. Following is a simple chart that should give you a basic idea of what breed might suit you best.

If This Describes You . . .	Think About These Breeds:
I am very active. I like rollerblading, biking, hiking, and swimming.	Dalmatian, German Shorthaired Pointer, English Springer Spaniel, Jack Russell Terrier, Weimeraner, Vizsla, Irish Setter, Doberman Pinscher, Brittany, Alaskan Malamute, Airedale Terrier
I am somewhat active. I jog short distances, I often go on long walks, I like light exercise.	Golden Retriever, Labrador Retriever, German Shepherd Dog, Beagle, Rottweiler, Standard Poodle, Boxer, Siberian Husky, Cocker Spaniel, Shetland Sheep Dog, Australian Sheepdog, Great Dane, Collie, Chinese Shar-Pei, Chow-Chow, Saint Bernard, Mastiff, Chesapeake Bay Retriever, Newfoundland, Bloodhound
I am less active. I like to watch movies, go for a nice stroll, garden in the backyard.	Poodle (Toy or Miniature), Dachshund, Pug, Boston Terrier, Miniature Pinscher, Scottish Terrier, West Highland White Terrier, Cairn Terrier, Bassett Hound, Maltese, Bulldog, Pekinese, Bichon Frisé, Lhaso Apso, Corgi (Pembroke and Cardigan)

You should still consult your breeder who can help you with specific nuances, such as which dogs will do better with certain types of exercise. Now let's look at the same chart in reverse. The following will let you know which dogs are probably a bad match for specific activity levels.

If This Describes You . . .	These Breeds Are NOT For You:
I am less active. I like to watch movies, go for a nice stroll, garden in the backyard.	Dalmatian, German Shorthaired Pointer, English Springer Spaniel, Jack Russell Terrier, Weimeraner, Vizsla, Irish Setter, Doberman Pinscher, Brittany, Alaskan Malamute, Airedale Terrier
I am very active. I like rollerblading, biking, hiking, and swimming.	Poodle (Toy or Miniature), Dachshund, Pug, Boston Terrier, Miniature Pinscher, Scottish Terrier, West Highland White Terrier, Cairn Terrier, Bassett Hound, Maltese, Bulldog, Pekingese, Bichon Frisé, Lhaso Apso, Corgi (Pembroke and Cardigan)

Your Environment

Just as there is a dog for every activity level, there are several dogs that can fare well in all sorts of home environments. Truth be known, pretty much any dog can do well on a farm—whether it be the most active border collie, or the tiniest Chihuahua—but certain dogs just fit in certain places better. Following is a chart to help you choose a dog that will fit right in with your living environment.

If This Describes You . . .	Think About These Breeds:
I live in an apartment in the city.	Poodle (Toy or Miniature), Dachshund, Pug, Boston Terrier, Miniature Pinscher, Scottish Terrier, West Highland White Terrier, Cairn Terrier, Maltese, Bulldog, Pekinese, Bichon Frise, Lhaso Apso, Corgi (Pembroke and Cardigan)
I live in a townhouse in a city.	Any of the above, Basset Hound, Rottweiler, Standard Poodle, Boxer, Cocker Spaniel, Australian Sheepdog, Chinese Shar-Pei, Chow-Chow, Chesapeake Bay Retriever
I have a suburban home.	Golden Retriever, Labrador Retriever, German Shepherd Dog, Beagle, Rottweiler, Standard Poodle, Boxer, Siberian Husky, Cocker Spaniel, Shetland Sheep Dog, Australian Sheepdog, Great Dane, Collie, Chinese Shar-Pei, Chow-Chow, St. Bernard, Mastiff, Chesapeake Bay Retriever, Newfoundland, Bloodhound
I live in a rural area.	Dalmatian, German Shorthaired Pointer, English Springer Spaniel, Jack Russell Terrier, Weimeraner, Vizsla, Irish Setter, Doberman Pinscher, Brittany, Akita, Alaskan Malamute, Airedale Terrier

CHAPTER 4
Where to Buy a Puppy

Buying a dog isn't like buying a new shirt. Even if you are dead set on getting a specific breed of dog, you should not simply rush into this kind of purchase. Although careful breeding makes each individual in a breed share a set of common traits, there are still subtle and not-so-subtle differences between individual dogs. In addition, some less scrupulous breeders have overbred and inbred many purebred dogs, creating low-quality specimens.

Breeders

When I started looking into buying my first dog as an adult, I naturally considered the types of dogs I had had growing up. This is what we all do. I decided to talk to some dog professionals. I happened to be working for a company at the time that had a pet division. Some of the people who worked in it were dog show judges as well as breeders themselves. I talked to those professionals, and they helped guide me to several breeds and then pointed me in the direction of some qualified breeders.

I eventually went to Nancy Campbell, a German Shorthaired Pointer breeder who also ran the rescue league and fostered several homeless dogs. She asked me more questions than I asked her. I felt like I already knew it all. She was talking with concern in her voice, and I feigned knowledge and confidence in my decision. Then she really started asking me about all kinds of things. How big was my apartment? How often do I exercise? How late do I work? How long does it take me to get home? And then she said no!

You can imagine my surprise! She felt that I was not prepared to take a puppy into my home and raise it properly. I had a career and often worked late. She felt that I wouldn't be there enough to socialize the dog. In short, she would never sell me a puppy and urged me to reconsider my desire to get a dog.

ESSENTIALS

While there are many excellent and qualified breeders around, there are always a few trading on trust that are not as reputable. Whether a purebred or a mixed-breed, you should be suspicious of any breeder who doesn't want to show you health records on the parents, who won't show you the parents, or who wants you to take a puppy before eight to ten weeks of age.

Not being one to take no for an answer, I called her back several days later and told her I had thought it through, come up with some realistic answers and wanted to discuss it with her again. When I was okay with her demands, she was convinced I was responsible enough to take a dog, and I got Exley, an eighteen-month-old rescue dog.

Nancy was an excellent example of a responsible breeder. As she put it, she wanted to make sure that I was committed to the dog and that I understood the responsibility I was taking on. She didn't want to take the dog back, not because she didn't like the dog, or would ever refuse one of her own, but rather, there were already enough homeless dogs. She sent me home with Exley's papers and instructions for care. She also gave me her phone number, and asked me to call her if I ran into problems or had questions. When I did in fact call her for advice or with questions, she was always very friendly and of great help.

Not enough breeders are that responsible. There are plenty of breeders that don't ask the tough questions. That's why it's important to find a reputable breeder whom you can trust. Many breeders are willing to take the time to ask you the right questions. If they don't, you should wonder how much care they take in breeding their dogs.

Your Purebred Dog's Papers

A responsible breeder should give you two pieces of paper with the sale of a puppy: a pedigree and a registration form. The pedigree tells you the dog's family background, and usually goes back five generations. The registration form must be turned over to you the very day you purchase or acquire your puppy. This form allows you to officially register your dog. The breeder should have registered the litter when it was born, at which time he or she received individual registration forms for each of the puppies in the litter. It is then up to you to fill out your pup's registration form and send it in with the required fee to the registering body.

Remember, just because your dog is a registered purebred does not mean his health or worth are guaranteed in any way. You will know the value of your dog by discussing his pedigree with your breeder. If there are no champions or dogs who've earned working titles in his line, then you shouldn't consider breeding him. In fact, your breeder will probably insist you sign a spay/neuter contract. If you want to show your dog, you need to find as much out about showing as possible before you try it, otherwise you may come away frustrated and broke.

Questions to Ask a Breeder

1. How long have you been breeding these dogs?
2. Did you breed any dogs other than these? If so, for how long?
3. When's the last time you showed one of your dogs?
4. Are either the sire or the dam finished champions? May I see their pedigrees?
5. Do either of them have working titles earned in obedience or other performance events?
6. Have the dogs been tested for hip dysphasia, eye problems, heart problems or whatever genetic conditions relate to the breed? (Breeders should be only too happy to show you pedigrees and health certificates. If they're reluctant or say they'll show you when you come to pick up the puppy, don't trust them. These documents should be readily available.)
5. Are either of the parents on the premises, and if so, may I see them? Ask about other siblings, too.
7. Have the puppies had their shots? What shots and when?
8. Is the litter registered? Will I go home with my puppy's registration? (If not, again, suspect trouble.)
9. May I have the names of references to call?

ESSENTIALS

One of the nice things about good breeders is that they will take the time to speak with you on the phone after you've brought Junior home. Many good breeders will tell you to call them should you have any troubles. The great thing about this is that breeders know the ins and outs of the breed, and know their peculiarities and family history.

Pet Shops

Are the dogs you can buy in a pet shop any different than the ones you can buy from a breeder? More times than not, absolutely. A breeder takes care that they have bred two dogs who complement each other in order to breed the best possible dog that would be most emblematic of the breed standard or ideal. Responsible breeders ask you a lot of questions before they agree to sell you a puppy, and they try to match yours and their puppies' personalities.

Bulldog

Photo by Mary Bloom©

Many pet shops get their dogs from puppy mills. These breeders produce dogs with little or no concern about breed standards, temperament, or health problems. As a result, unsuspecting buyers don't know what they're getting. These dogs are as purebred as the dogs you get from a breeder, because purebred only means the mother and father are registered purebreds. These puppies are also as cute as the ones you'll see at a responsible breeder's, though they may lack the energy or robust appearance of the responsible breeder's pups.

Pet shops know that puppies are most appealing when they're six to eight weeks old. That means that to get them to the store by that age they are usually separated from their mother and littermates at four to six weeks of age—far too early. These pups miss the nutritional and behavioral benefits of staying in their first family for as long as they should, and their new families pay the price in health and behavior problems later in life.

If you do buy a puppy from a pet store, ask the staff a lot of questions about its background and whether the store provides any guarantees on the puppy's health. Take the puppy to a veterinarian right away for a first physical, and if the vet suspects any problems, speak with the store staff immediately.

FACTS

Responsible breeders understand the dynamics of early puppyhood and use that knowledge to match puppies to their future owners. The breeder may decide that a family with active, assertive children may intimidate a lesser-ranked pup and want to pair that family with the "alpha" puppy. Similarly, an alpha pup in a reserved, family may grow to dominate them. Puppies need to be with their mother and littermates for at least eight weeks. Anyone who encourages you to take a puppy younger than eight weeks old is not allowing enough time for the pup to develop fully.

Purebred Rescue

A "rescue" dog is a purebred dog who has been "rescued" from a former home or from a pound or shelter and is currently homeless. Most AKC breed clubs sponsor purebred rescue groups. When a dog is dropped off at the shelter or taken into the dog pound, if that dog is believed to be purebred, that local shelter calls the contact person for the local rescue group. If the rescue coordinator believes the dog is a purebred of the breed in which he or she is involved, that dog is taken from the pound and housed in a foster home until the rescue organization can find the dog a home.

Many of the dogs in rescue groups tend to be mature, older dogs. However, you would be surprised to know how many dogs are really actually puppies! They have many dogs that are under eighteen months of age. And they often have some under the age of twelve months too.

Rescue is run generally by breeders who are very concerned about dogs in general. They make no money from this, and usually work on a volunteer basis. Much of the cost of fostering is picked up by the family that is sheltering the dog in their house. Each breed has a specific network of these people who have extremely big hearts, and only want to see the dogs find a good home.

Do these dogs have something wrong with them? Generally speaking, no. Sometimes these dogs end up in rescue because their owners have not been able to adjust to having a puppy in their lives. Or, they have been housed by people who no longer were able to properly care for their animals. Rescue coordinators bail out abandoned or unwanted dogs and evaluate them before seeking new homes for them. Many rescue dogs need some stability to help regain their confidence, and foster owners spend a lot of time working with such animals to ensure that they'll adjust to a new home.

They then list the dog with a national or regional network, where the dog will eventually be placed. All kinds of dogs pass through this scenario. Generally speaking, they tend to be a little older than puppies. They can be anywhere from eighteen months to ten years old. They come in all shapes, sizes, and temperaments. The only thing they have in common is that they are all purebreds.

Because they are rescue dogs, they also tend to be cheaper. The rescue associations usually ask you to make some kind of donation to defray the costs of operating the rescue group and the costs of the individual dog. These groups are run by loving individuals who are looking earnestly for the right home for the right dog. You should seriously consider this venue as a means for getting a dog.

Shelters and Pounds

One place you can always find either new puppies or slightly older puppies is your local dog pound or animal shelter. Many people will bring animals to these places because they know that the animals there have a better chance of finding homes than they might in their current circumstances. It is not uncommon that a box of puppies has been left on the doorstep of a shelter with a note, and sometimes, but rarely, a donation. Other times, the puppy has been brought in because the puppy doesn't fit in with the family situation or lifestyle. Obviously, they also house many older dogs too.

Many local animal shelters are in operation all over the United States. Some dogs are brought there by their current owners, or by the families of those persons. Sometimes the dogs are found on the side of the road and are brought in by a concerned citizen who can't shelter the animal, or they are brought in by the local animal control department.

Jack Russell Terrier

Photo by Mary Bloom©

Many times these dogs are perfectly fine animals who just need a home. In many cases, the animals take a little time to adjust when you first bring them home. Dogs want to be part of a pack. Being moved from pack to pack undermines a dog's self-assurance. As pack position is very important to how a dog sees him or herself, being separated and then situated into a new pack definitely plays games with poor Rover's head. The longer period of time a dog spends with you, the more secure it will become in its surroundings and the more comfortable it will feel with you.

Sometimes the shelters have lots of information on a particular dog, and sometimes they have none. But many of the people who work in shelters are there because they love animals and spend great amounts of time with them. They are often the best judges of how these dogs are and what they like and don't like. They can tell you how they respond to certain things and other dogs.

In short, if you don't care about purebred vs. mixed breed, there are plenty of puppies and older puppies that need a good home in these shelters. When you bring them home, they need a little extra loving and space before they can become more confident, but will make it up to you with love and admiration.

Questions to Ask at the Shelter

Make sure you learn as much as you can regarding the puppy you want to adopt from the shelter. Questions to ask include the following:

1. Why is the puppy up for adoption?
2. Who were the previous owners?
3. Was the animal abused?
4. Are its littermates present? If so, may you see them together?
5. Is the mother here? If so, may you see her as well?
6. May you spend more than a few minutes with the puppy in order to decide?
7. Has the puppy been checked by a veterinarian for potentially serious illnesses?
8. Has the puppy been vaccinated?
9. Has the animal shown any signs of antisocial or aggressive behavior?

Pound vs. Shelter

- The dog pound is usually an animal control center, where strays have been picked up by the local animal control unit. These operations are usually funded by local government.
- The shelter is usually a local animal care unit that is funded in part by state or local government monies, as well as by donations.
- No-Kill shelters are shelters that don't destroy animals. This is a bit of a misnomer. Many of these No-Kill places just don't accept animals they don't think are adoptable. These dogs are then brought to the local animal control unit for adoption or destruction.

Friends and Neighbors

This is probably one of the most unlikely places you will or should go to get a dog. How much does your friend know about breeding dogs? Has great fashion sense? Knows all the newest, hottest bands? Hangs out with cool people? Has a great job? But what do they really know about dogs?

Dalmatian

Photo by Mary Bloom©

Many times people who have puppies that they are giving away have a dog that has gotten pregnant. Sometimes they have bred her to another dog, and sometimes she has a beau of her own. However, while dogs may think they're picky, you should know that dogs don't differentiate by breed. They either like another dog, or they do not.

In many cases, you really don't know what you're getting. And that's when you have to ask yourself, "Is my friend really good to his or her dog? Did they read up on what to do with a pregnant dog? Did they go to their veterinarian and get his or her advice? Do I like my friend's dog? Have I spent enough time with that dog to know whether or not I like it?"

E SSENTIALS

Pet shops are certainly one of the largest suppliers of dogs to the general public in North America. While many pet shops are negatively labeled, because they use breeding farms called puppy mills to supply them, many pet shops do in fact use better suppliers. Regardless of whether you buy directly from a breeder or from a pet shop, ask for as much information as possible.

Another way that friends come up with dogs is when they find a stray and try to find it a good home. This is more common than you think. Make sure to ask as many questions as you can. Try not to be moved by the sad story. You need to find yourself a pet that you can live with for a long time. While many fine pets have been found this way, make sure to think about it before you bring one home. In short, if they're a real friend, they won't try to sell you a dog you don't need. Think about the person who's trying to give you the dog as well as about the dog itself.

Picking the Best Puppy for You

Obviously, this is the moment of truth. What kind of animal will you pick? There are several important things to remember when picking a new puppy, especially if the puppy is part of a large litter.

First, we're going to break down the decision process into two stages. The first stage is observing the puppy with the rest of the littermates. Sometimes this is not possible, but sometimes it is. This part can tell you a lot about the puppy's personality. The second decision process involves you and the puppy alone together. This is also a very important moment.

SSENTIALS

There are three things to remember when evaluating puppies before choosing:

- Position in the pack
- Sociability with humans
- Intelligence

A Puppy and Its Littermates

Watching how a puppy interacts with other dogs, especially its littermates, can tell you a lot about the puppy in question. Judging a puppy's position in the pack is extremely important. Is it the dominant puppy? Is it the weakling? These are both dogs novice owners should avoid. Dominant puppies usually turn out to be dominant dogs. They can be difficult to control and train. They will require someone with more experience in raising and training dogs. They, in fact, will require a dominant master.

Many people are moved by watching the litter's weakling puppy. They want to rescue it from the rest of the pack and nurse it. This is the beginning of our obsession with the underdog, quite literally. These dogs present their own problems. They usually lack confidence, both in the canine and the human world. This can lead to trainability problems and problems with human interaction later on.

Are either of these two dogs ever going to find a home? Yes. A more experienced person can take home these dogs and can many times bring them around. A puppy somewhere in the middle of the pack is probably a good choice. You want one who is neither pushed around too easily, nor too dominant. The middling puppy is the smart move if you have the choice.

Human Interaction

The next thing to judge is, how does the puppy respond to your presence? You probably shouldn't go for the first one who comes rushing at you. Neither do you want the one who won't come at all. You want one of middling temperament. A follower? That's a good dog. You certainly don't want your dog to be a leader. That's your position.

A little pup too busy to come over to you or too afraid to come over to you probably isn't a good bet. While socialization with dogs is important, socialization with people is also key, since your puppy going to be living night and day with you and your family, and not his.

Breeders are constantly amazed by how rough some prospective buyers can be. Remember, these are baby dogs. Be gentle. Don't pick one up by the ears. When you pick up a puppy, place your hand, palm up, under the belly of the dog, and lift gently. Your other hand should be supporting the dog's backside.

Intelligence

This is probably the most difficult to figure out. You want one who will make the effort to understand you. Calling the puppies in a friendly voice is the best way to get their attention. Do not command them, as you will probably frighten them at best should you attempt it. Which one understands? Which ones return your interest? The ones who don't understand your entreaty are probably not for you. Again, do your best to judge not the boldest, but the smartest.

Even if you weigh ninety-five pounds, you are a giant to a newborn puppy. The best way to entreat a little puppy to approach you is to bend on one knee and place your hand lower than their head. The idea is to offer something that is not so intimidating. You're trying to get a read of the dog's personality. You are not trying to scare the poor little thing.

What you're really trying to judge here is how well these puppies will take to obedience training. You want a puppy that is interested in human interaction—not just playing, but understanding.

Just You and the Puppy Alone for a Minute

This is the second part of the choosing process. What is it about? The idea is to see if the puppy responds to you alone, when it is not being distracted by its littermates. What would be best is if you can either go out in the yard or at least in a separate room for a moment, so that you can judge the little one. Some breeders will want to be present. That's fine. What you're trying to do is just get a little face time with the pup with as few distractions as possible. Here are some questions to ask yourself:

- Is the puppy responding to you?
- Is the puppy too distracted by other things to interact with you?
- Is the puppy responding to your entreaties?
- Is the puppy willing to play with you?
- Is the puppy too shy to respond to you?

These questions will help you to be better prepared to make a final decision.

Final Comments on Choosing a Puppy

Many of us are attracted to different things. But our tastes are consistent. What we need to do is think about what we need instead of what we like or find cute. While you maybe attracted by personality to the dominant dog, or the submissive one, or the litter clown, you should be choosing none of these. Are these bad dogs? No, but you are probably not the best persona equipped to deal with the personality traits being exhibited by those dogs.

Certainly one of the things most important is the energy level. Again, you should not look for the least or most active dog that is available for choosing. What you should be considering are the puppies of moderate tendencies.

CHAPTER 5
Puppy-Proofing Your Home

When you are firmly set on getting a puppy, you must take special care to make sure your home is safe for your new arrival. Even if you choose to get an older dog, the environment will be new, which will pique any dog's curiosity. You may decide to restrict your puppy to a specific area at first, which is highly recommended. However, dogs are master escape artists, so even if the new fella is restricted to one room at first, take the time to make sure the entire house or apartment is safe.

The Puppy's Own Space

The first thing you want to do with a puppy is limit the amount of space he has to run around—especially when you're not home. What many people do is limit them to a room or group of manageable rooms in the beginning. We recommend the kitchen as their first room. If you're crate training, and you should, the kitchen is a very good first place to crate. If you're not, then the kitchen should be their room, at least at first.

There's no way around it, if you're getting a puppy and you want to limit its space, you need a baby-gate. You can't escape it. Any other wacky concoction is a craps shoot. Dogs are obstinate. They know something better is on the other side of this contraption. If there is a weakness in whatever divider you put up, they will probe long and hard until they find it, and exploit it. Buy the baby-gate(s) and save yourself a lot of time and aggravation.

Why do you want to limit Spot's run of the house? In the beginning it's a very good idea. Firstly, when you're not home, it limits the amount of damage he can do to just one room. It's easier for you to look around and either move valuables or hide things away that might otherwise cause him harm.

Brussels Griffon

Photo by Mary Bloom©

Once you've put the baby-gates up, you need to look around the room. And you have to ask yourself the following question: If you were a dog, what would you chew on? Don't hesitate to answer in this way: everything. And that's your problem. If there are exposed wires, cover them up or pull them up. Eventually they will be chewed on. Antique chairs around the kitchen table. I don't think so. Put them in the attic for now. You may not want to take any chances. Are all bottles and cans out of the way? Cleansers and other toxins—put them away. And most of all, hide the garbage—under the sink, in the pantry, in the basement. Don't leave anything out. No large, tall container. No covered can. Garbage is the dinner of the gourmet dog. Everything wonderful and edible is in the garbage and your puppy knows it. Move it or come home every day and wonder what condition your house and your dog are going to be in. And believe us, your dog isn't going to help you clean up.

In short, clear the room. Proof the entire kitchen as best you can. What can't be moved, especially anything that's made out of wood, spray with a product called bitter apple. It leaves a very bitter taste on things. That way it deters chewing dogs because of the bad taste it leaves in their mouths.

Of course, you want to leave things for them to purposely chew on, for example, a toy, a chew hoof, a bone, etc. Make sure there a few of these things to distract your puppy from the things you don't want him chewing on.

When you are home, give the dog or puppy more space to roam around. Close all the doors to other rooms and limit his exposure to the upstairs. But give him more room than you do when you are not at home. If you have children, close the doors to their rooms, as well as closing the door to the garage, the den, etc. Some houses don't have lots of doors. Maybe you want to close off the living room or dining room. Buy even more baby-gates.

The idea is that the dog should only incrementally increase the amount of space he is able to live in as he gets a little older and starts to understand the rules of the house. Also, the less space you give him, the easier it is to manage him. You'll be able to keep a better eye on him.

The idea is to keep the dog away from things that look good to chew on. And remember, to a puppy, everything is chewable.

ALERT

There is nothing more exciting or interesting to a young puppy than a houseplant. It's natural. It's leafy. There's dirt! If you have any houseplants on the floor, get rid of them now! They are an accident waiting to happen.

Living Room and Family Room

Whatever you call it, the place where you and your family spend the most time will be the place your dog most wants to be. Such things as knitting materials, game pieces, any kids' toys, and any other small items are not meant for dogs. Also, if you are a smoker, be sure to keep the ashtray empty and the cigarettes out of reach.

Things like potted plants and delicate end tables will get knocked over. It might be a good idea to store them away for the first few months until your puppy can learn to behave properly. Electrical cords need to be coiled and sprayed with bitter apple to prevent chewing. Anything wooden or seemingly chewable should also be protected from chewing.

Even with these precautions, it is recommended that you only let your puppy into your living room with supervision. This way, you can properly teach him how to behave so someday you can move some of your finer and more delicate furniture back where you want it.

ALERT

Dogs like to chew on houseplants sometimes. There are many ordinary house and garden plants that can be toxic to your dog, even in small amounts. Here are a few of the more common, yet deadly, houseplants:

- Bean plants
- Cactus
- Dieffenbachia
- Hydrangea
- Ivy
- Lily

Bedrooms

As tempted as you might be to let the new puppy hang out in the kids' rooms, you must take extra-special care. A child's room is usually the most cluttered, especially with little things that may have been handled by fingers sticky with ice cream and other treats (this makes the most basic little doodad seem like a tasty treat to a mouthy puppy).

Under no circumstances should a puppy be allowed on a bunk bed! Your puppy is not a cat and will probably not land on its feet. In addition, a puppy's curious nature and inexperience in terms of coordination will almost guarantee a fall.

This can work to your advantage. Most children will do just about anything to be able to have the dog in their room. Let them know it will be okay so long as the entire room is puppy safe. Be sure to stress that it is for the puppy's health, otherwise your child might not think it such an important task, and simply stuff things under the bed where just about any puppy will be able to get at.

Posters should be tacked up high. A low hanging poster can be pulled down, possibly letting loose a tack which could be harmful if stepped on or swallowed. Deflated balloons and other small, soft items have a texture that will make your puppy think they are edible and could cause serious problems.

As for the adult bedrooms, nylons, loose change, make-up, and medications can all pose serious risks to a dog's health and should be kept secure and hidden. Waterbeds and puppy paws can be both devastating in terms of home damage, and deadly to a little puppy. Night tables, especially ones with lamps, should be made as sturdy as possible.

Onyx was a six-month old Labrador Retriever who was more than happy to drink out of the toilet bowl. However, she wasn't really tall enough to do so. One day, Onyx was really thirsty. She tried and tried as much as she could, but her height did not allow her to get to the water. So she climbed up on the toilet seat, but still could not reach the water. So she dove in or fell in, her owner wasn't sure. But the thump in the bathroom was loud enough. Onyx made quite the racket because she could not get out. Imagine what might have happened if her owner were not home?

Kitchen and Bathroom

Although it was recommended earlier that the kitchen is a good first room for your puppy, there are also many dangers that need to be addressed beforehand. Cabinets should be secure, if the doors tend to swing open, you will need to get some child locks. Place garbage cans out of reach—either in a cabinet or closet. If this is unfeasible, a tight-fitting lid will help.

Towels, rags, and other cloth items are super fun for any puppy to chew on and tear apart. The problem is the little pieces that result can get lodged in its throat and also cause digestion problems.

As for the bathroom, anything that smells nice—soaps, perfumes, shampoos, shaving cream—must be kept out of reach. Remember that even though you may try to keep the bathroom door closed and the puppy out, you will most likely forget once in a while, so it is better to be safe than sorry. You need to be extra careful with sponges and body scrubs because their chewy texture make them very fun for puppies of all ages and they can harbor residual chemicals and bacteria. The toilet seat should be kept down—a small puppy might be able to crawl in but not be able to get out. Rubber duckies and other bath toys may look like doggy toys, but they won't withstand even a puppy's chewing and can pose a choking hazard.

While you probably don't want your pooch eating your food anyway, it should also be known that a lot of food, such as chocolate, should essentially be considered poison to a dog.

Basement and Attic

Unless you are specifically setting up some space for your puppy in either of these areas, you should probably make a habit of restricting these areas. However, a loving puppy will want to follow you everywhere, and will probably find itself in either of these spaces.

Most likely, these rooms contain a large amount of stored items—holiday decorations, old baby items, and lots of junk you just haven't been able to let go of yet. All of this should be stored in secure containers and placed together where it will be difficult to knock anything over, or rummage through. Small spaces between boxes or boxes and walls should be avoided—your puppy will try to squeeze into small spaces and might not be able to squirm out. Laundry and other cleaning supplies must be secured. Dirty laundry, which will smell just like you, will get scattered around by a bored puppy if given the opportunity.

Garage

This is another area that should be kept relatively off limits to the four-legged members of your family. Dogs love both the smell and taste of antifreeze, which is deadly in even small amounts. Also, many rat poisons and other pest control products are designed to kill without tasting bad.

Nails, screws, paint, petroleum products, fertilizer, sharp objects, tools, electrical outlets, and things that could be knocked over—like bicycles, motorcycles, ladders, and furniture—are all serious hazards that need to be secured before your puppy can be allowed to roam this area.

The Yard

**Australian
Shepherd**

Photo by Mary Bloom©

The backyard can be one of the most dangerous places for a dog. Common yard plants like rhododendrons, azaleas, laurel, crocuses, daffodils, lilies of the valley, irises, amaryllis, and delphiniums are all very poisonous to your dog. Symptoms of plant poisoning can include watery eyes, runny nose, convulsions, depression, anxiety, listlessness, vomiting, and death. As many of these plants as possible should be removed from your gardens and surrounding property, but also keep a careful eye on what your dog takes interest in while in your yard and on walks. Veterinarians, the National Animal Poison Control Center, and even gardeners and landscapers can all provide you with info on what is poisonous and what isn't.

Another major concern is the use of pesticides. Even "semi-toxic" and "non-toxic" alternative chemicals can be very harmful. Remember, just because your dog doesn't seem to eat any of the plants outside, it doesn't mean he won't come in contact with pesticides. Most dogs will absolutely love scurrying through any shrubbery they can get at. They also like to roll around on the ground. If there are chemicals on the plants, then they will soon be on your dog. The dog will then ingest the residues when he bites at an itch. This can also cause skin and eye irritation.

As horrifying as the thought may be, there are other dangers to your dog lurking in your yard. An estimated 2.5 million pets are abducted each year. The fate of these poor creatures is grim, including being sent to a puppy mill or even sold to an animal research lab. If you live in an area where you think dog theft is a possibility, do not leave your pet outside for any considerable amount of time, especially at night. These areas include any heavily populated areas, or any area with a history of pet theft.

CHAPTER 6

Making Way for a Smooth Transition

You've actually picked a dog and the arrival date is near. Now comes one of the most important parts: preparing for your newest little bundle of joy. Whether you've done this before or not, it's important to review the materials you'll need to own a dog. The basic things are obvious—leash, collar, ID tag, crate, food, and bowls for water and food. And don't forget toys! However, there are things you need to know about each one of these, before you go out and buy one and then find out it doesn't work for you.

Plan the Ride Home

The first thing you and your puppy will do together is drive from the shelter or breeder to your home. Remember, this will be not only a strange new environment to the puppy, but also its first lengthy period of time away from its family and first home. Although dogs rarely suffer from what we call motion sickness, the noise, vibrations, and sudden movements can cause lots of anxiety. Some dogs will develop lifelong anxiety associations with driving and will vomit or urinate in a car even before the engine starts.

Labrador Retriever

Photo by Mary Bloom©

You should try to find someone else who can drive you, so you can comfort the puppy. In general, you should use a crate for traveling with your dog. However, for this first trip you should keep the puppy on your lap so you can provide constant comfort. Bring a towel or blanket as well.

Before you put your puppy in the car, make sure it goes to the bathroom. Not only do you want to prevent accidents, but it is also very important not to stop at rest stops with a dog area. A puppy hasn't yet had ample opportunity to build up its immune system, and common dog diseases could be very harmful.

Walking Supplies

If you've spent any time in a pet store, you know that there seem to be as many different contraptions for walking a dog as there are dog breeds. What's best or your dog? A lot of times you can get this information from the breeder. If you aren't comfortable with the breeder's suggestions, you can also consult your veterinarian or a salesperson at a reputable pet store.

Leash

Generally speaking, it's best to actually have two leashes. The first one is the leash you'll use for walks around the block, and most training, especially when working on the command "heel." Leashes or leads come in a variety of colors, textures, and styles—many tend to be made of either leather or nylon. Make sure you get one that's strong enough for the adult you're going to have. And make sure it's not too long. Five to six feet is more than enough.

The second leash you may be required to buy is called a training leash. These are usually very long—maybe eight to ten feet. Many trainers will want you to use this kind of leash when training for obedience. Usually you would use it outside. You teach the dog to stay or come at some distance, letting the leash drag on the ground. If the dog races past you or won't come near enough, you step on the leash and then slowly wind the dog in, praising him as he gets nearer. Again, some trainers use them, some don't. Just be aware that it exists.

Flexi-leads

Flexi-leads are an interesting new twist in the dog-walking world. These operate like the adjustable clotheslines of bygone eras. However, you're holding the contraption, and the dog is at the other end of the line. The idea is that it lets the dog have some freedom in roaming and when it comes nearer to you, the line automatically withdraws and recoils. There is also a button that can stop the flow of the cord at any minute.

These leashes provide people with the opportunity to run their dogs with greater freedom in open spaces where dogs are not allowed off-leash. The only problem they present is a possible burn to those who come too near. If the dog encircles you, or someone you're with, the cord whips around and may run across your unprotected skin, giving you either a cut or a rope burn. You must be alert to any changes of direction, etc. However, they add a fun dimension to the dog-walking experience.

Collar

Like leashes, collars come in various styles and colors, as well as materials. Unlike the leash, however, you will need to buy a collar to match the dog at his current size. You want something that goes around his neck comfortably, that won't slide off the head, but that is comfortably three fingers loose. To measure this, put the collar on, and make it somewhat loose. Your dog needs to breathe. Then see if you can put three fingers between the collar and your dog's neck. Don't pull on the collar to make the space, it should be slack enough that it happens without creating too much tension.

There are many types of collars. Let's talk about the four different kinds: traditional notch collar; choke chain or slip collar; the pronged training collar; electronic barking collar. The traditional notch collar is what we would recommend for the first collar. However, for beginner training, when you get there, a traditional slip collar or choke chain is often preferred. Basically this is a slip-knotted, smooth metal chain that comes in various sizes. The idea is that as the dog pulls harder, he inhibits himself from breathing. He has to stop pulling to breathe. Used properly, this is not cruel at all, and will save you years of wear and tear on your arms and shoulders. This collar should be used only during training, and should not be the collar you use all the time. If you properly train your puppy in the beginning, you will eventually not need this collar. If your dog still strains under this collar after training, then you should go back to school and find a new trainer.

The last two collars are often the refuge of the defeated. The pronged training collar operates like a choke chain, in that it tightens around the dog's neck as he pulls harder. But the pronged collar has dulled metal prongs that poke him in the neck the harder he pulls. Many people use this for dogs they can no longer seem to control when they are walking them. These collars are especially favored by owners of large, furry dogs, like German Shepherds, Alaskan Malamutes, Samoyeds, etc., as sometimes traditional chokers don't work on these breeds. They are also used by people with very strong dogs like a Rottweiler or St. Bernard. The thing that you have to remember is that your dog is stronger than you, and you are using the collar to control him. You're not fooling anyone, though, because both he and you know you're not the one in control. If you have resorted to this collar, see a professional dog trainer and get help for you and your dog. Any good trainer can get a dog on the right path without resorting to these collars.

The last and most well known of collars is the electronic barking collar. When the dog barks, he automatically gets zapped. I am not a personal fan of this type of collar, but I have known people to use them with great results. I have also seen people abuse their dog with one of these contraptions as well. If barking is that big an issue to you, make sure you pick a relatively quiet breed. Especially avoid dogs in the toy or hound groups.

QUESTIONS?

How tight should a dog's collar be?
The collar should not be too snug, nor too loose. The generally accepted rule is that it should fit well, leaving enough room for two to three of your fingers to easily slip between the collar and the puppy.

Head Halters

Head halters should only be used with older animals, and are not recommended for puppies. These are essentially harnesses that slip over and around a dog's head. The theory behind them is that a dog can be led more easily by the head than by the neck (which is usually a very strong part of a dog's anatomy). These halters are very effective, but they have some drawbacks. Firstly, they look like a muzzle, and make poor Spot look like the canine version of Hannibal Lecter. Many people think they are cruel, because they look so cumbersome. It also makes people think that your dog is somehow more dangerous than other dogs, because it looks like he needs a bit more harnessing than others.

Sleeping Accommodations

You should not let your dog sleep on your bed, unless you plan on having it sleep there every night. Even then it is not recommended for puppies, who can be injured from being rolled on. You will most likely need more than one sleeping area for your puppy, who will need lots of short naps.

Crates

Ten years ago this was considered one of the cruel ways to train a dog. Today it is one of the most popular, and rightfully so. It gives the owner a way to control his puppy, and the puppy gets his own room. Dogs are den animals by nature. They like closed spaces that offer protection and when he wants, on his own terms, isolation. There are many puppies today that are much happier than they might have been had they not been crate trained.

Yorkshire Terrier

Photo by Mary Bloom©

Proper crate training starts with the right crate, correctly appointed. Firstly, you want to buy a crate that will fit the adult. Now, you have a puppy. The puppy doesn't need all that space. You want a divider so that you can limit the space to just what the puppy needs.

From there, you want to create the perfect den. By placing towels around the sides and back of the crate, you've just given Fido his own room. Now he needs a bed. Especially for puppies, a few properly folded towels will do. Now it's comfy.

Next the crate needs to be furnished. Give him a few toys and a treat when he goes in. Maybe in the beginning, anytime you give him a treat, it's in his crate. The idea is to create as positive an environment as possible inside the crate.

Crates are made for several different uses. There are crates that are made just for training. These tend to be light-weight aluminum. They're good enough to use for travel if you're talking about traveling with your truck or station wagon. Other crates are made from high-stress plastics, and are quite sturdy. These tend to be the kind that are used for airline travel, etc. If you don't intend on doing any heavy-duty traveling with your dog, a training-quality crate will be just fine.

It's also important to note that crate prices vary greatly. You can often pick up crates cheaply from friends, in the classifieds, or at tag sales, as many dogs outgrow their crates when they get older.

FACTS

There are two basic types of crates: the wire mesh crates that can be taken apart for easier storage, and the hard plastic crates that are typically referred to as airline crates. Both have advantages. The wire crates allow your puppy to see all around him and feel more a part of things; when you want to limit distractions, you can put a sheet over this crate. The crate also folds down when you're not using it, making it easy to store. The airline-type crates offer a ready-made den environment.

Beds

There are a number of well-made dog beds available. Many are inexpensive. They are generally comfortable and vary in quality. Beds are better than folded blankets or a carpet remnant. Remnants can't be cleaned as thoroughly, and folded blankets may end up being a play toy and will require constant folding. The only recommendation between the different doggy beds is that the bed you choose should have an outer shell that can be removed. Many have zippers. Unzip that shell and toss it into the washing machine three or four times a year.

Dog Houses

Usually these are made out of wood or high-impact plastics. They tend to be made for outside dogs. If you are going to keep your dog outside, then you want to make sure the dog house is dry and has some sort of bed. People who keep active sporting and herding breeds consider this an acceptable way to keep a dog, although experts tell us that dogs want to be a part of the family and suffer psychological damage if they spend too much time alone. Active dogs, who spend their days with family members and other dogs probably don't suffer this trauma. However, if you commute and no one is at home during the day, and you keep your dog outside night and day, why do you have a dog?

If your pooch will stay outside during the day, though, you should provide him or her with a dog house, to keep them cool in the shade in summer; out of the cold winds of winter; and dry during April showers.

Identification

One of the most important things that your puppy could ever have is an ID tag. There are numerous ways that cannot be anticipated in which your puppy can become separated from you. Proper identification is extremely important. It's also the law!

One time we had a friend whose dog was in a state park, and he took off after some deer. This was a well-trained dog, with obedience training, but he disregarded his owner when the smell of venison beckoned. As it was late in the day, the owners were soon looking for the dog in the dark. They were out there for many hours before they found out the dog had been hit by a car some time earlier. The police could not contact the family because the dog had no tags on when he was lost.

FACTS

Remember, all dogs six months of age or older require a collar and license by law.

Sometimes things happen that seem to be beyond our control. We take things for granted. Make sure you get ID tags that give the puppy's name and your address and phone number.

With dognapping becoming more and more prevalent, other ID methods have gained in popularity. Another way to permanently ID your puppy is to put a tattoo on him. Many people tattoo their puppies with their puppy's AKC or CKC registration number. Other people use their driver's license number or their social security number. These are usually done somewhere on the underside of your puppy.

Another identification tool gaining in popularity is the microchip. These are usually implanted with a needle. The injection of it, however, looks worse than it is. These chips are permanent for the life of the dog, and are easily scanned. In the past, competing technologies made these difficult to scan, but today systems are better. Fees can range from twenty-five to fifty dollars, and the process can be done quickly and easily.

Toys

All you have to do is go to pet and toy superstores and spend five minutes in each to know that there are almost as many toys for pets as there are for children—and you will have fun choosing from among them. Some of our personal favorites are things like Kongs, tennis balls, Nylabone Frisbees, and plush toys that squeak. When buying plush for a dog, make sure it's manufactured to take the beating that a dog will inflict on it. Kongs are cone-shaped rubber pieces that are seemingly indestructible, and dogs love them. Frisbees are a lot of fun, and dogs love them too. But most Frisbees, while they feel pretty strong to you and me, are made out of a plastic that just can't take the pounding that a dog's teeth can dish out. That's why the Nylabone Frisbee is the best. Your dog can play Frisbee with you all day long and not puncture it. It also has a little bone-shaped handle on the top, so it makes it easier for your dog to pick it up. And of course your dog will need tennis balls to fetch. Tennis balls are especially good because they float.

ALERT

Toys you don't want to buy include those meant for children, action figures, plush, any plastic object with a liquid center, footballs, basketballs, soccer balls, kickballs (they will puncture and destroy these four), baseballs (they'll rip the hide cover off and then who knows what'll happen to all the insides), anything made of glass, and balls of twine.

Preparing Time with Your New Friend

A puppy away from its mother and littermates will suffer some form of separation anxiety its first couple of nights home. In the past, some suggested leaving the puppy alone for a while to allow it to adjust to its new surroundings. This is unnecessarily cruel. It has been found that by providing a new puppy with abundant initial attention—for the first three to five days—will help socialize your pet, reduce or eliminate separation anxiety stress, and can dramatically speed up the housebreaking process.

If at all possible, it is urged that the puppy be given lots of attention its first few days. Basically, the only time the puppy should be left alone is when it is eating, sleeping, or happily playing on its own. This doesn't mean everyone in the household must constantly be there—all the better if you have multiple people taking turns caring for the puppy. This will help the puppy get used to different members of the house and meeting different people in general.

If you are alone in your puppy-adopting endeavor, you should consider taking a few days off from work, maybe around a weekend. If you absolutely cannot spare a specific day, you should at least try to find a suitable sitter to fill in. This shouldn't be too hard; who wouldn't want to spend a day with a puppy?

ESSENTIALS

For a chew toy to be effective, it has to be interesting. What may seem interesting to us won't necessarily be interesting to a puppy. What IS interesting to almost all puppies, though, is food. Choose toys that can include food somehow. The best are hard rubber Kongs or sterilized, hollow bones. Stuff or smear the insides of these with peanut butter or a bit of dog food. Put the food where it will be a challenge to eat but certainly an enticement. This can keep a puppy busy for hours!

Getting the Whole Household Involved

Training my dogs was hard enough, but watching my family do things that might diminish my training efforts was even harder. Since I wasn't allowed to have housedogs, opportunities for encouraging begging and overexcitability were, thankfully, minimal. And fortunately they paid relatively little attention to my dogs. Aside from not wanting to burden anyone with my responsibilities, I was terrified to let my family care for my dogs in my absence. In their limited interactions with the dogs, I found they were too casual and trusting. I worked hard to keep my dogs well groomed, socialized, and mannerly. My family construed my conscientiousness as being cruel or overprotective. Consequently, they would occasionally, in their goodness, take the dogs out for a run in a burr-filled field, or be unaware of how closely dogs should be watched when around strange children, or fail to stop foolish adults from giving unfamiliar dogs bear-hugs or staring them down while making growling and barking noises. They'd also leave the dogs outside unattended and unsupervised in the unfenced yard.

Frustrated as I was, my dogs and I survived. But what can you do if your family consists of difficult, contradictory personalities?

ESSENTIALS
There is nothing cuter than children and puppies. But children, especially young children, are not experienced in handling such small animals. They don't know their own strength and how delicate puppies are. Puppies are not stuffed animals. You really need to tell your children not to squeeze too hard and hurt the newest member of your family.

Perhaps one is a wimp who tries to talk you out of doing nasty obedience that will ruin the dog's free spirit; each time you enforce a rule, he commiserates with the dog. Maybe another is a loudmouth, giving what he thinks is much-needed training advice, demonstrating his expertise by yelling commands to you and the dog. Maybe there's a talker who is always jabberjawing and saying nothing, then wonders why he gets treated like an inanimate object by the dog. Or perhaps there's a secret saboteur who watches what you do, and figures out methods to undo your hard work by feeding table food during meals, letting the dog pull on the leash or hang his head out of the car window, or inviting him on the furniture.

I wish people problems were as easy to solve as dog problems. Each family situation is unique. But in general:

- Express and demonstrate your concern for the dog's well-being by taking charge of his training, housing, supervision, and care, including health, exercise, and grooming.
- Make arrangements for someone trusted to handle these tasks when you are unavailable.
- Assign duties, with specific details as to how to perform them, to interested household members.
  Remember:

1. No matter how common your philosophies, no two people will agree 100 percent on how to raise a dog.
2. Expect to be annoyed, sometimes, by family members.
3. Understand that what others do can't sabotage your authority. The dog will learn what YOU expect from him, by the way you react to his behavior in your presence.

ESSENTIALS

For owners who desire their dogs to have access to the outdoors, a small doggy door built into the back door can be useful. At first, keep the doggy door propped in the open position, and lure the dog through with a favorite treat. Once the dog is going through regularly, begin to gradually close the door, a bit each day, until after a week or so the door has been completely closed. If you do this gradually enough, the dog will learn that it can pass through the door with its head to gain access to the outside. The only disadvantage is that it does not discriminate between dogs. You may even find that other than dogs, raccoons, or squirrels might figure it out!

Wrap-Up: Complete List of Puppy Supplies

The number and variety of supplies for dogs and puppies can be somewhat overwhelming. Don't sweat about it too much. If you ever find yourself lacking something, it's only a quick jaunt to the pet store away.

You will also find that different dogs will need different things. Consult with your breeder for any special items your puppy may need.

Essential Items

- Puppy food
- Food and water bowls
- Collar and lead
- Crate or carrier
- ID tags

- Toys
- Brush
- Nail trimmer
- Toothbrush and dog toothpaste

ESSENTIALS

In addition to a nail trimmer, be sure to get some styptic powder. Styptic powder will quickly stop the bleeding that can result from accidentally trimming your dogs nails too short.

There is one simple rule with dog bowls. Make sure you buy a bowl with a wide enough base that is difficult to tip over. Especially with puppies, bowls can become playthings. You want to avoid letting this happen. With smaller dogs, obviously, you don't want to have too small a bowl. With larger dogs, make sure the bowl is not just bigger, but a little heavier. Many are made from high impact plastic, and have bottoms that are weighted with sand. Others are heavy ceramic or stainless steel. They are all about the same. You need two bowls: one for water, one for food.

Other Items You Should Consider

- Training treats
- Bitter Apple (a foul-tasting spray that keeps dogs from chewing things)
- Doggy bed
- Pooper scooper
- Baby-gates
- Lint brush or pet-hair remover
- Newspapers for accident control

CHAPTER 7

Your Puppy's First Month

The most important thing to remember during your first month with a new puppy is to establish routine immediately. The way you treat your puppy now is the way your future dog will expect, even demand, to be treated later. Everything from where your dog will sleep, to when it is first fed, to what behaviors are acceptable should be set in stone from day one. You must also set it in your puppy's mind that you are the alpha member of the household. Spoiling a puppy can give it a sense of superiority that can cause problems later on, including aggressiveness.

The First Day Home

The first time you bring your puppy home it's the equivalent of the Oscars for the puppy. The excitement is palpable. The oohs and aaaahs begin. There's lots of laughter and cooing. Everyone wants to handle the new little feller. Plus there are the sights, sounds, and smells of the new house. All of this can be a little overwhelming for a little guy.

One of the first things you want to watch out for is not to overstimulate the poor little puppy. While everyone will want to hold on to the little one, one of the best things you can do is to minimize this tendency and to let your puppy wander a little. Letting the puppy explore and understand his or her surroundings is the best way to establish a relationship with the little pup. It will also help to stimulate and solidify his confidence in himself and his surroundings.

Establish Routine Immediately

The first day is when you need to begin to establish the routines that will carry you for the rest of your puppy's life. You should remember to establish consistent feeding times. You should also get your new puppy used to the collar and leash. While playing out in the backyard is fun and nice, it is important to establish walking routines. A walking routine will help Junior get used to the collar and the leash quickly. Going for a walk will also help you when it comes to socializing your puppy.

Establishing water, food, and sleeping arrangements will help your puppy be a more confident and happy dog who will be a friend and companion of value for many years to come.

ALERT

Leave the water out! Do not try to limit your puppy's water in an effort to curtail his or her urination cycle. This could have deadly consequences. Leave the water out and let him drink!

That First Night

Let's get this first thing right out there in the open. No puppies sleep with you on your bed. It's the wrong thing to do. When a dog sleeps on your bed, you're confusing them. They think you're top dog, especially coming into your house. If you let them sleep on the bed, they think they've moved up the ladder of success. You need to stay on top, especially in the beginning. The dog stays on the floor, if not in his crate.

ESSENTIALS

Here's an idea to help your puppy to sleep more soundly. One trick that several trainers have told me works very well is to place a clock that ticks, wrapped in a towel or blanket, in the crate with the dog. The constant tick-tock of the clock simulates the heartbeat of another dog, and will help your dog to nod off much more effectively.

Sleeping Dogs Don't Lie

While your puppy will be as excited as you when it comes to his homecoming, by the end of the night, much of the realities of the day will come crashing down on him. Puppies require plenty of sleep to begin with. But the first thing to consider is where to place the crate.

Many people's inclination is to place the crate in the kitchen. It's the floor that can take the most abuse and the place where everybody meets. However, many dog experts will tell you that, especially in a family where the house will be empty for a large part of he day, you should let your dog sleep in the same room as you—but not in the same bed. Since dogs are den animals, sleeping in the same room with you counts as spending time with you. So, placing the crate in the bedroom is a good idea. However, if you want the dog to remain in the kitchen during the time you are away from home, then maybe that's where you would prefer to put it.

The Big Cry

Now, regardless of how wonderful you are, and how wonderful your family and home are, your puppy is going to be miserable on the first night. It will dawn on your little puppy at the end of the day that his brothers and sisters and mother and former owner are not with him. He is alone with these strange people, in these strange surroundings, in this strange cage. Where is everybody? So concerned will he be with their location, he will start calling out for them—or you. He just doesn't want to be alone.

Petit Basset Griffon Vendéen

Photo by Mary Bloom©

The worst possible thing for you to do would be to console him. This would be spoiling him. Your dog is going to have to be able to sleep alone at one point or another. The longer you postpone the big cry, the more difficult it will be to cure Rover when he gets older.

The second worst thing you could do is to scold the poor little fellow. There is no doubt in any dog behaviorist's mind that this would cause more trouble down the line than you would care to imagine. By coming to the crate you are reinforcing the idea that if he calls out, you will come.

For this reason, some experts will combine the first two ideas and suggest the following: for the first week or two, let Junior stay downstairs until he's worked out this whole crying thing. Then you can bring him upstairs. He will make some noise his first night, but once he gets the message that he's not going to get up on that bed with you, he'll eventually settle down and go to sleep.

Regardless, you will feel heartless not rescuing the puppy, especially on that first night. Be strong, and both of you will sleep better in the nights to come.

The First Week Home

The most important thing to remember to do in the first week is to establish routine. If you want your dog to succeed, you really should establish a routine, so that Junior knows what you want and when.

You want to establish a routine for the entire day. You want to establish a schedule. A walk in the morning? Then breakfast? A walk in mid-morning? A walk just after noon? A walk around the late afternoon? After dinner? Two walks and then bedtime? Regardless of when you want to establish the walks, you should do your best to make them happen at the same time every day, as much as possible.

Crate time should also be regimented. Much as Rover doesn't want to, sometimes going to bed is just what the doctor ordered. Getting the proper amount of sleep is very important. You can throw in a few toys, and maybe a treat. If the puppy doesn't go to sleep at first, don't worry. And don't rescue him or give in if he begins to whine.

Naming Your Puppy

There are a lot of things you need to take into account when you name your animal. Certainly names go in and out of fashion. Spot and Rover and Fido are not as popular as they once were. King, Baron, and Major are still some of the most popular names. Benji isn't as common as it used to be. Neither is Lassie. However, there are some practical considerations when deciding on a name for your new family member.

The most important rule when naming your family pet is KISS: Keep It Simple, Stupid. I have heard of some of the oddest names for pets of all kinds. But dogs, more than most, are the animals that require the most interaction. So before you name your dog Phillipedes (the guy who ran the first marathon), or Bacchus (the god of wine), remember it's got to be a name the dog will be able to respond to, or one that you will be comfortable saying over and over again.

Something short, no more than three syllables, is generally a good idea.

ESSENTIALS

A dog will actually be able to recognize a two-syllable name better than a single syllable. One of the reasons is that single-syllable names often sound like many other sounds your dog will hear. So if you decide you want to name your dog "Sam," consider calling him "Sammie" as a general rule.

Teaching the Puppy Its Name

This is the easiest thing you will do. Call the dog, energetically. Every time the dog responds by coming to you, offer it a treat. You don't have to give it a Big Mac, just give it something small—a part of a small treat, a liver treat, something soft and edible. Make sure it's something the puppy likes. Repeat this as often as you like. Eventually, you want to keep calling the puppy, only offering treats occasionally, until the dog approaches you without treats.

Of course, the dog, whether with treat or without, should be highly and generously praised each time he or she comes to you, responding to your entreaty.

If only everything were that easy!

Changing the Name of an Adopted Puppy

Sometimes, when you adopt an older puppy, you might be horrified by the name someone else had given to your dog. Such was the case when I adopted Exley. I named him after my favorite writer, Fredrick Exley, who wrote a wonderful book called *A Fan's Notes*. While I will admit that Exley is an odd name, it was far better than the one he came with—Spike. I really disliked the name Spike, and discussed it with the rescue person. I was happy to find out that you could teach a dog a new name.

First, you would follow the same pattern as described previously. The training method itself doesn't change, what you say changes. In the beginning, you want to call the dog by its given name. Then, after about a few days, you want call the dog by both names. Use the name you want to change it to first. For example, I used to call out, "Exley, Spike," and when the dog came, I rewarded him. I stopped using the name Spike after about three or four days. But I practiced a lot in that time.

I did this in the home, or training in the park in a dog run, and in the backyard. I never let my dog go off lead during this period without being in an enclosed environment. It was only after several weeks of this kind of training, and when I was absolutely sure of the completion of this training, that I began long lead exercises, which we will discuss later.

Dogs are not actors or rock stars. You cannot constantly change your dog's name. Once in a lifetime is probably enough. Constant name changes will lead to confusion and difficulties where training and obedience are concerned, as well as a host of other problems.

FACTS

Adopted puppies experience a lot of stress. They have been separated from their mother, their litter mates, and the last home they knew. Usually these dogs will act out different things, in order to get attention or gain acceptance. Sometimes they will repeat behaviors you think are unacceptable, but may have been acceptable in their previous home. Have patience with the adopted puppy. He desperately wants to be accepted, though there are times when you may question it. Usually these dogs crave attention and are thrilled to be in your home. They require a little extra leeway and in return will repay you with a lot of extra love.

Handling Your Puppy Properly

The easiest way to pick up your puppy without risking injury is to reach under his chest (brisket) between his front legs with one hand and place the fingers of your other hand between his two rear legs, keeping your thumb under his tail. As you straighten your knees to stand, smoothly bring him into your chest so he is leaning into you. Puppies can get wiggly when you least expect it, so make certain his weight is fully supported by your hands, fingers, and forearms. Young children and awkward people shouldn't pick up the puppy and, instead, should either get down on his level or let him sit on their lap if he is small and calm enough. Many puppies do not like to be carried, but all should learn to tolerate being picked up and held briefly.

Beagle

Photo by Mary Bloom©

As for general handling by you and others, gentleness is key. Rough handling, even under the guise of play, can hurt even the sturdiest looking puppy, and can create bad habits in the future. It is very important that "strangers" meet your puppy, this will help your dog learn to accept strangers in stride rather than show signs of timidity or aggression.

Practice Proper Habits from the Start

It cannot be stressed enough that you need to maintain proper habits from the start. Almost all "bad dog" habits result from the first couple months of the puppy's life in its new home. Practicing good habits with your puppy will help it grow up to be a well-rounded member of the family. It is virtually impossible to "punish" a dog. Even when you catch a dog in the act of doing something wrong, it will more likely just develop fear of cruelty, rather than associate punishment with deed.

Australian Shepherd

Photo courtesy of Mary Bloom

Labrador Retriever

Photo courtesy of Mary Bloom

German Shorthaired Pointer

Jack Russell Terrier

Shetland Sheepdog

Photo courtesy of Mary Bloom

Dalmatian

Photo courtesy of Karen Taylor

Miniature Schnauzer

Photo courtesy of Karen Taylor

Brussels Griffon

Photo courtesy of Mary Bloom

Miniature Dachshund

Photo courtesy of Mary Bloom

Great Dane

Cavalier King Charles Spaniel

Shih Tzu

Cairn Terrier

Boxer

Border Collie

Pug

Photo courtesy of Mary Bloom

Petit Basset Griffon Vendéen

Photo courtesy of Mary Bloom

Bichon Frisé

Photo courtesy of Mary Bloom

Chihuahua

Weimaraner

CHAPTER 8

Puppy Nutrition

There are many puppy formulas out on the market today. Do you need to feed your new friend a puppy mix? Not necessarily. But if you want the best results and you want your puppy to have the best chances of growing up strong and healthy for years to come, it's a good idea. Each brand available in the marketplace today has its specific advantages and disadvantages. However, they all tend to be higher in protein than other brands. This is good. The idea is that it's providing the minerals, nutrients, and proteins that growing dogs need to establish strong bones and muscles.

FACTS

Puppies get to eat more often than adult dogs, because of their special nutritional needs.

- Four times a day in small amounts; usually this is from age one to six months
- Three times a day from age six to eleven months
- Twice a day thereafter

Foods to Start Your Puppy With

The breeder you buy your puppy from will be able to clue you in on what type of food is best for your puppy. How long should you keep your puppy on a puppy formula? Again, many of the manufacturers will recommend a specific time to switch over to a more normal, adult diet. However, a good rule of thumb would be that at approximately eighteen months, it's probably a good time to wean your dog from a puppy formula.

Maintain the Breeder's Food

When you buy your puppy, ask the breeder, pet store, or shelter what kind of food the puppy has been eating and try to maintain that food, at least for the beginning. If you are buying a puppy from a good breeder, she'll insist you use her dog food for a while. You are best off listening to her advice. Many times, you'll be bringing a puppy home, and he's bound to be nervous already. You are trying to keep things the same, for a smooth transition. Since dogs sometimes have adverse reactions to sudden changes in diet, it's best to try to maintain some kind of continuity, so as to keep him as calm as possible.

Make Changes Gradually

If you are going to change dog foods, you really want to try to do it gradually. If you are feeding two cups in the morning, and you want to change Fido's diet, you should do this in stages. Give him one cup of old food and one cup of new food for several days, and then make the switch. Again, the idea is to keep mental continuity as well as physical continuity. A sudden change in diet may elicit adverse reactions, either emotionally or physically. Make this kind of transition as painless as possible.

FACTS

When you feed your dog for only ten minutes twice a day, you are encouraging your dog to think of you as the alpha dog. In the wild, a dog eats according to his station, and the alpha dog establishes that rotation. You establish and keep your place as alpha when you establish the eating time.

What Dog Food Contains

This is as simple as shopping for yourself: look at the ingredient list. You're looking for some basic factors here: proteins, carbohydrates, vitamins, minerals, fats, and preservatives.

Proteins could be any type of meat or meat by-product, such as chicken, lamb, beef, or chicken meal. These are best for your dog. Many foods, however, use vegetable proteins. These are harder for your dog to digest, so while you will invariably find them in his food, make sure they are not a sizable source of that food's ingredients. Rice, corn, or other some other grain should also be in the top four ingredients.

Carbohydrates in small quantities are good for dogs. Providing lots of carbohydrates in a dog's diet could result in bloat at the worst, and a busy day following Rover on the sidewalks. Wheat and soy can sometimes trigger an allergic reaction in dogs. Be aware of this.

Fat is good—for dogs anyway. You can give them the oils of roasted meats, etc., in moderation. These fats contain oils essential to help keep up healthy skin and a shiny coat. Don't let those drippings go to waste, but also, let's not feed Spot a dish of this stuff either. You can drizzle a meal here and there with pan drippings. Some breeders and other dog experts give their dogs fat, like lard, bacon fat, etc. The problem is that this stuff goes bad easily. I've heard of plenty of dog people who've given their dogs rancid fat. Stay away from this. This is an easy thing to remember—when you're on a fat-free diet, make sure you throw Spot a few extra calories. Just don't overdo it. What some responsible dog owners do is put one or two teaspoons of vegetable oil mixed in with their food.

Vitamins and minerals are an important part of your dog's life, especially if you have a puppy. Many foods are vitamin and mineral fortified; however, vitamins tend to lose their potency very easily. It's not a bad idea to supplement your dog's diet with a vitamin regimen, especially if you have an active dog.

Preservatives are important in ensuring the quality of the dog food for a specific amount of time. Manufacturers use these ingredients to try and maintain some sense of freshness, taste, and texture. However, you want to make sure that many of the preservatives are listed toward the bottom of the ingredient list. Just like you, your dog doesn't need that many preservatives.

It's important to look at the order in which the ingredients appear. Make sure that the higher-quality ingredients are at the top of the list. You really want two proteins (neither of which is vegetable based) before you get to the carbohydrates. Any kind of chicken, beef, or lamb, or any kind of meal from those meats, is a good bet. Any kind of additives should also go toward the bottom. Some additives cause an allergic response.

FACTS

When dogs eat, they are telling you a lot about themselves. Maybe they don't like the food. Maybe the food is spoiled. Maybe the dog isn't feeling well. If one of our dogs ever walked away from his or her dish, the first thing we'd do is take that dog to the vet, if we hadn't already noticed something strange.

Types of Food

There are so many puppy foods on the market today that trying to do a synopsis would be insane. For the most part, as long as you buy a brand name dog food, you are probably in good hands.

Many years ago, this may have not been the case. There were a handful of manufacturers that dominated the industry—Kal Kan, Alpo, and Purina were among those dominant giants. They manufactured safe dog food. It wasn't exactly exciting, but then again, no one was going to die eating it. Over the years there have been changes. Challenges by new products like Gaines Burgers occurred, but the status quo was maintained. Then upstarts arose and found footing. First there were gourmet foods, and then "scientifically engineered" foods. Today it is a billion-dollar industry. However, as the pet food market has grown, many of the old standbys had to regroup and repackage.

So today, most of the brand names are of pretty good quality. Generics are still very questionable, and are better off avoided. Today, manufacturers spend millions on research and development in order to find some edge in this very competitive marketplace. Capitalism has benefited our canine friends, as they now have a healthier, better tasting, and wider variety of foods than ever before. However, that does not mean that all dog foods are the same. There many different things you need to look for depending on the age and circumstances of your dog.

FACTS

Kal Kan for years was one of the top dog food brands in America. Back then not too many people really cared what was in dog food. With the onslaught of heightened competition between the major manufacturers, and the new high-end foods coming out, Kal Kan was losing major market share. What's a dog to do? The execs came up with a plan. They made the food more nutritious and recast the food as an upscale brand—and thus Pedigree was born. Today, Pedigree is one of the best-selling dog foods in America.

Dry vs. Wet

Of course the first question anyone asks is should they feed dry food or wet—meaning dry food or canned meats. As was stated before, you should ask your breeder what she feeds her dogs. But not all of you bought from a breeder, and so you are wondering what would be the best possible thing to feed your hungry new addition to the household. Canned food and dry food are formulated to provide your dog with the same types and mixtures of proteins, fats, carbohydrates, vitamins, and minerals. However, canned food is more expensive because it is better, right? Wrong! Canned food is more expensive because it costs more to package and ship! In many cases, while dry food contains the same thing canned food does, it's different because all the water has been taken out of it.

Shih Tzu

Photo by Alice Su©

I have talked to many breeders and dog experts, and the general consensus is that most high-quality dog people feed their dogs commercial, name-brand dry dog foods and supplement those foods occasionally with canned food. There's no denying that canned food adds great flavor to a meal, and a little added meat, which dogs love. However, as we talked about earlier, mixing in food may adversely affect their digestion. Be careful, and monitor their reactions. In some dogs, this change may cause diarrhea or vomiting. If this is the case, don't do it. However, there are also those dogs who have a constitution that would allow them to eat an entire side of beef and it wouldn't bother them in the least. If your dog does have a sensitive digestive system, then keep them on one type of food (the one that causes them the least trouble) for a majority of the time.

With dry food, there are things you need to watch out for. The first thing to keep in mind is freshness. Your first inclination may be to hop in the car and to run to some price warehouse so that you can buy some industrial-sized bag of dog food, enough to feed all the dogs in New York City for a week, and save a few dollars in volume. That way you won't have to go buying this stuff all the time. Well, hold on there, Dollar Bill. This is the worst of all the possible options you could face. The one thing you don't want to do with dry food is store it for a long period of time. First, the vitamins, which we talked about earlier, are fragile, and may break down very quickly sitting in your basement or pantry. You need to keep this stuff in a COOL, DRY place. The idea is to keep the food as fresh as possible for as long as possible. The longer you keep it, the worse it gets. And it will go stale if you decide to warehouse vast quantities of it.

The Dog Food You Use Depends on Your Dog's Stage and Activity Level

As we talked about earlier, twenty years ago all dog foods were essentially the same, no matter what kind of dog you had. Oh, there were a few high-end brands only breeders or sportsmen bought, but now there are numerous brands and types available to the average person. Are they necessary? Some are. Read the following to see which one suits your dog.

FACTS

Free feeding encourages picky eating. Some dogs learn that if they don't eat what's there, if they wait long enough, you'll break down and feed them something homemade. Do not do it! They'll eat the next time, don't worry.

Puppy Food

Is it really important that I buy Rover some kind of puppy food? Aren't all dog foods really the same? All dog foods are not the same. Puppy foods are specially formulated to help develop strong bones and good muscle mass. If you read the ingredients, you'll see that puppy foods tend to offer more protein and vitamins than normal dog foods, and are formulated for excellent health at this very important developmental stage.

If it's so good for him, shouldn't I then just keep feeding it to him even after he's grown up? No! It's like being a human. You drink lots of milk when you're growing up, to help develop properly. But as you get older, milk become less important, and too much milk, when you're older, may lead to some minor health problems. When your dog is old enough, you should switch him to a food more appropriate for his situation.

Maintenance Diet

After your puppy has grown, and is older than eighteen months, then you'll want to switch him over to an adult diet. This is just regular dog food, more or less. In this category, though, there is a multitude of choices. There are high-protein formulas, natural formulas, lamb and rice, chicken and rice, beef, liver, etc. There are a few different things here to consider. If you have a happy, healthy, active pet, these foods are for you. Some are designed for very active dogs, and some are better for less active dogs. Regardless, you can't go too far wrong in this category with a healthy, adult dog. If you think your dog might need something different, or if you have any questions, maybe you should talk to your veterinarian.

Lite Formula

Uh, oh! Rover's had too many snacks! Does your dog look like a barrel with four legs? Does it look like Fido suddenly went from happily bounding up the stairs to trudging breathlessly while his stomach drags over the corner of every step? Then you need a lite formula dog food to get Rover back into good shape.

FACTS

Don't start feeding your puppy a lite formula because you think he's getting fat. Lite formulas are for adult dogs. Feeding a puppy lite formula dog food can deprive your puppy of much needed and valuable proteins, vitamins, and minerals. No dog under the age of two should be eating lite formula. If you're going to cut back on anything, it should be the treats.

Unfortunately, Americans have brought their battle of the bulge to their dog's doorstep. And many major manufacturers have joined in the fray. Lite foods are meant to delivery the equivalent number of vitamins, minerals, and proteins as other dog foods, but with reduced calories. Follow the directions and don't overindulge your dog with treats. Remember, while you can be reckless with your own health, you shouldn't be reckless with someone else's—especially your dog's!

Make sure to note that these formulas are not meant as a long-term solution to you overfeeding your dog. Read the directions carefully. These are usually very good, and thoroughly researched by the pet food manufacturers. Sometimes, less active adults who are not seniors may go on these diets for longer stretches than others. Ask your veterinarian for his advice.

Hypoallergenic Diet

Prescription diets are available from your veterinarian. Many of these foods are available from large pet superstores or feed warehouses, if not from your veterinarian. The labels on these foods will explain what they contain, and what allergies or illnesses they are meant to deal with. Never attempt to put your puppy on any kind of restrictive diet without first consulting your veterinarian.

When and How Much to Feed

As always, there are no hard-and-fast rules about how many times a day a dog should be fed. The idea is to maintain a desired body weight—not too heavy, not too thin. It's the amount of food they're eating that remains the most important thing. Other indicators of a happy and healthy dog are the brightness of the eyes, the shininess of the coat, and the activity level of the dog.

Dogs by nature are worse than humans. Many of them would eat to the point of bursting. I've certainly known my share of humans who would do that too, but dogs do like to eat, in general, and many experts believe that twice a day is correct. It's fun for them as well as a good way for them not to fill up on one meal.

Some experts would argue that instead of making both meals of equal size, you should vary the size between the two feeding times—say morning and evening. These experts argue that you should feed them the larger meal in the morning. It will give them more time to digest it, and maybe burn it off. Others argue that especially if you're gone all day, you may not want to load your dog up, and that way they might be a little sleepier and better behaved while you're off at work.

The following houseplants can be deadly to a mouthy puppy:

- Mistletoe
- Nightshade
- Oleander
- Philodendron
- Poinsettia
- Potato leaves

How Much?

How often you feed your dog is one thing. How much you feed your dog is another! Different dogs require different amounts of food. You would not feed a Shih-Tzu the same as you would a Retriever.
You really should feed a dog what he or she can eat in ten or twelve minutes' time, twice a day. Any more than that is probably not necessary. Some dog foods include feeding instructions on the backs of their packages. You might want to look at this as a guideline when you begin. You'll soon learn if you're feeding them too much, as they will start to grow a little heftier. You should immediately cut down on their rations if this occurs.

A dog whose diet is high in vegetable sugars (from things such as apples, onions, and any product containing corn) will probably have an unusual amount of gas. Dogs cannot digest many plant sugars, which means those sugars are left to the naturally occurring bacteria in their intestines. When this bacteria gets ahold of the sugar, that all-too-familiar gas is produced. The best way to avoid this problem is to avoid giving your pup people snacks, especially the sweet ones!

What if my dog doesn't finish? Too bad. Scheduled eating times force picky eaters to eat when they're hungry. If you're dog doesn't finish this time, then they will the next time. If they don't, then maybe you should try a new food.

Snacks and Treats

From organic cookies cut in fun shapes to beefy chewsticks and beyond, dog treats come in every size, shape, color, and flavor imaginable. There are animal parts (ears, noses, feet, etc.) that dogs love, and the venerable Milk Bones. The idea is that these treats make dogs' lives fun and extra tasty. However, the word on treats is MODERATION!

Unlike you, your puppy cannot feed himself. So, if he develops weight problems due to overeating, especially with things like treats, only you are to blame.

Basset Hound

Photo by Mary Bloom©

Look, let's be honest, the urge is incredibly strong to treat our dogs, especially puppies. However, weight gain is a problem for puppies and dogs just like it is for humans, and may cause all kinds of illnesses. Treats are not as nutritionally balanced as they are tasty. All treats are bad for your dog in excess, however, they usually are not harmful in (you guessed it) moderation.

Treats are especially useful during training of any kind, whether it's the simple sit/stay or something more difficult like agility training etc. Treats are a wonderful way to get your dog's attention and encourage good behavior.

Water

The same as it is for humans, water is one of the most important elements in a dog's life. It may be even more important. Man has the ability to sweat, which is an involuntary function of the body that cools the body off in times of extreme heat. The dog does not sweat. The dog tries to cool off his body by staying out of the sun, sleeping in a cool dry place. He also pants a lot, trying to draw in cool air to replace the hot air in his body. But the main thing a dog does when he's hot is drink. This cools him off better than anything.

> Some dogs are allergic to plastic! Just to be on the safe side, stainless steel or ceramic bowls should be used.

ALERT

It's important to leave out a clean bowl of water at all times for your puppy. Never regulate their water supply. They can't tell you when they're thirsty, so it's vital that you leave it out. When they're thirsty, they'll drink.

Another thing, don't let your dog drink out of the toilet. This is not a substitute for a water bowl. I've known few dogs who have died from it, but there are all kinds of bacteria in there. And while your dog has very strong enzymes that might break down lots of organisms that our bodies can't, it's still not a good idea, no matter how funny or harmless it may seem. You never know, maybe they could pass on some of these germs to you.

CHAPTER 9
Grooming

Grooming your puppy is very important, because the more time you spend taking care of your dog, the happier and healthier it will be. You may look at your puppy and think that you don't have to worry about most of the grooming chores until it's older. Not true—it's a good idea to start grooming immediately. A puppy is easier to handle, and since the initial grooming will be very light, you can be extra gentle. The idea here is that grooming is not only about making a puppy pretty, it's about health maintenance—defeating problems before they arise.

ESSENTIALS

There are several types of brushes available depending on what kind of coat your dog has. Ask the store manager which is best for your dog. You may want a variety to get through the undercoat and the longer hairs. Some grooming tools are listed as follows:

- Slicker brush
- Pin brush
- Bristle brush
- Mat rake
- Shedding blade
- Curry Comb
- Hound mitt
- Metal combs with wide teeth, medium teeth, and fine teeth

- Styptic pencil
- Cotton balls
- Ear Cleaner
- Shampoo
- Conditioner (optional)
- Extra towels
- Flea comb
- Toenail clippers (guillotine-style, scissors style, or grinder)

Brushing

Now, why do you suppose that many dogs would stand by you all day long and let you pet them, and not let you brush them for a few minutes? More times than not the average owner is using the wrong comb, especially in the beginning. Brushing is a great thing to do. It helps keep the coat in good shape, which also promotes better skin care. Brushing also eliminates things like burrs and matting, and will alert you immediately to the presence of fleas.

FACTS

Just because you've chosen a shorthair breed doesn't excuse you from brushing your puppy. There are many benefits to brushing—and your puppy will love the attention.

Brushing is also a way to work with your dog and examine more closely his coat and skin. If there are inconsistencies or infections or rashes, you'll see them a lot more quickly and be able to counteract them much more effectively if you treat your dog to regular brushing. In many cases, brushing is the time when many owners find out about things that are seriously wrong with their dogs, like tumors (usually in older dogs) as well as melanomas.

Boxer

Photo by Mary Bloom©

Puppies don't have a lot of hair, so make sure to use a soft brush. Some experts use very soft human brushes, especially in the beginning. Otherwise you're just scraping the skin and hurting the dog. Especially early on, many people buy those little metal combs and go raking it over poor young Spot's back. Ouch! You'd wrestle too! Remember that during these sessions, you want to be making as many happy, cooing noises as possible. Hollering and spitting out commands is a bad way to try to get your dog to work with you on this. And as the puppy grows up, you want the little devil to have a good experience with this, so that it is not a struggle throughout both of your lives.

FACTS

You've seen them—the poor, hideous creatures with the summer cut. An English Sheepdog shaved down in summer. An Afghan hound shaved down. Listen, if your dog wanted a summer cut, dogs would find a way to do it themselves. Many experts agree that summer cuts are not in Rover's best interest. It is thought that many hairier dogs don't suffer nearly as much as we think. It is believed that their undercoats tend to keep them cooler in summer than man originally imagined.

Burrs and matted fur are the two enemies of longhaired dogs. These are problems that need to be dealt with. If you don't understand why, then put a great big wad of bubble gum in your hair and try to live with it for a week. It's a real pain. That's the way dogs feel about matting and burrs. In some cases, you can work these problems out. Sometimes pouring a little vegetable oil on the spot will help you work burrs out of longer hair. Otherwise they need to be cut. For the most part, you should just cut out matting as well. Trying to work out matting is a difficult and painstaking job, with few rewards. If you cut the fur, it's less painful for Spot, and in the end, the hair will grow back.

Baths

Dogs react differently to water in different scenarios. Take the beach for example. Exley, our German Shorthaired Pointer, can't wait to get out of the car. He races up and down the beach, excited as can be. Throw the ball into a wave? No problem. Exley races at top speed, puts his head into the wave, comes up for air, finds the ball, and brings it back to land. Of course, he wants you to throw the ball again, and again and again. Our German Shepherd, Chelsea, got hit by a wave once, and she refused to go near the water again. Soaking wet, she walked around the beach as far from the water as possible, with her tail between her legs. Eventually, she came up to the water's edge to try to wrestle the ball from Exley. That was it. Near a pond or pool they invariably act the same.

Switch scenes. We are now in the backyard of the DeVito house, or worse yet (for my wife and me) in the bathroom, with the tub running. Chelsea is not thrilled, but she can be commanded toward the water (running or not). Once in the tub, she will sit or stand and patiently submit to this unhappy exercise. Exley, on the other hand, has to be dragged. Somewhere long before we got him, bathing was a very bad ordeal. He has gotten better with coaxing (dog biscuits, liver treats, cookies). Even so, once in the tub, without a hand on him, Exley will look for the first opportunity to escape. Many scenes that would have seemed hilarious to us on film have left their less than funny marks down our halls and in our living room.

You need to do everything possible to make bathing a pleasant experience for your dog. Some knowledgeable dog people start by bringing the dog in by use of treats, etc. Treat the situation as if it were any other kind of training scenario. The idea is to get your dog to equate good things with having a bath—not bad. There are many good dog shampoos available on the market. Many of them are made for different kinds of coats. They are all formulated to not irritate a dog's skin, and for that reason are recommended.

Before you wash your dog, it's usually a good idea to brush the dog, especially during the shedding season. First wet down the dog with water. Then start with a big gob of shampoo on your hands and start at the base of the neck working your way along the body towards the tail. Rub in a circular motion. Don't be too rough. Make sure to work the dog thoroughly under the chest and his hindquarters. Make sure you get the tail. Be sure to wet his head before applying a small amount of shampoo that you have rubbed between your hands. Do his ears, forehead, and snout gently.

Golden Retriever

Photo by Mary Bloom©

Rinse your dog with clean water. I can never for the life of me figure out why you would want to try to rinse your dog with the dirty bath water you just bathed him in. Sometimes it's a good idea to fill up a bucket of clean water and leave it on the side, so that you can rinse him off with clean water. I know many people who turn on the shower. Many dogs don't like this because they don't appreciate the fun of a shower. If you want to, you can close the shower curtain and let your dog shake. Believe me, you'll towel him again and again and not be able to dry him as well as when you let him shake once in an enclosed area.

After a bath, you probably want to let them dry off. Give them some thing to lie down on if they don't already have someplace. In the summer, we put the dogs out on the deck, and they lie in the sun and dry off. In the winter, we put a baby gate up in the kitchen doorway and let them sleep on a rug under the table. When we bathe the dogs, we also take the time to wash the covers of their beds on the same day. Who wants a nice clean dog that's going to go and lie down on something dirty? What's the point of that? After a bath is usually a good time to brush your dog. Much hair that hasn't actually come off (and a lot does) may have been loosened up. A quick combing will make their coat that much nicer and keep that much fur from collecting in the corners of your house.

Clipping Toenails

Growing up, my parents always had professionals cut the toenails of my dogs. Then I went and got my first dog and decided I was going to clip his toenails. I did the first and second claws correctly. The third one I cut to the quick and blood went squirting everywhere like a bad comedy skit and my dog started howling and pulling away. In the end my kitchen looked like a Quentin Tarantino set. I swore I would never do it again. Eventually I relented. I watched friends who also had dogs and watched them cut their dogs' nails. I watched and learned. Some of us have that opportunity and some of us don't. If you do, take advantage of it.

QUESTIONS?

What is the "quick" of a dog's toenail?
The quick is the soft, fleshy part of a claw. It resides within the nail, near the base. It's a little easier for those dogs that have white nails, as you can see the quick (it's the dark shading about half way up the nail). With black nails it's pretty much guess work. Better to be conservative.

Why do we cut our dog's toenails? Because if you didn't, the nails would grow so long that eventually it would hurt your dog just to watch. I have actually seen it happen. The toenails continue to curl and when the dog steps down on his foot, The nails are pushed into the paw, and the dog actually walks like he's pulled up lame.

So how is it done right? You have to be patient with your dog and you have to be careful. The idea is never to get too aggressive about cutting the toenails. You just want to clip the end off, no matter how long the nails are. Even if they still look long after cutting off just the tips, don't worry, ten days later you can have right back at it, because as you cut the toenails, the quick will recede within a week's time.

So, how do we go about cutting the dog's nails? First, you need to get the dog used to your handling his feet. Many dogs don't like this. What you want the dog to do is lie down on his side and allow you to pet each one of his paws, gently. Say nice things to the dog. Calm his nerves. Give him treats for his good behavior. Do this several times. Then on the appointed day, have him lie down on his side. Reward him. Then take one paw at a time and start to clip. Remember, don't cut too far down—just the tips. What I do is leave a cookie just beyond his reach, near his head. It usually takes the edge off. In the beginning, I used to give him a small treat for every paw.

What do you do when you have cut the quick? Well, there are different types of clotting agents that are available at the pet supply store. If you don't have any of that, corn starch is usually pretty good. It also acts as a clotting agent. Try putting direct pressure on the wound, with a clean cloth. Make sure there's plenty of the agent before you apply the direct pressure. The bleeding usually stops in a few minutes. If you just nicked the quick, the scary episode will be over quickly. However, if you do real damage, you might want to rush your dog to the vet immediately.

Remember—just cut off the very tips. Don't try to do too much in one clipping.

Ears

The first thing you need to know is that dogs with floppy ears tend to need more attention than do those dogs with cropped or short ears.

Why? Because it gets hot and ugly in there. There's not much good circulation of air in those spots. Bacteria build up, parasites build condos, and bingo, smelly, gross ears. Some of the first signs of ear problems are the three following traits:

1. The dog is shaking his head constantly.
2. The dog is scratching his ears often.
3. You can smell those ears from across the room!

If your dog is showing (or emitting) any of those clues, then it's time to clean those ears.

Pomeranian

Photo by Alice Su©

Do not use Q-tips or other cotton swabs to clean your dog's ears! If you can, go to your nearest pet store and find a good ear-cleaning solution. Then go home. Load up a cotton ball with some solution and start gently swabbing the ear. Don't go too deep. Clean what is known as the outer ear. If your dog is having a problem, it might take three or four cotton balls before you're able to clean his ears out completely. Try not to be grossed out by the balls as you extract them from his ears. They won't be pretty.

After the ears have been cleaned, you might want to squirt a little cleaning solution into the ears and rub the ear. Read the directions to properly apply your particular brand. Afterwards, you and your dog will be much happier, and you'll avoid costly veterinarian bills from having to deal with ear infections.

It's important to note that dogs who suffer from problem ears tend to be repeat offenders. In other words, if your dog has ear problems once, they are more likely to reoccur. So, keeping your dog's ears clean is a very important thing.

Eyes

The most important thing about the eyes is that they are the window to your dog's soul and his health. Your dog's eyes should always be alert and clear. In terms of hygiene, it's always important to wipe away the crust that builds up in the corner of your dog's eyes. While you might not think it bothers them, it does indeed. Left unchecked, it often is the source of irritation, or worse, may help to breed an infection. Make sure to wipe your dog's eyes whenever possible.

Dogs will wipe their own eyes on carpeting and furniture if the crusty buildup becomes unbearable. This is not only unpleasant for you, but it can cause more problems for the dog than solutions. Dirt and scratches may result. Some breeds, such as the Pekingese, can have their own facial hair actually grow to the point where it pokes them in the eye. This is painful for the dog and can result in infection. If you see this happening with your dog, very carefully use a pair of blunt-ended scissors to trim away the hair near the eyes, trimming parallel to its eyes.

Teeth

Proper dental care can add as much as five years to your dog's life. In addition, the quality of your dog's life will be much higher, especially in its later years. Proper dental care will also do wonders for eliminating doggy breath. Ideally, for the best dental care you should clean your dog's teeth every day and have its teeth professionally cleaned at least once a year.

It is best to ease your dog into this routine. Even puppies will show their best squirming talents during a tooth brushing. Start by just using your plain finger to gently rub the surfaces of your dog's teeth. Once your puppy seems okay with this, start using a soft cloth or some gauze for a while. From there you should begin using a regular dog toothbrush.

In addition to regular cleaning, you should take care to observe the dental health of your puppy. Though most problems won't show up until later in life, it is a good habit to get into from the start. Once a week, you should check to make sure none of your dog's teeth are loose. You should also look for discolorations of the teeth and gums, as well as lumps on its tongue. Any of these problems can be serious. Dental infections can quickly spread to other parts of your dog and can cause death.

If you try to examine your older dog's teeth for the first time, use caution. As a general rule, dogs don't like anyone messing around with the inside of their mouth. And if there is a problem in there somewhere, and you poke at a tender spot with your fingers in the dog's mouth, the pooch may inadvertently bite down.

Professional Groomers

Especially for longhaired breeds, you will want to use the services of a professional groomer at least twice a year. They are experienced and will make sure all the proper things are done to your dog. They are expert at cleaning his ears, cutting his coat, clipping his nails, and in general making sure he looks like the dog you want him to be. There is no shame in leaving your dog with a groomer. You can't possibly be called upon to know the many tricks and intricacies of grooming as these people do. Do it for your puppy and for yourself.

CHAPTER 10
Housetraining

The first thing every new owner should know before bringing a puppy into the house is how to teach him where to relieve himself. The good news is that all puppies can be housetrained. The bad news is that a puppy rarely becomes housetrained by just letting him out several times a day. This comprehensive housetraining plan requires dedication—but it's simple and foolproof.

The Basics of Housetraining

- Confine your puppy to his crate when you can't watch him so he won't relieve himself where he's not supposed to or while you're not looking (if you prefer, use a baby gate to confine him to the kitchen or laundry room while you can't watch him—just make sure the room is puppy-proofed).
- Supervise your puppy when he is out of his crate (umbilical cord or shadow).
- Feed him a high-quality diet at scheduled times and limit treats.
- Take him to his potty spot as soon as you return home, soon after meals, and when he wakes up from a nap.
- Teach him to eliminate on command by saying "Go potty, good puppy" in an excited voice while he's doing his business.
- Clean up his accidents immediately (remove debris or moisture, then treat with neutralizer and cleaner).
- Never correct him after the fact.
- Keep a log of his habits (when and where he pooped or peed, and when and how much he ate and drank).

Crate Training

Until a puppy is perfectly trained, he needs a safe place in which he can do nothing wrong. So when you can't keep your eyes glued to your puppy and monitor his every move, confine him to a place where inappropriate behavior—soiling, stealing, shredding, chewing, or scratching—isn't an option. I suggest crating because it eliminates the risk of him damaging woodwork, flooring, wall covering, or cabinetry.

 **SSENTIALS**

Crates are not cruel. Remember, dogs are naturally den animals. They normally take to crate training very naturally, if you take care to properly set up the crate.

Assuming you ultimately want your puppy to enjoy freedom in the house, crating is almost a rearing necessity. Crating is widely accepted by behaviorists, puppy trainers, veterinarians, and knowledgeable puppy owners as a humane means of confinement. Provided your puppy is properly introduced, you should feel as comfortable about crating him in your absence as you would securing a toddler in a highchair at mealtime.

Whether the enclosure is a room, hallway, kennel, or crate, it should be:

- *The right size.* It should be large enough that when your puppy is a full-grown dog he'll be able to stand without his shoulders touching the ceiling of the crate. This sized crate will be far too large for your puppy at first. Use a divider to limit the amount of space your puppy has; for the first month or so, one-third to one-half the crate should be fine.
- *Safe.* Homemade enclosures may save you money, but you would feel awful if he poked himself in the eye, stabbed or hung himself, or swallowed wood splinters or material like wallpaper or blankets because you ignored potential dangers. Make sure there are no protrusions or sharp edges, and no ingestible components.
- *Puppy-proof.* If he is prone to chewing, scratching or jumping up, prevent access to any woodwork, linoleum, furniture, counters, garbage, or windows so your home doesn't become a victim of your puppy's destructiveness during his training period.

FACTS

One sure way to ruin the crate-training method is to use the crate as a means of punishment. If you lock your puppy up as punishment, you will soon lose the advantage of a dog who enjoys the comforts of his own room in the house.

Introducing Puppy to the Crate

Though your puppy will come to think of his crate as his sanctuary because it satisfies a puppy's denning instinct, he may not like the idea of going in the crate at first. If you reinforce his objections to the crate by making his early associations with it unpleasant, he may never adjust to it. And that will be a setback for both of you. Go slowly, and praise every positive step along the way.

Make the crate a safe and cozy place for your puppy. Put it somewhere your pup will have some privacy, but not where he'll feel all alone. A corner of the kitchen is usually a good spot. Line the bottom of the crate with newspaper for extra insulation from the cold floor, then put a soft blanket or piece of fleece on top of the newspaper. Hopefully your puppy will never eliminate on his sleeping material in his crate, but don't bet on it, especially not in the first few weeks. The blanket or fleece should be machine washable, and of course the newspapers can be thrown away.

Black Lab

Photo by Mary Bloom©

Get your puppy into a good chew toy habit right away by putting an appropriate chew toy in the crate. Puppies need to chew, so unless you want them to go to work on your shoes, furniture, floor—whatever—turn them on to puppy-appropriate toys early.

When his crate looks like something you might want to curl up and nap in, call him over to it. Let him sniff it. Don't push him toward it or into it. Let him discover it in his own time. Make it interesting for him by putting some small bits of something really tasty like cold cuts or cheese near the entrance. When he shows interest, toss a goody into the crate. If he runs in and gobbles it up, tell him what a good puppy he is.

Don't shut the door on him the first time he goes in the crate. Let him go in and out a few times, continuing to praise when he shows interest. After all this stimulation, take him to his potty spot. This is his first introduction to the crate.

Later, feed your puppy in the crate. Place him and his food inside and sit with your back blocking the doorway of the crate. Don't close the crate door. For his next meal, prop the crate door and sit at the opening with your puppy. Keeping his food in the bowl, place a few pieces of kibble in the crate, then feed him a few pieces from your hand outside the crate. This way he associates being fed as something that happens in the crate and out. Feeding your puppy from your hands is also an excellent way to teach him that your hands mean good things. Your puppy (and later, your dog) should always associate your hands (and any person's hands) coming toward him as a good thing. There may be times when you have to grab his collar or take his food away or when strangers want to pet him.

Going to Bed

Next, teach your puppy to enter and exit the crate on command. Put his paws right in front of the opening. With one hand on his collar and the other pointing into the crate, say, "Bed." Gently guide him in by the collar as you place your hand under his tail and behind his rear legs to prevent him from backing away. If necessary, gently lift him in. Immediately invite him out by saying, "Okay," and praising him for coming out to you.

Practice several repetitions of this routine—without being enclosed. If you shut him in and leave him every time he is put in the enclosure he may develop a bad association with crating. But when he learns to go in the crate on command as a result of frequent practice, he is more likely to also accept being enclosed.

If you reserve his favorite toy for the times he spends in the crate, he may actually look forward to crating as an opportunity to play with it. Leave food and water out of the crate; puppies don't need it in there and most will dump or scatter it instead of eating or drinking. Create a peaceful environment by covering the crate with a sheet or, if his tendency is to pull it in, surround the crate with a couple of stiff panels for a more enclosed, denlike atmosphere.

FACTS

A crate is not a cage unless you make it so. Crate training relies on your making the crate into a den. To crate train successfully, you need to remember to make the crate a comfy room. The crate is not a house of punishment. The more denlike it is, the happier your puppy will be. Make sure it is clean and properly covered. This will make your puppy naturally enjoy its crate.

What to Do If Puppy Barks in the Crate

Sometimes a puppy will bark, yodel, whine, or howl when crated. Unless he is trying to tell you he has to go potty, ignore any noise he might make. Most pups will quiet down if you ignore their pleas. If yours doesn't and you or your family members are losing sleep or sanity, startle him into being quiet, use a word for it ("Shush") and praise for the quietness.

To startle your barking or crying puppy, your timing has to be good. While he's in full voice, throw an empty soda can at his covered crate or clap your hands sharply twice. You can also create an earthquake by attaching the leash to his crate and giving it a quick jerk as he barks. Do these things where your puppy can't see you. You don't want him to associate you with things that startle or scare him. As soon as he's quiet, come in and say, "Shush." If he stays quiet, say, "Good Shush" very enthusiastically. You may need to do this a number of times before he learns what Shush means. He'll still try to get your attention by barking or crying. Combine ignoring the noise and startling him until he figures out that you only praise him when he's settled down.

A crate-trained puppy is not housetrained. Your puppy is likely to do things you're not going to like when loose in the house and, therefore, needs plenty of supervised exploration to learn the house rules. If your puppy is out of his crate, keep your eyes glued on him or, better still, umbilical-cord him so when you can't follow him, he'll follow you; this affords you the opportunity to curtail misbehaviors before they become habits.

Here's how it works: Tie his leash to your belt on your left side. Give him only enough slack to keep him at your side without your legs becoming entangled. If he attempts to jump up, chew, bark, or relieve himself without your approval, you'll be able to stop him instantly by tugging on the lead to distract him. You'll also be able to tell him what a good puppy he is when he trots after you or sits by your side as you work around the house or sit down to do something. Umbilical-cording is a fantastically simple technique and important training tool, which every able-bodied household member should use. You can even umbilical-cord two puppies at once. Or when one pet is trained and the other isn't, you can cord the untrained puppy while giving the reliable one his freedom.

Crate Soiling

Although dogs normally won't mess in their crates, some do. Occasional accidents shouldn't concern you, but if it happens every other day or more, try these suggestions:

- Remove all bedding in hopes he'll be repulsed by having nothing other than his body to absorb the mess.
- Use a smaller crate so he only has enough room to turn in place.
- Teach him to enter and exit his crate on command. ("Go to your bed/spot.")
- Put his food and water in the open crate to encourage a better association about being in there; remove it when he's enclosed.

Maintaining a Schedule

Most puppies leave their litter to enter their new home at about two months of age. At this age, the pups eat a lot, drink a lot, and have limited ability to control their elimination and no comprehension that that might be important. Feeding and potty times should be adjusted to help puppy reach his potential in the housetraining department as quickly as possible. At two to four months of age most pups need to relieve themselves after waking up, eating, playing, sleeping, and drinking. At four months, the puppy may be developed like an adult internally, but expect him to behave like a puppy.

To housetrain effectively, you need to establish a schedule that works for your family and will help your puppy learn the rules quickly. You will be amazed at how quickly your puppy learns if you stick to a schedule that has fixed times for eating, sleeping and exercising.

Sample Schedule

6:30 A.M.	Take puppy out immediately when you wake up
6:45 A.M.	Feed puppy breakfast
7:00 A.M.	Take puppy back outside
7:15 A.M.	Play with puppy while getting ready for the day
7:45 A.M.	Take puppy outside
8:00 A.M.	Crate puppy when family leaves
Noon	Take puppy outside
12:15 P.M.	Feed puppy lunch
12:30 P.M.	Take puppy outside
12:45 P.M.	Play with puppy
1:00 P.M.	Crate puppy if leaving the home again; use umbilical cord training method if doing things around the house
5:00 P.M.	Take puppy outside
5:30 P.M.	Feed puppy dinner
5:45 P.M.	Take puppy outside
6:00 P.M.	Play with puppy for remainder of evening, with trips outside every few hours

Just before bedtime: Take puppy outside. No more water after this for the rest of the night. Crate puppy for the night. (Very young puppies may have to be taken out once during the night.)

Diet and Feeding

Feed specific amounts of high-quality puppy food at specific times. Pups should be fed three times a day up to three or four months of age, and after that can be fed twice daily for the rest of their lives. If your schedule requires you to be gone for six or more hours at a time, feedings can be disproportionate. Consider feeding a larger portion when you will be home for a few hours and will therefore be able to give him the opportunity to relieve himself.

Look for signs that the food you've chosen agrees with your puppy. He should maintain the proper weight and muscle tone, have a healthy sheen to his coat, and have plenty of energy. Gas, loose stools, constipation, itchy skin, bald patches, or listlessness indicate a problem that may be diet-related. Investigate possible solutions by consulting with your veterinarian. When switching food, do so gradually over a period of at least five days. To maintain the firmness of his stools begin with a 20:80 ratio of new to familiar foods, and switch the ratios by 10 to 20 percent daily.

FACTS

What you feed your puppy is as important as keeping him on a schedule. Ask your breeder or veterinarian for a recommendation. Buy a dry kibble made of nutritious, easily digestible ingredients, minimal fillers, and no food coloring (these will stain your carpet if the puppy has an accident. You may pay a little more, but your puppy won't have to eat as much to get the nutrients he needs, and he will therefore eliminate less.

Water

Puppies should have free access to fresh, clean water at all times except while crated and about two hours before bed. Always allow your puppy ample opportunity to drink at least five times a day (perhaps give water every time he goes out to ensure adequate hydration).

For pups who urinate frequently, try restricting access to water. But before doing so, tell your veterinarian about your plans to see if he or she wants to perform any diagnostic tests to rule out bladder or urinary tract problems. In severe cases where, despite a clean bill of health, the pup still continually urinates, offer water only before taking him out to relieve himself. With pups who just can't seem to hold it throughout the night, withhold water for three hours before going to bed.

Puppies can dehydrate very easily and very quickly. It is extremely important that you give your puppy ample access to water. Restricting your puppy's water as a means of potty training should only be done as a last resort and only after consulting with your puppy's veterinarian.

The "Potty Spot" and How to Eliminate Immediately

Teach your puppy to eliminate on command. This lesson is handy both when he is too distracted and won't potty or when he's on a surface that he's inclined not to potty on—for example, a kennel run, wet grass, or where other puppies have been. Others will go potty only if they're in a particular area or taken for a walk. By teaching your puppy to eliminate on command, you can get him to go where you want, when you want, and simplify the housetraining process. Here's how to do it.

Leash your puppy and take him to the Potty Spot. When he begins the sniffing and circling ritual that immediately precedes elimination, start chanting a phrase like "Potty, hurry up." What you say is unimportant, but it should sound melodic and should always be the same phrase. Use the same words for defecation and urination. After a week begin the chant as soon as you enter the potty area. Always praise when he does what you want and give him an extra-special reward of playtime in the yard or a stroll around the block.

If you take your puppy to his Potty Spot and he doesn't eliminate right away, take him back inside for a few more minutes until you're certain he needs to. Don't take your puppy outside, ask him to do his business, and take him for a walk whether he does or not. Teach him that going potty right away means getting a walk. If you dash back inside after puppy's gone potty, he'll learn that the only way to get a walk out of you is to hold it—and the only way for you to take him out is to go in the house. Remember, reward him for doing the correct thing: pottying in his spot when you ask him. Then and only then should he be rewarded.

Dealing with Accidents

No matter how careful you are, occasionally inappropriate elimination happens. If your puppy has an accident do the following:

- Never correct the puppy after the fact. Do scold yourself by saying, "How could I have let that happen?"
- If you catch him in the act, startle him by saying, "Ach" loudly or picking him up in midstream and carrying him outside to stop him.
- Clean up messes immediately. Remove debris and blot up any moisture, then use a cleaning solution, and finally treat the soiled area with an odor neutralizer.

Until your puppy is perfectly potty-trained, remember:

1. Puppies who can hold it for long periods while they're in their crate or at night are not necessarily well on their way to being housebroken. Don't judge his capacity by his behavior while crated. Metabolism slows down with inactivity, so even a totally untrained puppy may not soil for up to twelve hours when he's crated.
2. Puppies enjoy playing, observing, and investigating, and often forget about going potty when they're left alone outdoors. Don't let your puppy out without supervision and assume that he did his business.
3. Puppies often indicate when they want to go outdoors and play, instead of when they need to potty. Don't rely on or encourage him to tell you he wants to go out. Many puppies will indicate frequently and always eliminate when taken to the potty area. This causes bladder and bowel capacity and control to be underdeveloped.

Common Housetraining Problems

Leashing your puppy during potty breaks will enable you to keep your puppy moving and sniffing within the appropriate area, and thus speed the process of elimination. If you sense your puppy is about to become distracted from his duty of looking for a potty spot, use a light, quick jerk on the leash as you slowly move about the area yourself. If you don't get results within five minutes, take puppy back inside and put him in his crate for another ten minutes or so. Eventually he'll have to go, and then you can reward him for going outside in the designated spot.

He Takes Forever to Go

Only give your puppy a few minutes to potty. If you give him twenty minutes, he is likely to demand thirty next time. After a couple minutes, put him back in his crate long enough to make him thankful for the next potty opportunity you give him. As stated earlier, have your puppy earn playtime by pottying first and playing afterward. Potty breaks will be much less time-consuming if your puppy learns to associate the initial act of walking outdoors with the act of going potty, not playing.

Cutting Back on Taking Your Puppy Out

Many owners make the mistake of continually taking a puppy out before he really needs to go. Although they do so hoping he won't soil the house, they are actually preventing him from developing the capacity to hold it. Since housetraining is a matter of teaching the puppy to control his bladder and bowels until he has access to the outdoors, taking the puppy out too frequently slows the housetraining process. When you think he doesn't need to go out but he does, try umbilical-cording or crating him for a half-hour before taking a walk.

How Long Will It Take?

Plan on a year or more to complete the housetraining process. Although your puppy may be flawless for days, weeks, or months, under certain conditions any puppy can backslide. Seemingly benign events such as these can cause housetraining regression:

- Changes in diet
- Weather changes (too hot, cold, or wet, or noisy thunderstorms) can make outings unproductive potty times

- New environments (vacation homes, new house, or friend's house) may be treated as an extension of his potty area
- Some medications (like allergy medications) and certain conditions (like hormone changes associated with estrus) can cause more frequent elimination

Submissive Urination

If your puppy wets when he greets people or is disciplined, he isn't having a housetraining problem. Uncontrollable and unconscious leaking of urine is common in puppies and certain breeds. If your pup has been given a clean bill of health by a veterinarian so that you know his problem isn't health related, work on the problem by:

- Never yelling, striking, or showing anger toward him
- Making your entrances and greetings devoid of emotion
- Avoiding eye contact, talking, and touching during emotional states
- Withholding water if you're going out for a short period of time, and giving lots of water after you've been able to take him out to relieve himself

Avoid vigorous petting, impassioned tones of voice, and strong eye contact. Only interact with a superficial, brief pat, calm word, or fleeting glimpse when his bladder is empty. When he consistently responds without tinkling, test his control after he's had water. Gradually try a warmer approach, but be ready to turn off the affection and issue a command if it pleases the pee out of him.

Paper Training—Is It an Option?

Owning a small puppy offers lots of advantages. One of these is that if you don't want to walk him outdoors, you can teach him to eliminate on papers indoors. To start, get full-sized newspapers and a sixteen-square-foot, wire-mesh exercise pen, available from puppy supply catalogs or by special order from a pet shop. Place the pen on an easy-to-clean floor and line the bottom with newspapers opened flat out. For one week, keep your puppy in the fully papered pen anytime you aren't supervising or exercising. Then, put a bed in the pen and gradually reduce the papered portion to one full-sized newspaper, overlapping five sheets to ensure proper absorption. Once he is pottying on the paper, open up the pen within a small room or hall. When he consistently soils on the paper, gradually give him access to the house, room by room.

Once trained, some paper-trained puppies only go on their papers; others prefer the outdoors but will use papers if necessary. You can paper-train a previously outdoor-trained puppy and vice versa, but you'll avoid extra work by deciding what you want up front.

CHAPTER 11

Socializing—Raising a Friendly Dog

Puppy training begins the moment your puppy comes into your house—whether you want it to or not. Soiling, biting, jumping, barking, and running are natural behaviors; as a new puppy parent, it is up to you to show him where and when those behaviors are appropriate and, more importantly, where they are inappropriate. Begin teaching and socializing your puppy as early as eight weeks of age if he is properly vaccinated and his good health is confirmed by your veterinarian.

Meeting People

Socialize your puppy to people, making sure he gets plenty of experiences with both genders and a variety of races and ages. Go to the park, a parade, the beach, or outside of a shopping center. Bring some of your puppy's kibble or some other tasty treats and have strangers ask your puppy to sit for a greeting and a treat. If you do this often enough, your puppy will start to think, "If I sit when I see someone coming I'll get a treat." Not a bad thought!

Occasionally, leave your puppy in the care of a trustworthy, levelheaded friend for a minute, an hour, or a day. Your objective is teach the pup to be self-assured in your absence; therefore, don't say good-bye or hello to the puppy. Treat the situation as a nonevent so your puppy is less likely to experience separation anxiety.

Think about items people carry and equipment they use. Expose your puppy to wheelchairs, canes, bicycles, lawn mowers, roller skates, vacuum cleaners, etc.

FACTS

When you're out and about with your puppy, remember that he's a baby. Praise him when he actively and willingly explores something, but don't push him or coddle him if he reacts with fear or great reluctance. Your role as puppy parent is to help him feel safe about the world, not scared by it.

Getting to Know the World

Take your puppy as many places as possible so he becomes a savvy traveler who is accustomed to elevators, stairways, manholes, and grates. Acclimate him to walking on a variety of surfaces such as gravel, wire, sand, cobblestone, linoleum, and brick. Because some puppies prefer to eliminate only in their own backyard, teach him to eliminate on command in different areas, so weekend trips and the like won't be a problem.

If you want to foster enjoyment of the water and your puppy isn't a natural pond-puppy, walk him on-leash on the shoreline. Once he is at ease with that, venture into the water. Gently tighten the leash as you go, forcing him to swim a couple feet before you let him return to the shoreline. Never throw a puppy into the water.

QUESTIONS?

Why is confidence so important when it comes to training and raising your puppy?
A confident dog allows guests in the house with little fanfare, but will be alert should something go wrong. The confident dog does not shy away from people. He is sure of himself, and can be depended upon for a steady temperament. He is not overly aggressive toward strangers or other dogs. A skittish dog, a dog that lacks confidence, is one who is unsure of people or other dogs. His behavior can be unpredictable. He can be overly wary of strangers.

Meeting Other Animals

Let him get to know other animals—cats, chickens, horses, goats, birds, guinea pigs, lizards, and of course, other puppies and dogs. Often upon meeting a new species a puppy is startled, then curious, and finally some become bold or aggressive. For his own protection and for the protection of the other animal, always keep him leashed so you can control his distance and stop unwanted behaviors by enforcing obedience commands.

Whatever you are socializing your puppy to—animals, objects, or people—approach the new thing in a relaxed manner and avoid any situation that would intimidate the average puppy, like a group of grade schoolers rushing at him. Be prepared for three reactions: walking up to check it out and sniff, apprehensive barking, or running away.

No matter his response, remain silent. In the first (and, by the way, best) scenario he is thinking rationally and investigating his environment—don't draw attention to yourself by talking, praising, or petting. Allow him to explore uninterrupted. This good boy is entertaining himself and being educated at the same time. If your puppy lacks confidence or displays fear, don't console him because this will reinforce his fear. Use the leash to prevent him from running away. If he is still slightly uncomfortable, drop some tasty bits of food (like slivers of hot dog) on the ground. Most puppies will relax after a nibble or two because the uncomfortable situation has been positively associated with food.

If loud noises frighten your puppy, desensitize him by allowing him to create a racket. Offer him a big metal spoon with a little peanut butter on it. It won't be long before he is creating hubbub and loving it. Of course, if the clamoring drives you nuts, feel free to limit his playtime with these items.

ESSENTIALS

When introducing a new puppy to your current dog or cat, remember that your established pet considers your home its territory. If possible, try and introduce the animals in neutral territory, maybe in a friend's yard. It's very important to make sure neither of the animals becomes afraid of the other, or the other pet will quickly become a bully.

Grooming and Examinations

Maltese

Photo by Mary Bloom©

This section addresses training your puppy to accept grooming and examinations. As to the specific grooming procedures, techniques, and products to use, talk to an expert like a breeder, handler, or groomer.

Begin by acclimating your pup to having all areas of his head handled. Look in his eyes, ears, and mouth, and check out his feet (feel the toes, pads, and nails) and body (run your hands along his legs, underbelly, chest, and tail).

Touch his gum line, his teeth (don't forget the molars), and inside his ears. Open his mouth as if you were giving a pill: gently grasp the upper jaw with one hand and the lower jaw with the other, fingers behind the canine (fang) teeth. Try all these things when he is standing on the floor and also when he is on a table or other slightly elevated surface, like the top of a washing machine.

Additionally, teach your puppy to accept being rolled on his side. Start by practicing the "Settle Position." Kneel on the ground at his side and reach around him as if you were giving a bear hug. Clasp his legs on the opposite side and gently roll him by moving his legs under his body and toward you. Then, with your hand holding the rear leg, slide his bottom between your knees and straddle him. Place your hands, palms down, on his chest with your thumbs facing one another below his armpits to prevent him from wriggling away. Remain still and calm. When he relaxes, release him by saying, "Okay," as you loosen your hold. Practice this procedure on seven- to eighteen-week-old pups.

Riding in the Car

As soon as your puppy is large enough, teach him to enter and exit the car on command. Practice this by leashing him, walking him up to the car, and commanding him to go in as you give him a boost. Invite him out of the car by calling, "Come," as you gently pull the leash. Practice several of these, several times a day until he goes in and out on command. Even before your puppy is ready for that lesson, decide where you'd like him to ride. Crating is the safest option. If it isn't the most convenient, try a puppy seatbelt, which is available at many pet shops or by mail order. Don't feed your puppy prior to riding if he has any tendency toward carsickness. It is also a good idea to keep the air temperature inside the car comfortably cool (if you roll down a window, choose one that your puppy cannot stick his head out of). Additionally, you'll reduce the chance of motion sickness by avoiding bumpy roads.

Some dogs end up loving riding in the car so much that their owners will take them for rides almost everywhere they go. It goes without saying that leaving a dog in an unattended car in the summer is extremely dangerous. Remember that just because it's cloudy now, doesn't mean the sun won't poke through any minute. Even cracking all the windows won't help much as the temperature in your car will climb well above 100 degrees quickly.

Final Comments on Socializing

Perhaps your veterinarian advised you against exposing your puppy while his immune system is developing, but you fear the risks of neglecting his socialization during this critical period. Though you may not be able to walk him around the big city, you can start a socialization program at home:

- Desensitize him to noises by letting him play with an empty plastic half-gallon or gallon milk jug or big metal spoon.
- Accustom him to walking on a variety of surfaces such as bubble wrap, big plastic bags, and chicken wire. Put a treat in the middle so he gets rewarded for his bravery.
- If his experiences with meeting new people will be limited, you can get creative with costumes. Wear hats, masks, and capes, walk with a cane, or limp, skip, and hop.
- Handle him as described in the grooming and examination section.
- Take him for car rides with permission from your veterinarian.

CHAPTER **12**

Basic Training

Basic behavioral training is essential for any dog. This isn't designed for teaching your dog to do tricks, but rather to give you the tools to keep your dog under proper control for its own safety and your peace of mind. Proper basic training will enable you to trust your dog at home alone without wondering what piece of furniture it is destroying.

Equipment

In order to get the most out of your training, you need to have the proper equipment. The most important pieces of equipment for basic training are a well-fitted collar, six-foot leather leash, and fifteen-foot-long line. Additionally, when working toward off-leash control, you'll need a tab (a short nylon rope) and a fifty-foot light line. All are described in some detail below. When you begin training, use the collar your puppy wears around the house: It should be well made and properly fitted. If it's not or he doesn't wear a collar, start with a snug fitting, buckle-type collar, flat or rolled. Consider switching to a slip collar, a prong collar, or a head halter if you've used the procedures recommended in this book but, because of his size or strength, would like an extra measure of control.

Don't use a prong collar on a puppy younger than six months! Puppies need you to teach them how to act. This painful collar is meant to be used with dogs that have failed to understand the lessons of heeling and other proper behavior. Most qualified trainers never have use for them. You really shouldn't either.

Slip Chain Collars

When using this type of collar, take advantage of the quick slide and release action of a slip chain with flat, small links. It should be only ½ to 2 inches larger than the thickest part of your puppy's skull. Although collars this small can be difficult to slide on and off, snug collars deliver timelier corrections. This type also stays in place better when properly positioned—high on the neck, just behind the ears, with the rings just under the puppy's right ear.

Puppies grow fast. Don't choke your dog by forcing him or her to wear a collar they've outgrown. Your puppy will wear through several collars before growing to full size.

So that the slip collar will loosen after corrections, it's important to put this collar on correctly. To do so, slip the collar through one of the rings and form a "P" with the loose collar. Put the collar over your puppy's head with the tail of the P attached to the leash. You'll know if you've got the collar on correctly if the links slide easily when tightened or loosened.

Nylon Slip Collars

Neither round nor flat nylon slip collars offer the slide and release action of a chain, but they do deliver stronger corrections than buckle collars. As with any collar, the nylon slip should only be tightened momentarily while correcting; because the pressure is always the same, constant tension means the puppy isn't being told when he's doing well and when he's doing poorly.

Prong Collars

Strong or easily distracted puppies may benefit by use of a prong or pinch collar. The prongs come in four sizes-micro, small, medium, and large. The length is adjustable by removing or adding prongs. Since many brands of these collars will fall off without warning, when you're working in open areas, consider fitting your puppy with a buckle or slip collar in addition to the prong, and attach your leash to both.

Some people think prong collars look like instruments of torture. If you're turned off by the appearance of the prong collar, look for another tool to aid you. But if you are both apprehensive and curious about this collar, it's actually a very humane tool when properly used. Ironically, some harsh trainers abhor them and some soft trainers embrace them. Cruelty or kindness isn't linked to whether a puppy wears a prong collar but rather to the tactics employed. If you want to use one, have an experienced trainer show you how to properly fit and work with it.

Collar Transitions

If the collar you use for training is different than the one your puppy usually wears, he is likely not to obey well when he isn't wearing his training collar. Treat him like an untrained puppy and be prepared to enforce all your commands so he'll behave regardless of which collar he's wearing.

FACTS

Traditional length lead is approximately five feet. However, many trainers will also recommend training your dog on a long lead once you begin training outside. Long leads can be up to ten feet or more. The idea is to let your dog run free with the long lead still attached to the collar. You should then practice calling your puppy. With the lead dragging, you can always step on the lead to stop your puppy if he doesn't come to you.

Leashes and Lines

To teach commands and mannerly walking, and to umbilical cord your puppy, use a six-foot leather leash. Use a $\frac{1}{4}$-inch width for puppies up to fifteen pounds; use a $\frac{1}{2}$-inch width for puppies sixteen to forty-five pounds; use a $\frac{3}{4}$-inch width for puppies forty-six to seventy-five pounds; and use a 1-inch width for puppies over seventy-six pounds.

Dalmatian

Photo by Karen Taylor©

To train your puppy to accept the leash, start by putting on his buckle-type collar and lightweight leash. For ten to thirty minutes, three times a day for a week, watch him drag it around the house or yard. Better still, attach the lead prior to playtime with another puppy or a favorite toy. He'll step on it, scratch his neck, refuse to move, or maybe even scream, all of which you should ignore. Since many puppies like to chew the lead you may need to thoroughly spray it before each session with a chewing deterrent like Bitter Apple.

When he is comfortable about dragging the leash, pick up the handle and coax him to walk on your left side by carrying and squeezing an interesting squeaky toy. If he really fights you, attach the leash handle to a doorknob and let him struggle with that while you drink a cup of coffee. Watch him out of the corner of your eye to confirm that his antics aren't endangering him. Repeat the procedure for five or ten minutes at a time until he is relaxed before attempting to walk with the leash in hand again.

Long Line

Many exercises, including sneakaway and advanced distance stays, are done on a fifteen-foot nylon cord called a long line. Since many pet stores don't carry them, just go to a hardware store and buy a swivel snap and fifteen feet of nylon cord—$1/4$-inch diameter for a medium-sized puppy and $1/8$ inch smaller or larger for small and large puppies, respectively. Tie the snap on one end and make a loop for your thumb on the other.

Light Line and Glove

The light line is a fifty-foot nylon cord. Use parachute cord for large puppies, Venetian blind cord for medium or small puppies, and nylon twine for tiny breeds. The light line is tied to the tab and used as you make the transition to off-lead work. When you're working with the tab and light line, wear a form-fitted gardening glove to ensure a better grip and to prevent rope burn.

Head Halters

Head halters can control a puppy's head and nose more effectively than other collars. One strap rests behind the ears and another fits around the muzzle. If your puppy's trachea or esophagus is sensitive when pressure is applied, the head halter won't irritate the condition but will give you great control. And you can easily stop a large puppy from lunging or pulling by turning his head toward you, even if you lack strength.

Retractable Leashes

These popular leads come in lengths from eight to thirty-two feet. You can let the puppy venture away and explore without getting his legs entangled, thanks to a constant, slight amount of tension. The buttons on the easy-to-grip plastic handle allow you to lock it at a length as short as four inches for some models, or as long as the total length or any length in between. Sounds great, but unknowingly, owners are teaching sloppy behavior. Allowing a puppy to dart and criss-cross the handler's path puts them in danger and tells the puppy that he's in charge.

To make your puppy adapt to your pace and stay by your side using a retractable leash, lock it in the shortest position. The plastic handle allows you to give a stronger tug than the leash allows, which is especially useful if space is limited or footing is bad. When you arrive at his potty area or meet up with a canine playmate, unlock the lead and, with your permission, let the puppy pull out the length.

Establishing Rules and a Schedule

1. Decide what you'd like your puppy to do.
2. Decide what clear visual or auditory signal you will use to initiate the desired action.
3. Give verbal commands using the right tonality, inflection, and volume (don't plead, mumble, or shout).
4. Preface verbal commands with the puppy's name. The name and command should sound like one word ("Buster heel," rather than "Buster . . . heel"). Just one exception: Don't use his name in conjunction with the "Stay" command, since hearing his name infers he should be attentive and ready to go.
5. Say the command only once.
6. Make an association: While teaching, give the command as you make the puppy do the action (for example, say, "Sit" as you pull up on the collar and push down on the puppy's rear).
7. Give commands only when you can enforce them, otherwise you risk teaching disobedience.

8. Decide on reinforcement: How are you going to show the puppy what to do? Unlike the other eleven steps, this will change depending on your puppy's stage in training.
9. Show your appreciation with precisely timed praise.
10. End every command by releasing with the "Chin-touch Okay."
11. Test your puppy's understanding by working him around distractions before progressing to the next level.
12. Don't take obedience for granted—puppies forget, get lazy, become distracted, and inevitably fail to respond to familiar commands. Especially if he rarely makes a mistake, correct him so he understands the rules haven't changed and neither should his behavior.

Before You Get Down to Lessons

I've found the following exercises to be effective warm-ups to the work of more formal training. Try them and see.

- *Running Sneakaways:* Practice until the puppy is following you attentively regardless of distractions.
- *Leash Length Sneakaways:* Leash Grip—Hold leash by placing your right thumb through loop of leash. Put slack in right hand, too. Remove left hand from leash and walk with puppy at your left side. Practice by dropping the slack and running to correct forging. Walk briskly ahead to correct lagging and crossing behind.

Clicker and Treat Training

Clickers are often used for training service dogs and for teaching tricks. Simply put, when the puppy does something desirable, he is given a signal (usually a distinct sound) that the behavior is right, offered a food reward and, eventually, taught to do it on command possibly without the food. It has long been used to train a variety of species, including dolphins, birds, and monkeys. Many trainers use the click of a tin cricket to signify the appropriateness of a behavior. For instance, if the objective is to teach a puppy to sneeze, the trainer would wait for him to do that, click the tin cricket and offer a treat or other reward. Because of the power of association, soon the puppy will react to the sound of the clicker with as much delight as the treat. Therefore, if the puppy is working far away or retrieving and can't be given a treat, the clicker communicates that he is doing a great job. Of course, many people do the same thing with the word "Good!" instead of the clicker. With animals who are unresponsive to verbal praise—like rodents and farm animals—the clicker is an invaluable training tool, but a variety of methods are equally successful when teaching basic puppy obedience.

Using Treats to Train

Most trainers want their puppies to obey out of love rather than because they were beaten or bribed. But is your love motivation enough? Not always, and you certainly don't want to end up disciplining your puppy for something that you can be teaching him pleasurably with something he's motivated for: a tasty treat.

There are basically three ways to use food:

- As a lure to get the puppy to perform a task
- As a reward for completing an already learned task
- As reinforcement for behaviors offered by the puppy (click and treat training)

Most people use treats and body language as a lure because it is the fastest way to entice the puppy to perform a task. But beware: there is a huge gap between following a lure and obeying a command. To bridge that gap, learn how to enforce your commands with your hands and leash. This will also prove invaluable if your puppy isn't interested in the treat because he's full or distracted.

ESSENTIALS

If you prefer not to use treats, don't. Though using treats can enliven a puppy's response to an already learned command, I have never found it necessary to use food to teach a task. In fact, I've preferred to stay away from it so I can see when the puppy is actually learning commands rather than just performing actions.

Sneakaways

I use a method I call the "sneakaway" as the foundation for teaching commands and solving problems, and to teach a puppy to walk nicely on lead. This mesmerizing exercise teaches your puppy to be controlled and attentive despite distractions. Even without specifically addressing problem behaviors, you may find they magically disappear as your puppy learns his sneakaway lessons. At the very least, you'll find sneakaways improve his general trainability and therefore greatly reduce your workload.

Labrador Retriever

Photo by Mary Bloom©

To begin the sneakaway, put your puppy on the long line (the fifteen-foot nylon cord described under "Equipment"). Then take your puppy to an obstruction-free area at least fifty feet square. Put your thumb through the loop of the line and your other hand under it. Plant both hands on your midsection to avoid moving them and jerking your puppy. He may get jerked during this exercise, but it won't be because of your hand movement. The sneakaway is simple: when your puppy goes north, you go south. When he is thinking of things in the west, you head east. Sneakaways teach your puppy to watch you in anticipation of your speedy departure. As a bonus, your puppy will enjoy the sneakaway if he likes running with you. Being an astute observer of human behavior, it's easy for him to avoid the correction by "catching you" before the line tightens. So, sneakaways not only teach your puppy to walk nicely, he'll also watch you, have fun, and never be the victim of an unjust correction.

As you stroll with your puppy, watch him closely but inconspicuously. If he becomes distracted or unaware of you, immediately turn and walk briskly in the opposite direction. The line will tighten abruptly if he isn't following as you move away. After an hour of practice, split up anyway you like over the next two days. Your puppy should be keeping his legs tangle-free, be aware of your movements, and be willing to be near you.

Occasionally, even after an hour of practice, a puppy may refuse to budge. Others may throw their paws over the long line and shake their heads furiously or bite the line. With both types, you may be tempted to stop momentarily, carry your puppy, or quit. Resist the temptation; those actions just add to your puppy's confusion. Instead, create an umbilical cord for him by tying his leash to your belt. For two days, make him walk by your side as you perform your daily activities around the house and yard. After a few hours of umbilical cording, staying near you should be second nature. Now practice sneakaways again, using a slip chain or prong collar. If you do so for a total of three hours over the course of a week, he is likely to be following happily.

Whether as a result of panic or feigned helplessness, a rare puppy may jump, spin, and severely entangle himself in the line. Ignore his self-created dilemma and refuse to rescue him. After two or three days you will never see the behavior again.

Advanced Sneakaways

In step two, instead of walking away, pivot and run when your puppy's attention wanders from you. Once he's begun running after you, stop dead. Also, take inventory of your puppy's personality, desires, and fascinations. These may include noises, smells, certain activities, food, toys, different areas, or other animals and people. From now on we'll refer to these as distractions. Each time you practice, run a little faster as you sneak away and use more challenging and irresistible distractions.

Regular Leash Walking

Begin the next phase of your training once your puppy is content to be near you no matter what distractions are around. This step teaches him to walk on a loose leash at your left side. Attach the six-foot leash to his collar and put your right thumb in the handle. Enclose your fingers around the straps of the handle below. Hold the mid-section of the leash with the right hand, too, so your left hand is free. The leash should have just enough slack to touch the middle of your left thigh when your right hand is at your hip.

Great Dane

Photo by Mary Bloom©

If your puppy consistently pulls, try this: when your puppy forges ahead, open and close your hand to release the slack, then grip the handle as you pivot and run away. Do this when his shoulder is only inches ahead of your leg, rather than waiting until he is tugging at the end of the leash or lunging frantically ahead. When your puppy is running after you, pick up the slack in the leash again and stop dead.

If your puppy runs right past you, pivot once again and sneak away before he bolts ahead. If your puppy is a charger, watch his body language closely so it becomes easy to anticipate when to do multiple, direction-changing sneakaways.

If your puppy attempts to lag, reduce the slack by tightening the leash a bit—about one to five inches—as you briskly walk forward. The puppy may bump into the back of your legs for the next few steps but that, along with the fact that the leash tightens against your left thigh with every step, will encourage him to return to your left side. Remember to keep your left hand off the leash so nothing interferes with your thigh pulling into the leash.

Sneakaway Summary

The goal of the sneakaway is to maintain control, attention, and a slack lead around any distraction, as a foundation for all other training.

Days One and Two: Walk silently and quickly away from puppy when he is inattentive or attempts to wander more than five feet from you.

Days Three and Four: Same as first two days, but:
1. Run away when he is inattentive or wanders.
2. Use distractions.
3. Stop dead when line goes slack.

Days Five and Six: Same as three and four, but:
1. Run as fast as you can.
2. Use more tempting distractions.
3. Train in different locations.

The Learning Process

Everyone's idea of what constitutes a trained puppy varies. If your definition includes having the ability to control your puppy around distractions and obey heel, sit, down, stay, and come commands, the answer depends on how quickly you can learn basic puppy training skills. If you are willing to devote twenty or twenty-five minutes of daily practice for ten weeks, both you and your puppy are likely to achieve excellent results. Plan your training agenda being sure to note the number of repetitions and specific ways to practice each exercise. Some days it may feel you're getting nowhere, but the cumulative effect of this strategy never fails to develop a proficient team.

All Dogs Are Different

Just like people, all puppies should be evaluated based on their individual temperaments and characteristics. No breed has a patent on problems or virtues. Therefore, stereotyping breeds does more harm than good. You should heed warnings to be extra conscientious because of certain breed tendencies—teaching a sporting puppy to listen to you even in heavily scented fields rather than following his nose; being on the lookout for aggressive tendencies toward other puppies in terrier breeds; or socializing herding breeds a lot, especially when they are four to six months old, so they don't become skittish.

Keep in mind that puppies, like people, have different aptitudes. For people it may be language, not science, and for puppies it may be stays, not recalls. Puppies do learn how to learn, so that after ten weeks, it becomes difficult to separate the naturals from the initially confused or resistant.

Be Patient

Puppy training is an adventure of sorts: never predictable, sometimes elating, and sometimes tedious. Be optimistic about your puppy's potential but expect his progress to occasionally be slow or nonexistent. Don't, however, abandon your original goals and settle for meager results: Shoddy, half-learned obedience can cause annoying problems or allow them to fester. Many owners give up on training but later decide to give it another try—this time approaching it with far greater determination and achieving far better results. Whether this is your first time around or your last-ditch effort, recognize that a degree of frustration is part of the learning process. If frustration or doubt strikes, keep training. You may be five seconds from a learning breakthrough.

Learning anything new—including how to train your puppy—is challenging, so show yourself compassion. I've been training puppies for twenty-two years. I don't want to make mistakes when training, but sometimes I do. If I attempt to train, I may make a mistake. But if I never try, I'll never have the puppy I really want. Decide what kind of behavior you want and pursue it with patience and kindness.

Praise as a Training Tool

With some puppies, a word of praise goes a long way. Others appear unaffected by it. Gracious puppy trainers use lots of praise at the right time in the right way to acknowledge and congratulate specific actions, concentration, and worthy intent. Experiment with a variety of ploys to find what delights your puppy no matter what his mood. I've found quiet, interesting sounds, combined with scampering movement, gentle pushes, and vigorous, light, brief scratching with my nails usually elicit a good response.

ESSENTIALS

The "Chin-touch okay" can be a valuable signal to teach your puppy to realize when he did something right, and to let him know that it's time to relax. Start off by rubbing under your puppy's chin and saying "good boy" (or something similar). It's important to be very cheerful and excited to let the puppy know he did something good. As time progresses a simple yet affectionate little rub under the chin will be all the affirmation your pup needs.

Whatever you use, your puppy's reaction is the most important indicator that you are on track. Does your type of praise make his eyes bright and get that tail wagging? If he is bored by your technique, working to find out what he likes will improve every part of your relationship.

Never praise your puppy if he does his work in a distracted or preoccupied manner; he may think you are praising his inattention. Instead, do sneakaways to help him realign his priorities.

On the flip side, punishment will do little in terms of training a puppy, unless you want to train your puppy to be timid. Generally, a dog will not link punishment to doing something wrong. Regular punishment will only make your puppy afraid of your training sessions.

CHAPTER 13

Common Behavioral Problems

So, you thought puppyhood would be full of Kodak moments—the kids happily playing ball with the puppy, puppy curled up asleep in Dad's lap while he watches TV, a smiling, happy ball of fur scampering beside you to discover the world—and instead you've got a miniature terrorist on your hands. Does it seem like all your puppy does is get into or cause trouble? Is he playing too rough with your kids, barking or crying too often, roughly jumping onto people and making a speedway out of your home?

A Puppy Is a Puppy Is a Puppy

The first thing to remember is that a puppy is a puppy. Does that mean you just have to grin and bear this trying time? Of course not. But it does mean you need to look at and understand your puppy for what he is: a baby learning about the world. Like human babies, puppies explore with their mouths, their paws (hands), and all their senses. They are soaking up everything about their environment, including how their littermates and the "adults" in their world respond to it. If something's exciting to others in their pack, it'll be exciting to your puppy; if something smells good, tastes good, or feels good, he wants a part of it.

So what are you going to do about it? Like any good parent, your job is to teach your puppy the rules. Not by yelling, hitting, choking, or hurting your puppy—which only makes him afraid of you—but by truly teaching. Knowing what you want your puppy to do is the first step. Then set up small but achievable goals that you and your puppy can celebrate together.

FACTS

Miracle cures, gadgetry, and fads may propose easy solutions to difficult problems. Typically, attempts to solve problems with a single tactic or object usually fail. For example, using odor remover on your carpeting won't abolish house-soiling, and using a no-pull harness won't teach your dog to heel. On the other hand, multifaceted solutions are recommended and highly successful—like ridding your carpet of odor and using the housebreaking advice in this book. A new word, for example, may be a beneficial addition to your training program if it works for you and your puppy.

Review the basic training methods described in Chapter 12, because if your puppy knows to listen to you when you ask him to sit, lie down, come, and so on, he'll be responsive to your teaching when it comes to solving problem behaviors.

Problem-Solving Mindset

To teach your puppy good manners, which should minimize problems, remember the following: Teach fairly and wisely. Be the role model for your puppy (and your family).

Ask yourself how you're contributing to the problem. Remember, it's only a problem if you think it's a problem; your puppy doesn't think digging in the yard is a problem, he thinks it's great fun.

Ten Common Puppy Problems

These are the ten problems you're most likely to experience as a new puppy owner (besides housetraining):

- Mouthing and nipping
- Chewing
- Barking, crying, and whining
- Digging
- Jumping up
- Playing too rough, rowdiness
- Separation anxiety
- Submissive urination
- Begging
- Stealing food, clothing, or other objects

We'll address each of these in the rest of the chapter.

Many people think their puppies are so cute. And as such, when their puppies do something mischievous, we tend to sometimes laugh. Now, I don't want you to be a curmudgeon, but don't indulge your dog in things as a puppy that you would not want him to do as a dog. What a puppy does and can get away with becomes tiresome and annoying when he becomes a dog.

Mouthing and Nipping

Even if you've only had your puppy one day you've learned that he explores things with his mouth. This is completely natural; he can't help it! If your puppy came from a sizeable litter, he learned to roughhouse and play with his littermates using his mouth, body, and paws. So his mouth is his direct access to everything pleasurable, and his method of saying, "Enough" or "Back Off."

Cavalier King Charles Spaniel

Photo by Mary Bloom©

What you have to discourage is your puppy using his mouth to "maul" you or anyone with the sharpness of his teeth or the strength of his jaws. Here's how.

If your puppy chomps down too hard on your finger, hand, wrist, ankle—any body part—immediately cry out in pain. Say, "OUCH," and make it sound like you just got your entire limb bitten off by a shark. Don't raise your voice in anger. Don't strike out at your puppy. Don't shake your limb or pull it away from your puppy's mouth. Just let out a big YELP. That should surprise him enough so that he stops pressing down and looks up at you.

As soon as your puppy releases you, change your tone completely and warmly (not excitedly) praise your puppy. Hopefully you have a toy available nearby. Give that to him and tell him what a good puppy he is to take the toy. Instructed this way, most puppies quickly learn bite inhibition.

The biggest problem with a mouthy puppy and a family is that while it might be easy for you to control yourself and respond correctly when puppy gets you with those razor-sharp puppy teeth, it's usually not the way children respond. Their natural tendency is to pull away from the puppy or flail at the puppy—both behaviors that may incite the puppy to increase his attempts to nip because he thinks this is rough play.

Teach your children how to react to this situation by staging it with your puppy and demonstrating to them the response you want. Your puppy and your children will learn at the same time.

If you suspect that your puppy is acting inappropriately even when you've tried to teach him right, don't let him continue to mouth and nip so that he's harming anyone. Ask your veterinarian to refer you to a trainer or behavior specialist who can assess and diagnose your puppy—before it's too late.

Barking

Out of respect for other household members, neighbors, tenants, and anyone with a low tolerance for barking, correct this problem—otherwise, you may be forced to get rid of your dog or face eviction. Don't worry that your dog will stop barking all together. Teaching barking inhibition increases his value as a watchdog because when he barks, you'll know it's for good reason.

To correct barking, even if it is only a problem in your absence, teach the dog to be "Quiet" or "Shush" on command when he's standing next to you. The best way to do this is to also teach your dog to "Speak," or bark on command. Then you can teach him to "Quiet" or "Shush."

Teach "Speak" by getting your puppy's attention with a treat or toy. Get him excited by teasing him with the treat and saying in a barklike way, "Speak!" As soon as your dog lets out a woof, give him the treat or toy. Good puppy! Try this again two or three times. Your pup should catch on to "Speak" pretty quickly.

When you think he's got "Speak" learned, as soon as he takes the treat or toy (during which time he won't be able to make a noise), say "Quiet." He won't associate the word with his not barking for a while. You'll need to refrain from giving him the treat or toy for increasing amounts of time after you say, "Quiet" so he starts to associate that request with getting the reward.

If your dog will obey the "Quiet" command without you having to raise your voice or repeat yourself, no matter what the distractions, barking in your absence will usually subside. If it doesn't, you may be unintentionally reinforcing excessive barking by attempting to silence a dog by petting him or giving him a toy or by allowing him to be vocal without repercussion.

If your puppy respects the "Quiet" command and you never tolerate barking or try to appease him but he continues to vocalize in your absence, find out exactly when and why he is barking. Record him with a tape recorder when you leave, ask a neighbor about his habits and spy on him. If he is not barking at outside noises, separation anxiety is probably the problem. Read about handling separation anxiety later in this chapter.

Crying and Whining

Believe it or not, these two behaviors can bother you even more than barking. Why? Because it's so hard for your puppy to understand what you want him to stop doing when he's crying or whining. The best remedy is to completely ignore your complaining pup when he's doing either of these things. It will be very difficult for you. After all, a crying pup is like a crying baby—your instinct tells you to go and do what you can to relieve whatever the discomfort is that's causing the crying or whining. Remember the old adage that dogs do things to get what they want. If your dog has been adequately fed, exercised, and loved, the only other thing he could want is more attention, more food, or more exercise. But he's not the one who should be dictating that, because next thing you know he may decide he wants to stroll the block at 3 A.M. No, your puppy gets the things he needs because you oversee his environment responsibly enough so that his needs are taken care of. Therefore, crying and whining become behaviors whose sole purpose is to get your attention. Don't become a slave to them!

If your puppy is crying or whining for no apparent reason other than to get you to pay attention to him, try turning on a radio or television to block out the sound of his protestations. As hard as it will be, ignore your puppy's cries. However, the second he stops crying (eventually he has to stop), go to him and reward him with attention, exercise, or food. If you're trying to break a habitual cry or whine, you'll need to increase the time between when your dog stops and when you go to him so that he truly associates that he's being praised for being quiet. Another solution to crying or whining is to startle the puppy. This doesn't have to be a physical force correction; instead, it's intended solely to break the offensive action and try to redirect the behavior.

Chewing

The table. The chairs. The rug. The sofa. The car seats. The kids' toys. The garden hose. The swimming pool cover. The remote control. A cell phone. You name it and a dog has chewed it to bits. Is there a worse feeling than coming home and seeing your beloved sound asleep amid a cyclone of destruction? After all, you feed him, exercise him, buy him great toys, comfy beds, keep him up on his shots, and love him to pieces. And this is what you get in return?

You're not going to want to hear this, but 99 percent of the time the destruction is your fault. You allowed the puppy too much freedom while alone in the house. You didn't provide any puppy-friendly chew toys. You left the puppy alone too long. You left one of your favorite "things" (cell phone, remote, handbag, shoes, pillow, etc.) within reach of your inquisitive puppy—and don't underestimate the reach of a bored puppy. Next thing you know, your stuff's history.

What do you do when this happens? Yell at your puppy? Spank or shove your puppy? Isolate your puppy (to "show him")? No, no, no.

Please—for your sake and your puppy's. The first thing to do is take your puppy outside. He will probably need to relieve himself after all the fun he's had and the stuff he's eaten. If possible, leave him outside in a fenced area while you go back in to survey the damage. Make sure immediately that your puppy hasn't eaten anything that could be poisonous (prescription drugs, household cleaners, some houseplants) or damaging to sensitive body organs (pins, splintered bones, large buttons). If you find any remnants of anything dangerous in the debris, call your veterinarian immediately and ask him or her if you need to bring your puppy in for an examination.

Miniature Pinscher

Photo by Mary Bloom©

If the damage is just, well, damage, bring your puppy inside and put him in his crate. While you're cleaning up, you will probably want to cry or curse. That's okay, just don't direct it at your puppy. He'll pick up how upset you are, and if he thinks he's the cause, he may worry that you will always react this way to him. Then you have a puppy who hasn't learned anything except that Mommy or Daddy is very scary when they come home, which will make the puppy more anxious, which will lead to more destructive chewing.

After you've cleaned up, assess how your puppy was able to get to what he got into. Did you leave the garbage can where he could tip it over? Did you think it was safe to confine him to the kitchen and the den now that he's older? Lesson learned: don't do it again.

FACTS

Puppies need and love to chew, and it's up to you to give them the kinds of chew toys that will satisfy—or they'll invent their own! Getting your puppy into a good chew toy habit now will save you thousands of dollars in destroyed belongings. Puppies like soft, squeaky toys. Since they can chew the squeakers out of some toys, it's best to give these to your puppy under supervision. Then you can both enjoy the fun!

What you want to do is make sure that your puppy has chew toys he's really interested in. Smear peanut butter in a rubber Kong. That'll keep him busy. Add different sizes of treats and kibble so they fall out gradually over the course of a few hours or the day. (Remember to subtract this amount of food from his regular meals.) Get a cube or round toy that you can put treats into and that puppy needs to bat around to get the treats out. Puppies are most prone to get into trouble just after we leave and just before we come home. They miss us when we go and get excited to see us later. This time can seem like an eternity. But you can have your puppy loving to see you leave and well-behaved when you come home by getting him hooked on safe chews that earn tasty rewards.

Don't think your puppy will want to chew less if he's by himself outside or in his crate. He'll get bored just as quickly in these spots as he will the well-appointed living room if he doesn't have something to chew on to take his mind off things.

Digging

Digging is practically the only problem that cannot be prevented, lessened, or solved with obedience training (although sometimes training, because it relieves boredom, indirectly reduces the behavior). Dogs don't dig because they are dominant, belligerent, unaware of authority, or out of control—they do it instinctually to make a cool or warm place to lie down or to make a nestlike den for their puppies. And, yes, interesting smells in the soil, the wonderful feeling of vigorous burrowing, and dirt in their toes are hard for any dog to resist. Therefore, monitoring your dog and correcting digging attempts is an ongoing process—you aren't fighting your dog, you are fighting nature. Your best option is to never leave your dog unsupervised in an area with digging potential, but if you can't always do that.

The best thing to do is recognize and accept your dog's need to dig, and then give him a place where he can do it to his heart's content. Choose a part of your yard or garden that can be your puppy's sandbox, just as you'd provide for a child. Make sure the area is large enough and block it off with a border. Dig a small hole in the spot and put a cheese-smeared bone in it. Bring your dog over, and when he starts digging in the spot, praise him. If he gets rewarded for digging here, he'll probably return to check it out again. Refresh the goodies you stash in this spot occasionally.

Another option is to exercise him vigorously and regularly so he doesn't seek aerobic activity from digging. For some dogs that's still not enough. If you live near a beach or a park or someplace where digging won't permanently deface the landscape, encourage your dog to dig there.

Fill previously dug holes with dog feces. Most won't return to dig in that hole—especially if they're finding tasty treats by digging somewhere else.

Jumping Up

Some puppies have no desire to jump up. They are content to let you bend down to pet them. Others jump up either because they are very bold and sociable or because they have been rewarded for doing so with petting and attention.

Jumping Up on People

If you don't want your puppy to get into a bad jumping-up habit, or if you want to teach him not to jump up now, here's what to do. When guests or family members enter your house and shower the dog with affection, they teach the dog to jump up and act crazy. For good-sized, healthy adults, this can even be fun. But for elderly, frail people, young children, and finely attired guests or strangers, not only is it not fun, it can be very dangerous. This doesn't mean your dog can never jump up on someone to play. It means that he can do so only when asked, and always well after anyone has entered the house. Though play, fun, and enthusiasm are an important part of a well-balanced, bonded relationship, they should never be associated with people coming and going.

Great Dane

Photo by Mary Bloom©

Encourage visitors and members of your household to show self-control. Practice calm arrivals by making it a habit to busy yourself doing other things, oblivious to your dog's prancing, barking, jumping, or panting. As you walk in the door, if your puppy starts leaping on you, simply ignore him. Don't even make eye contact or say anything to him. Walk away. Listen to your phone messages, sort through your mail. Totally ignore him until he settles down. Then calmly say, "Good puppy," and gently pet and praise him. Ask him to sit, and give him extra petting when he does. Insist that guests and family members do the same. Within two weeks of practicing uneventful arrivals, usually jumping up entirely subsides.

If calm arrivals haven't cured your dog, continue practicing them but, in addition, try these strategies.

Teach your puppy to sit at the sound of someone at the door. This will not happen overnight. It's something you have to work on with your puppy, and you'll need the help of a family member, friend, or neighbor. Set up fifteen to thirty minutes to work with your puppy every few days for a couple of weeks. On the first lesson, you work with your puppy inside the house while your assistant plays the visitor.

With your puppy in a buckle collar and on the leash, and you with some small, handy treats in your pocket, have your assistant ring the doorbell. Calmly walk to the front door and, before opening it, ask your puppy to sit, praise and reward with a treat when he does. Open the door and hold on to the leash so he can't jump up high. With your assistant holding the door open, ask your puppy to sit. He probably won't want to listen. Get his attention with your treat, then lure him into a sit if necessary. Praise. Greet your assistant as a guest.

Instruct your assistant that as he or she crosses the threshold of the door, they are to respond to the puppy in one of two ways.

1. If the puppy is still trying to jump up, spinning around and acting overexcited, your "guest" should completely ignore him. Walk on by and inside the house. You stay by the door and wait until your guest is out of puppy's sight. Ask for another sit and praise when he does.

   Take your puppy, still on leash, into the other room. Ask him to sit, and have your assistant approach the puppy. Give your assistant a small treat and have him or her ask your puppy to sit. When the puppy sits, the guest gives the treat. Your puppy then associates sitting with a nice greeting.

2. If the puppy is fairly calm, give your guest a small treat and have him or her ask the puppy to sit. Treat and praise when he does. Give a warm, friendly greeting (nothing overexciting) and calmly go into another room.

By whichever procedure you've gotten there, once you're in the other room, sit down and calmly chat for a minute or so, ignoring the puppy. Then start all over again. Your "guest" should ring the doorbell and practice entrances with you for no longer than thirty minutes a few times a week. Vary the people you ask to be your "guests" so your puppy doesn't just think he only greets your husband nicely. If you work this way for a few weeks, then follow this routine every time you have a visitor, you'll be amazed at the results.

Jumping Up on Counters and Furniture

Many people enjoy having their dogs on the furniture with them, whether it's on the sofa, a favorite armchair, or the bed. Dogs love it, too, because not only does the furniture smell like you, it's comfortable and usually affords him a better view of what is going on both inside and outside. The glitch is that once you allow him on the furniture, his scent goes on it, too, and it becomes his domain, so don't expect him to wait politely for the next invitation. If he's sneaking on the furniture despite your consistent disapproval, provide your dog with his own piece of furniture—a very comfortable dog bed (store-bought or homemade).

ESSENTIALS

If he's still getting on furniture, you may find that compromise is your best option. Put an old sheet or throw over your pup's preferred piece of furniture. That way, when you're not there, he won't stain or shed all over the furniture. As often as you want, remove the sheet and throw it in the wash. This works for sofas, chairs, and beds.

Playing Too Rough

Many owners say their dog's favorite game is tug of war. And for many owners it's pretty fun, too—until your once fifteen-pound fluff ball is seventy pounds of adolescent muscle and will do anything to win. Or until he starts to growl whenever you come near any of his toys. This doesn't mean you can't play tug of war. It just means that, like everything else, you have to call the shots. You determine when the game begins and when it ends. This is where "Drop it" comes in handy again. If tug-of-war is turning into war, say, "Drop it" and stop pulling. If he doesn't let go right away, don't pull again. Say, "Drop it" again. If he doesn't, get up and walk away. It's you he wants to play with. Don't turn his resilience into a contest of wills. When he has dropped it, without saying anything, go get the tug toy and put it away where he can't reach or find it by himself.

If you keep tug games short and in control from the very beginning, you and your dog will be able to enjoy them within appropriate limits. Make sure the rest of your family understands these tug game rules, too.

The same goes for any kind of rough-housing, whether you're doing it with a toy, your hands, rolling on the floor, whatever. Start with fun, short sessions, and when you've had enough, say, "That's all," and calmly stop whatever you're doing.

QUESTIONS?

How do you know if you're playing too rough?
Never work him into a frenzy; instead, learn how to make games fun and low key. You should be able to stop the game at any time and walk away. Never use games to frighten your puppy or hurt him. Your puppy is going to get stronger and bolder as it ages. If your puppy doesn't develop an appropriate level of control, you run the risk of your puppy injuring someone.

Playing with Other Puppies

Rough play among puppies is usually harmless amusement for humans and canines. If generally friendly and tolerant of one another, puppies rarely inflict injury. They will get noisy and animated: growling, barking, squealing, tumbling, and dragging one another by convenient body parts (like ears and limbs) is common. Break them up only if one is being endangered or if the play occurs in a formal living room or while people desire quiet. Don't raise your voice to break them up. Instead, leash one or both puppies and give a subdued command to stop, then enticingly lure your puppy away from the action and reward him for following you by giving him a treat and telling him what a good boy he is.

Separation Anxiety

Having to leave a dog alone is worrisome if he gets frantically frustrated when he's separated from his owner. Overly dependent dogs commonly respond to separations by continually barking, whining, and howling, destroying his living space, and attempting to escape by chewing, digging, and jumping over fences and out of windows. In addition to causing expensive damage, many dogs injure themselves. When panicked, they are oblivious to the physical discomforts of laryngitis, bloody-raw gums and paws, broken teeth, self-mutilation caused by chewing and licking, and even broken limbs as a result of jumping out of windows.

How are you supposed to live with a puppy who practically holds you hostage by not being able to be left alone? Here's my advice: Avoid both after-the-fact corrections, which increase anxiety, and consoling tones or gentle petting, which reinforce the neurosis. Instead:

- Exercise your puppy vigorously and regularly.
- Improve his ability to handle all sources of stress by teaching reliable obedience.
- As you come and go, remain relaxed and refrain from addressing your dog.
- To directly increase his tolerance of separations, practice these three exercises:

1. *Random tie outs:* Insist that he remain quiet when you leave. Take your dog to indoor and outdoor areas, familiar and unfamiliar, filled with or absent of distractions. Silently tie his leash short to a stationary object and walk away for a few minutes. Sometimes remain in sight and other times walk out of sight. When you do return to him, praise him for being a good puppy. Practice every other day for a half hour until he'll be silent regardless of where you leave him, where you go and how long you're gone.

2. *Out-of-sight sit- and down-stays.* This is the same principle as the previous exercise, except you're asking your puppy to stay sitting or lying down as you leave for increasing amounts of time. Don't expect a puppy younger than six months old to be able to sit and stay for longer than a minute or so, same with staying down. But as you work with your puppy on the out-of-sight exercise, you can get in an occasional sit-stay or down-stay, and reward him for

doing so. As your puppy gets older, you can increase the lengths of time you ask your puppy to stay seated or down.

3. *Whirling Dervish Departures:* Dash from room to room grabbing your keys, briefcase, jacket, lunch box, etc. Rush out the door and to your car then back out of the driveway, motor around the block, pull back in the garage and saunter into the house. As you put your things away, completely ignore your puppy. After relaxing for a few minutes, repeat the frenzied departure and relaxed arrival over and over for an hour. Repeat this pattern three times the first week, then once a week for a month.

To reinforce your training, make it a habit to periodically confine your puppy while you're at home. Sequester him in a quiet area and place your recently worn sweatshirt or bathrobe on the floor on the other side of the closed door. If your smell permeates his room, he may not even realize it when you finally do leave. Give him his favorite toy only when you confine him. Then, when you do actually leave, follow the same routine.

FACTS

Many people leave the radio or TV on for their puppies while they're gone from the house. The idea is the noise will help them feel less alone. My advice is to avoid leaving a TV or radio on, because your puppy may become a victim of unsettling and noisy programming and advertisements. I tell owners they should replace that cacophony with white noise; the gentle whir of a fan puts puppies at ease (so long as it's not blowing cold air on them), or you could try an indoor fountain (one your puppy couldn't reach or get to), or a white noise machine.

Since separation problems can periodically return despite these precautions, reinstate these recommendations as needed.

Begging, Stealing, and Scavenging

It often takes only one tidbit for your clever puppy to be convinced that your meals are better than his and that you're willing to share if he begs.

If you've fostered this bad habit, it can be broken, but you probably can't be cured. You have to stop feeding him ANY human food any time around mealtime. I know your puppy is your best buddy, and if you've enjoyed your pizza, why not give him some of the crust? It sure makes him happy! The answer is: be aware of the repercussions. Don't expect your puppy to differentiate from the times you eat a pizza in front of the tube and gladly share it with him and the time you have your daughter's soccer team over for pizza and you don't want him underfoot or being fed by every member of the team then getting sick.

Differentiate your mealtimes and his by confining him in his crate or a separate room where he can't watch you while you eat. Give him a favorite toy so he's distracted and doesn't whine, cry, drool, or stare you down. Stay strong!

Stealing and Scavenging

If you were all alone in someone else's house, what would you do when you got bored? Would the thought of looking at their stuff or even rummaging through cabinets, closets, or the refrigerator tempt you?

Now you know how a dog feels. He is trapped and bored and has no hands with which to do arts and crafts, but he does have plenty of senses yearning to be indulged. When given too much freedom too soon, he will quickly discover the joys of hunting for household treasures too often left easily accessible by negligent humans.

Many dogs steal for amusement when you're home. They know the only guaranteed way to rouse you from the recliner is to show off the valuables that have been confiscated. Police your canine kleptomaniac by:

* Incarceration—crating
* Chain gang—umbilical-cording
* Surveillance—keeping your eyes glued to him

Don't be a victim, keep the garbage out of reach, close cabinets and closets and put laundry away, teach the "Drop it" or "Leave it" command, and dispense justice fairly. Only correct crimes in progress, never correct stealing after the fact. Upon discovering the infraction, leash your dog, invite him to make the same mistake, and correct it by redirecting his attention to something he needs to do to get a reward, such as praise and/or treats from mom.

Problem Prevention

Miniature Schnauzer

Photo by Mary Bloom®

Giving an untrained puppy freedom in your house can be deadly. Natural curiosity and boredom cause them to chew electrical cords, ingest toxic substances, and destroy valuables. When given freedom too soon, puppies who don't accidentally execute themselves often become homeless because of damage the owner is angry about but could have and should have prevented. Puppies are opportunists. This doesn't mean they are bad; it just means we are foolish if we walk out of the room leaving goodies on the coffee table and truly believe our puppies would never even think about touching them.

If you don't know where your puppy is, he is probably into something he shouldn't be. Save your valuables, your sanity, and your puppy by watching his every move, umbilical cording him, or confining him to a safe, destruction-proof area.

CHAPTER 14

Obedience Training

Here, you will learn how to get your puppy to obey your wishes. While basic training will teach a puppy how to behave properly in general, obedience training will give you the ability to get your dog to do what you want, when you want it to. Not only that, but obedience training is the foundation to more advanced tricks.

Sit and Sit/Stay

There are a couple of ways to teach "Sit" effectively. I prefer the first method, but I encourage you to try both to see which one works best for you and your puppy. You could even alternate to see if your puppy is really learning the command or just the associated actions.

Method 1: Teach the "Sit" command by putting your puppy on your left side, holding his collar with your right hand and putting your left hand on his loin just in front of his hip bones and behind his rib cage. Command "Sit" as you pull upward on his collar and push downward on his loin. Talk, pet, and praise, but don't let the puppy move. When necessary, reposition him by pushing him back into the sit as you tighten up on the collar. After a few seconds, release with "Chin-touch okay." If he is rigid and won't budge then move him forward and walk him into the sit.

ESSENTIALS

"Sit" is something you can ask your puppy to do many times during the day, so it's easy to practice. Remember to keep these training opportunities short, focused, and enthusiastic. Ask/train your puppy to sit before any meal; before you put his collar on; before you open his crate door; before you give him a hello or good-bye petting; when he approaches you to play; before you let him jump on your lap or share the sofa with you; or just at random.

Method 2: With a small, yummy treat in your hand, like a sliver of hot dog or cheese, get your puppy's attention. When his nose is sniffing at the treat in your hand, without letting him eat it, keep your fingers close to his nose and raise your hand up and back. In order for his nose to follow your hand, your puppy will have to raise his head, which will naturally cause his hindquarters to go down into a sit. Say, "Sit" while you're moving your hand, and as soon as puppy is in the sit position, give him the treat and praise, saying, "Good sit!" Do this only two or three times, then take a break.

Vary the Environment

To proof the "Sit," ask your pup to sit on a strange-feeling surface—plastic bubble wrap, gravel, or a wire grate. Place him in the "Sit" if he refuses, then try a more normal surface like wet black top, slippery linoleum, or sand. Then ask him to sit on something really comfortable like a thick rug, plush carpeting, or a pillow. Practice several times a day on the most difficult surfaces first, then medium, and finally easy. Consider the command mastered when he willingly obeys the first "Sit" on the strangest surface.

Advancing to Sit/Stay

Before asking your puppy to sit and stay, your puppy should be a champ at sitting on command and waiting to be released with the "Chin-touch okay."

Rhodesian Ridgeback

Photo by Mary Bloom©

To start off, hold the leash taut over puppy's head. Say, "Stay" in a firm voice, then take one step back from him. While looking at your puppy, count silently to three, then release with a chin-touch okay and praise your puppy. Do this once more, and if your puppy stays for the whole count of three, give him a big hug and do something else for a while. If your puppy moves his head or wags his tail, that's acceptable, but you should correct scooting forward, rotating, and attempts to stand by pulling up on the leash and repeat "Stay" firmly.

If your puppy tries to lie down, tighten the leash enough to prevent him from lowering comfortably into the down position and give him praise as he realizes he doesn't have enough slack to lie down. Loosen the lead and prepare to repeat this sequence many times during the next week of training if your puppy is one who is inclined to recline.

You may be wondering why you should care about lying down on the sit stay if you're not thinking of doing any competitive obedience. The answer is simple: you need your puppy to sit, not lie down, so you can look in his mouth, administer medication or ear ointment, or wipe dirt off his paws. Say what you mean and mean what you say to avoid confusion in all areas of training.

Sit/Stay from Farther Away

Once your puppy understands stay with you close in front of him, you can start increasing your distance from him while still expecting him to stay in a sit. To do this, ask him to "Stay," and take three of four steps back. Silently count to three, then release with "Okay" and praise your puppy. Increase both the amount of time you ask him to sit/stay and the distance you walk away from him until you can walk out to the end of the leash and he holds a sit/stay for seven or eight seconds. What a good puppy!

When he's solid with sitting and staying from a distance, introduce distractions like stepping side to side, bending down, pulling forward lightly on the leash, or dropping food or toys in front of your puppy. This teaches him that no matter what your preoccupation or what activities surround him, he stays put. While creating distractions, as long as your puppy remains in the sit/stay, tell him "Good stay."

Stop movement immediately by 1) sliding your free hand down almost to the snap of the leash as you step toward your puppy; 2) quickly maneuvering your puppy back into place without saying a word; 3) pulling upward on the leash; or 4) moving back to the end of the leash.

Enforce sit/stays while you 1) address a postcard, 2) read the headlines, 3) pop in a video, 4) empty the garbage, 5) download a computer file, 6) tie your shoes, 7) wrap a gift, 8) get stuck on hold,

9) weed a flowerbed. When you no longer need to allow spare time for corrections, your puppy has mastered the sit/stay.

Basic Guidelines for "Stays"

- Just before leaving your puppy, use a hand signal along with your "Stay" command. To signal, flash the palm of your free hand, fingers down toward his eyes.
- Use distractions—people, places, movement, food, toys—to test him and confirm he's learning.
- Be acutely attentive, and move in to correct the instant your puppy begins leaving the "Stay" position; otherwise, he'll wonder what the correction was for.
- Correct silently. If your puppy didn't listen the first time, repeating yourself will only cause further confusion or disobedience. Let your hands and leash alone amend his error.
- Adjust the strength of your correction to your puppy's size, level of training, why he moved and how excited or distracted he is.
- Leave instantly after the jerk.
- Finish all "Stays" by walking to the puppy's right side, giving praise, then using the "Chin-touch okay" release.

Down

Again, there are a few ways to teach your puppy to down.

Method 1: While your pup is sitting, place your thumb and index finger behind his shoulder blades and on either side of the backbone. Say, "Down" as you push down on his back and shoulders. When he's on the floor, praise by scratching his tummy, then release him with the "Chin-touch okay."

Method 2: With your puppy in the sit position and a tasty treat in your hand, hold the treat near his nose so he gets interested in it. Without letting him eat it but so that his nose follows your hand, start to slowly lower your hand toward the floor and toward you. The idea is to get his front end to come down toward your hand and then follow your hand out until he's lying down.

Many puppies stand up while they follow the lure with their nose. You can either keep a hand on his hindquarters to keep them down, or you can sneak the food lure under a chair so that he has to scooch on his tummy to follow it. As soon as he's down, feed the treat and say, "Good down!" Then release with the chin-touch okay.

If your puppy braces when you try Method 1, use your right hand to pull his head down to the ground as you push. Another option is to push with the fingers of the left hand as you use your right hand to lift the front paw that is bearing most of his weight. If you still simply can't get him down, discontinue work on the down and concentrate on perfecting the sit/stay around distractions; rare is the puppy who resists the down after becoming completely cooperative on the sit.

Once your puppy knows what down means, practice rapid-fire downs by commanding "Down," giving praise and releasing with the chin-touch okay and repeating the sequence for one minute, three times per training session. Exceptional puppies may learn the verbal "Down" command in a week. With an average of twenty repetitions per day, most puppies will down 50 percent of the time after one month.

But getting certain puppies into the "Down" can look like a scene from all-star wrestling. It's better to deal with these shenanigans in your house than at the veterinarian's office, where similar protests will be common if you haven't done this homework to abolish tantrums.

ALERT

Many puppies try to weasel out of the "Down" with their paws and mouth. Though they aren't actively threatening, the owner may be advised to wear a sweatshirt, pants, and gloves so flailing nails and teeth can't scratch the skin. Three ten-minute sessions practicing down, release, down, release, over and over usually teaches compliance.

Testing Your Puppy on the Down

- Eliminate your body language by putting your hands in your pockets and evaluating yourself in front of a mirror. Your mouth is the only part of your anatomy that should move when commanding "Down."

- Whisper the "Down" command.
- Turn your back and look over your shoulder at your puppy to give the command.
- Stand in the shower (without running the water), sit in your car, or lie on a bed, stairs, or sofa, ask your puppy to down, and see if your command still has authority.

Advancing to Down/Stay

The down/stay command is an excellent one for your puppy to know. Then you can tell your puppy to lie down and stay for grooming and examinations, during meals, or as guests arrive, or just to calm your puppy. Don't move on to this unless your puppy can do a leash-length sit/stay around distractions and can "Down" on command.

To start, ask your puppy to "Down," then say "Stay" in a firm voice. While he's down, examine his ears, eyes, teeth, and paws. Use a pull on the leash or a two-finger push to correct movements like crawling, rolling, or ascension. Praise him frequently when he cooperates, and return to his right side to praise and then release him with the chin-touch okay.

Although there is no need for the puppy to stare at you while he is in the down stay, you should correct grass munching, sniffing, or licking himself by saying, "Ach" in a startling way to get his attention back on you. Praise when he looks at you, and reinforce the "Stay."

Heel

Like the skill and art of dancing, the benefits of heeling stretch well beyond the exercise itself. Dancing is a wonderful form of recreation on the dance floor, but the posture, alignment, controlled energy, balance, and poise practiced in dance movements sashay into everyday tasks.

The heel command teaches the puppy to walk on your left side regardless of your pace or direction and to sit when you stop. Gone are the days of him pulling ahead or dragging behind, weaving from side to side or getting underfoot during walks. As the puppy learns to heel and you learn how to teach him to move precisely, a deeper learning takes place for both of you. To remain in position, the puppy's awareness, watchfulness, and willingness grow. Since you need to watch your puppy very intently during the process, you'll develop a sense of knowing what the puppy is going to do before he does it—otherwise known as "reading" your puppy. Trust and respect develop as you and your canine partner master the art of heeling. This newly formed bond will help you channel the puppy's energy more efficiently no matter what the task, challenge, or obstacle.

Your goal is to teach your puppy to maintain heel position, on your left side, with his shoulder aligned with yours, and his body three inches from your leg. The position is the same whether you're moving forward, turning, or standing still. When you stop, your puppy should sit automatically.

Before you begin, practice sneakaways (steps 1–3) for at least one week, until your puppy is attentive to you despite distractions.

To begin, hold the leash in your right hand with your right thumb through the loop and four fingers holding the slack just as you did during leash-length sneakaways. Say, "[puppy's name], heel" as you begin walking. Prepare to stop by grabbing the collar with your right hand and using your left to place his rear end into a sitting position so his right front foot is alongside your left ankle.

As you walk along preparing to halt, control your puppy's position using the fold-over maneuver. Grab the leash with your left hand and hold it taut over puppy's head, then use your right to grip the braiding or stitching of the leash just above the snap. Next, take your left hand off the leash and use it to place puppy in a sit in perfect heel position as you halt.

If your puppy forges ahead, do a leash-length sneakaway. Drop the slack of the leash, grip the handle, hold your hands at your waistline, and run away. As the puppy returns to your side, return to the original leash grip, holding the slack, as you continue walking.

If your puppy lags behind, say, "Good puppy!" as you spring ahead by taking a puddle jump with your left leg first. As you do this, your left thigh will pull the leash, and your puppy, back to the heel position. The jump ahead will also prevent the puppy from crossing behind you to the right side.

Going from Heel to Sit

Before you begin this, your puppy should reliably sit 80 percent of the time when you ask him. He shouldn't need to be touched or retold. What you want him to do is stop heeling and go into the sit position. Here's what to do.

1. Command, "[puppy's name], heel" and move off on your left foot.
2. Prepare to stop by gathering the leash in both hands.
3. As you finish your last step, pull up on the leash, and say, "Sit." You'll need to practice this over and over. Don't wear yourself or your puppy out. If he doesn't get it the first time, try once more and, if you're successful, end on a positive note. If he doesn't get it the second time, go on to something else and start again later.

Learning to Heel with Turns

You'll need to practice turning while you're heeling. This helps stop tendencies to heel too far from or too close to you, and to correct slight forging and sniffing of the ground. You want to practice turning sharply.

Use the "Jackie Gleason left turn" to stop slight forging, crowding, and sniffing of the ground: Turn ninety degrees to the left, then step perpendicularly into your puppy so your left foot and leg slide or step behind his front legs. Shuffle into him until he becomes attentive and moves back to the left side. Practice slowing your pace abruptly, then turn left immediately if your puppy's shoulder is even one inch ahead of yours. If your puppy attempts to cross in front of you to the right side, tighten the leash with your left hand as you continue to step into him.

To stop wideness, sniffing, or lagging, use puddle jump following a right turn. Pivot ninety degrees to your right on your left foot, take a large step in your new direction with the right foot and leap forward with your left leg as if you were jumping over a puddle. As you jump the puddle you should feel the leash against your left thigh, pulling the puppy forward. Steady your leash by holding your right hand against your right hip as you leap.

Jump and praise simultaneously to motivate your puppy. Hold the leash in your right hand so the slack will remain in front of your thighs as you jump.

Come

One of the most frustrating things for dogs owners is a dog that won't come when called. So that you don't become one of those owners, you want your puppy to learn that when he comes to you when you call him, he will be made to feel like the world's best dog. Coming to you should always be a positive experience. Reward your pup with exuberant praise, tasty treats, a game of fetch, more time on your walk, whatever it takes to let him know that he did the right thing. Your puppy will learn this if you make it easy for him to succeed by starting with short "comes" and progressing to distance "comes." Your sneakaway training should have taught him that he gets the most praise when he comes to you.

Reeling in Your Puppy

Leash your puppy and take him for a walk. If he begins sniffing something, gazing around, or meandering off, call "Buddy, come!" Immediately back up quickly as you reel the leash, praising enthusiastically. Kneel down when puppy arrives, heaping him with verbal praise and occasionally slipping him a super-tasty treat. Release with the chin-touch okay and continue practicing the sequence.

Some puppies will come toward you but stay out of reach or dart right past you. Some owners, without realizing it, encourage the puppy to cut his approach and stay further away by attempting to cradle, caress, or hug the puppy. Petting the puppy as he arrives can create or worsen these recall problems because extending your arms makes it appear you are protecting the space in front of you. Instead, use verbal praise to acknowledge, encourage, and congratulate the puppy's arrival and keep your hands to yourself until he's right with you.

After practicing your reeling recalls twenty or so times, your puppy is probably running toward you faster than you can reel. Now see if he'll leave distractions when you stand still and call, "Come." If he doesn't respond promptly, use a sharp, fast, horizontal jerk toward you as you praise and back up. If he does respond to your command, praise and continue to back up, praising as he nears you.

Standard Poodle

Photo by Karen Taylor©

The goal you want to reach next is to teach your puppy to stop and come when called even if he's running away or you're following him. That sounds like asking a lot of him, doesn't it? But remember again, if you practice asking him to come several times a day and you make it rewarding for him every time he does so, why wouldn't he want to be attentive to you?

Here's what to do: Three times this week create a situation that will cause your puppy to forget his training and pull toward a distraction. For example, ask a fellow puppy owner to go with you on a walk. Instruct him to walk his puppy about ten feet ahead of you. Your puppy is likely to want to catch up to them. As you are walking directly behind your puppy, ask him to come. If he responds, what a good boy! Praise and crouch down to reward him, then release with the chin-touch okay. If he doesn't respond, tug on his leash, back up, call him again, and praise when he turns toward you. Then reel him in.

If your puppy stops when you call him but he doesn't come to you, stay put. Don't chase after him. Pull the leash to let him know you want him to come toward you, then ask again. He should do what you want.

If you intend to call your puppy from a distance, first attach a long, lightweight line to your puppy's collar. When he's distracted, position yourself over the line and call him. Praise him the entire time he's coming toward you, from the time he begins taking his first step toward you until you release with the chin-touch okay. If the puppy ignores your request, correct him by grabbing the line and using "wrap, run, and praise"—wrap the line around your hand twice just above where your thumb attaches to your hand, make a fist around the line, and anchor your hand on your waist as you run away from your puppy. When the line starts to pull him, he will have to follow you. Praise all the way that it takes for him to reach you, then release with the chin-touch okay when he gets to you.

Reliability on the Recall

The goal of this is that whether his last recall was a minute ago or a week ago, he will reliably obey the come command. Before you begin, perfect sneakaways around distractions and practice your recalls with distractions as described previously.

Twice weekly, for thirty minutes, take your puppy to a new location, one he will eagerly explore and continually investigate. Try parks, fields, a friend's yard, or anywhere you know he'll want to investigate. Attach a very long 50- to 200-foot light line to his collar and allow him to roam. Put on your gloves and every five minutes or so, when he least expects it and is running away, call and "wrap, run, and praise."

Basic Guidelines for "Come"

- Don't put your authority at risk by calling come when your puppy may not obey and you know you can't enforce.
- Standardize your voice, always using the same enthusiastic tone that suggests urgency, to say, "Buddy, come!"
- Appeal to your puppy's chase instinct and help ensure a faster recall by moving away after calling come.
- Praise enthusiastically while he approaches. If you wait until he arrives, your lack of commitment will reduce his commitment to the process, too.
- Squat to acknowledge his final approach and arrival.

- Make him come all the way to you. If you suspect your puppy isn't going to make a direct approach, move opposite from the puppy's line of movement so he gets pulled toward you.
- To reward a good response, release immediately with the chin-touch okay. Periodically delay the release as your puppy's recall becomes faster and more reliable.

Wait

A request that comes in very handy around the house is "Wait." Use this to ask your puppy to wait at the door, go in or out of the door, or when you're out of sight.

The "Stay" command means freeze in the sit, down, or stand position and, therefore, is very restrictive. The "Wait" command, though, allows your puppy to move about, but only within certain areas. You can use it to keep your puppy in the car or out of the kitchen. The only thing "Wait" has in common with "Stay" is that both last until the next direction is given, twenty seconds or twenty minutes later.

ESSENTIALS

If your puppy waits but, when released, bounds through the door, mowing down anything in his path and dragging the unfortunate master gripping his leash, say, "Sit" following your chin-touch okay. Practice the pattern of "Wait, Okay, Sit, Come Inside" until he is responding on a slack leash. After inviting him through a main door, command "Sit" immediately following his exit. When he does it on a slack lead the first time through, start doing the same pattern with the leash dragging.

Teach the "Wait" command at doorways first. Choose a lightweight door and estimate how wide your puppy's front end is. Open the door two inches more than that as you command "Wait." Stand there with your hand on the knob of the partially open door, ready to bump the puppy's nose with it should he attempt to pass through the opening. Be sure never to shut the door while correcting. Instead, leave the door open with your hand on the door handle, ready to stop attempted departures with an abrupt and silent bump of the door. If necessary, butt him with a quick movement that makes it appear the door is snapping at him every time he tries to peer or charge out. Leash your puppy so if your attempts to deter him fail and he successfully skips across the border, you can step on the leash and prevent his escape.

Practice at familiar and unfamiliar doors as a helper tries to coerce your puppy to leave. Your helper can talk to the puppy and drop food, but your helper shouldn't call your puppy. As your helper remains on the opposite side of the door, engage in lively conversation to teach your puppy that even when you are preoccupied, the "Wait" command is enforced. When that lesson has been learned you'll no longer need the leash.

CHAPTER 15

Basic Care for Your Puppy's Health

This section will help you keep your puppy healthy and happy for years to come. Remember, the most important part of keeping your puppy healthy is the information you gather right there on the front lines. No one spends more time with your puppy than you and your family. Watch for signs like changes in appetite, general demeanor, and stool consistency. Know what the normal, everyday habits of your puppy are, so that if something changes, you'll be the first to know.

Finding a Veterinarian

There are many good veterinarians around the country. These people are usually dedicated animal lovers and have spent many years training to become a doctor in the animal fields. It takes more schooling and residency to become a veterinarian than it does to be a specialized people doctor. You should have the utmost respect for your chosen veterinarian.

Rottweiler

Photo by Alice Su©

However, all that said, your veterinarian is only as good as you are. The veterinarian doesn't know your dog. He doesn't know your dog's history, habits, or general disposition. Since puppies and dogs can't talk, your veterinarian can only work with what he sees in front of him and what you tell him. During any visit, any good veterinarian will ask plenty of questions. If you've been observant and paying attention, the answer to his or her questions will be found somewhere between your information and his or her examination of the dog. Make sure you know.

If you haven't been to a veterinarian recently, you'll be surprised by the abilities of these small medical centers and the host of animals they must deal with and treat. Today's veterinarians range from large medical complexes to vets who still make house calls. The type that is found in your area will depend on several factors. Veterinarians in rural areas tend to travel more than those in urban or suburban sections of the country. This is because they are used to traveling to farms in a wide-ranging region, where it's easier for the doctor to move around than the livestock.

If you've never had a puppy or dog before, or you are new to an area, finding a veterinarian is a very important step. One of the best things you can do is ask around. Friends, family, neighbors, and other dog owners are all very good places to start. Listen intently and ask plenty of questions. Do they keep good hours? Do you think the doctor spent enough time with you and your pet? What's his or her general disposition? Are they a busy firm? How long has the office been open or how long has the veterinarian been practicing? Does this veterinarian have a specialty?

Usually you will find camps of dog owners who favor one over the other. Some will swear by one and naysay the other. This is typical. But a concerned group of dog owners hanging out at a dog run will never tire of giving you their opinions on the local veterinary situation. Always consider the sources. Is there a person there who seems to be a good, concerned, conscientious owner? Or is it coming from some one who just seems to be blind to his own dog's actions and temperament?

Lastly, make sure you give the veterinarian you've chosen the benefit of the doubt. He or she has studied animal anatomy and physiology for years. They are very well trained. While it's important to be able to tell your veterinarian what you know about your puppy, it's also just as important to let him or her tell you what they know about animal medicine. Certainly, in extreme situations, you may want to seek a second opinion. That's up to you and how much you've come to trust your veterinarian or not. Since puppies, and animals in general, can't tell you what's bothering them, sometimes veterinarians are going to make the wrong diagnosis. These can be expensive, but are not usually life-threatening. Don't berate or start second guessing your veterinarian based on one diagnosis. Should it be habit forming though, you would be within your full rights to terminate that relationship.

An Ounce of Prevention

You love your puppy, so of course you want him to be healthy—alert, bright-eyed, with a lustrous coat and sweet breath. It's no fun for you or your dog to suffer with constant itching, hair loss, vomiting or diarrhea, or stinky dog breath. Believe it or not, it doesn't take repeated visits to the veterinarian or costly drugs to have a healthy dog. All it takes is common sense and vigilance. All it takes is regular preventive care.

What does preventive care mean? It means taking care of your dog the way you take care of yourself. It means:

- Brushing him regularly
- Checking his eyes, ears, and mouth regularly
- Keeping his toenails short
- Feeding him a high-quality food
- Making sure he always has access to cool, clean water
- Keeping his environment clean
- Giving him the attention and exercise he needs
- Spaying or neutering your dog
- Keeping him current on all his vaccines
- Taking him for a regular veterinary checkup at least once a year

Preventive care means you're in touch with your dog's physical and mental condition. Let's look at each of the areas of preventive care and see how they benefit you and your dog.

Regular Brushing

Regular brushing accomplishes so many things! First, it removes dead hair and stimulates new hair growth. It invigorates the skin and coat, adding shine while removing any knots that may be forming and any dirt or dead skin that's sitting in the coat. Brushing feels good to your dog, and he will look forward to having his coat brushed gently and thoroughly. Because your puppy will enjoy being brushed regularly, you'll enjoy brushing him. Grooming sessions are great bonding sessions! But even more important, they're your opportunity to check your dog's skin and coat for any problems.

By brushing your puppy regularly, you'll be able to spot fleas or the tell-tale sign of their presence, "flea dirt," which is the digested blood fleas excrete after a meal. Flea dirt looks like little flecks of pepper sprinkled on your dog's skin. If you wet a paper towel and rub the "dirt" with it, you'll find it dissolves to a rusty red color—blood. If you see flea dirt on your dog, the fleas are not far away, and you'll need to take immediate action to rid your dog and your home of the problem. (Learn how to deal with fleas later in this chapter.)

Brushing will also expose any ticks that may have gotten onto your puppy. There are all different kinds and sizes of ticks, and various ticks carry various diseases. Of course, you must remove any tick you find on your dog right away (learn how later in this chapter), but the sooner you find it the less likely the chance of infection.

You'll also notice cuts, scrapes, and patches of red, swollen, or hairless skin if you brush your puppy regularly, and again, the sooner you find them, the sooner you can treat and relieve them.

FACTS

Did you know the skin is the largest organ in the body? By being the largest organ, it's the most exposed part of the body, and is therefore subject to the greatest onslaught of environmental elements. Your puppy's skin and coat are prime targets for ticks, fleas, prickly seed pods, sharp objects like barbed wire or splinters, all sorts of allergens, and a host of bacteria.

Checking Eyes

It doesn't take a lot of work to check your puppy's eyes—after all, if you're like me, you spend so much time looking into them already that it's no big deal. But to keep your puppy's eyes free from infection, you need to see beyond his best begging look or his I-love-you-madly look and notice whether there's a buildup of excretion in the corners of his eyes, or whether there's any swelling or redness around the eye. It's even possible for your dog to scratch his cornea on sharp grass. To remove excretory buildup around the eyes, use gentle materials like tissues or a soft towel and cleansers specially formulated for use around the eye. Soap stings puppies' eyes, too! If you notice redness, swelling, or scratches, a trip to the veterinarian is warranted.

Checking Ears

Does your puppy have floppy ears or erect ears, long, hairy ears or cropped ears? If you have a prick-eared or cropped-eared dog, you will have to worry less about dirty ears that can lead to infected ears, because more air gets into the inner surfaces of the ear flaps. If your puppy's got floppy ears, no matter the length or thickness of fur on them, you'll need to make sure you check the inner surfaces frequently. The warm, moist environment under the dog's ear is the perfect host to dirt and bacteria build-up. Proper ear-cleaning procedures are described in Chapter 9. Study them and make a point of looking under your dog's ears every few days.

Checking the Mouth

Isn't doggy breath the worst? Make sure your family never has to suffer with it by taking the proper care of your puppy's teeth and mouth. Dogs form plaque and tartar just like we do, but until we teach them how to use a toothbrush, they need our help to keep their pearly-whites spic and span. Don't despair, it's easy to do. There are all sorts of brushes and doggy toothpastes available, or you can use a moist scrap of cheesecloth sprinkled with baking soda and get the same results. Don't use human toothpaste on your puppy! What you want to do is just run a toothbrush or the cheesecloth over your puppy's teeth near the gum line so you loosen the particles. No need to rinse—your puppy will do that when he drinks some water.

Another thing you want to check your puppy's mouth for regularly is to spot problems like chipped teeth, swollen gums, or any cuts. If you notice any of these, call your veterinarian.

Caring for Toenails

Keep those toenails short! Overgrown toenails can cause your puppy's feet to splay, can lead to bone and joint problems, and can even grow so long that they curl under the foot and into the foot pads. Not good!

There are a variety of doggy nail clippers you can use. Experiment to see which you're most comfortable with. (How to clip nails is explained in detail in Chapter 9.)

The Importance of Diet

A thorough discussion of diet and the kinds of foods available for puppies was presented in Chapter 8. You may want to review it to remind yourself just how important it is to the overall health of your puppy. Like us, a dog is what he eats. If he's eating doggy junk food, his whole body will suffer. If he's eating a high-quality food, his whole body will benefit.

Cool, Clean Water

Would you want to drink the lukewarm, slobbery water left in the bottoms of people's water glasses after a meal? No way! Well, your puppy doesn't know enough to not drink the canine equivalent that's often left in his bowl, and because he needs to drink to stay hydrated, he'll drink it anyway. So if you only fill the water bowl once a day or when you get around to it, don't be surprised if your puppy occasionally gets an upset stomach or diarrhea. He needs fresh water all day long. Change the water in his bowl several times a day, and make sure to wash the bowl.

Vaccines

For the rest of his or her life, your puppy will need to receive vaccinations to protect him from major infectious diseases like distemper, parvovirus, leptospirosis, hepatitis, and of course, rabies. Don't desert him now! Your puppy needs his vaccines updated regularly, and there's no excuse for missing them. Your veterinarian will make sure you know when your puppy's due, so make the appointment and take your pup in for his shots. These bacteria are responsible for some diseases that can also infect people, so the health of your puppy and your family is at stake.

Your veterinarian will want to see your dog at least once a year, not just to make sure he's up on his shots, but to give his professional opinion on the overall health of your dog. The vet will examine your dog from head to tail, including his eyes, ears, mouth, feet, limbs, chest, back, and anus. He will ask you about any lumps or bumps he might detect, as well as any swellings or tender spots. He'll let you know if your dog's teeth need a scraping (like ours do occasionally), and he'll advise you about your dog's weight and overall condition. If you've been following the preventive measures described here, you will be proud to hear your veterinarian tell you how healthy your dog looks and acts. Way to go! That's a compliment to the kind of care you're giving your best friend. Keep it up.

A vaccine is intended to work with the immune system to fight against invasive infections of bacteria and viruses. By injecting a harmless amount of the organism the body may someday need to fight off, the immune system is "jump-started" to respond to that organism again if it enters the body. Without vaccines, dogs are far more susceptible to contracting infectious diseases from other dogs and other animals.

Pug

Photo by Mary Bloom©

Veterinarians typically begin a vaccination schedule for a puppy at about six weeks of age. At this time the pup receives a shot for distemper and measles. Approximately eight weeks later, at fourteen to sixteen weeks of age, the pup needs his DHLPP shot, a combination vaccine for distemper, hepatitis, leptospirosis, parainfluenza virus, and parvovirus. The veterinarian may also vaccinate the pup against rabies at this time. Expect to take your dog in for his DHLPP shot every year thereafter, and for his rabies shot as necessary, depending on which vaccine your veterinarian uses (some need to be boosted more often than others). In some parts of the country, veterinarians recommend that dogs receive a vaccine for the tick-borne Lyme disease, too.

These are the deadly diseases you're protecting your dog against with his shots:

Distemper

This is a viral disease that attacks a dog's gastrointestinal (digestive), respiratory, and nervous systems. It can strike at any age, but is most deadly if acquired young, which is why it's one of the first shots a pup receives. A dog with distemper will secrete a thick, yellowish discharge from his nose and eyes. He'll run a fever and he will not want to eat. The pneumonia, encephalitis, and dehydration that can result can be deadly.

Infectious Canine Hepatitis

Another viral disease, this one attacks body tissue, particularly the liver, and most often strikes dogs under twelve months of age. Symptoms are mild and include increased thirst, loss of appetite, abdominal discomfort, and lack of energy. Death is sudden and there is no specific treatment.

Canine Leptospirosis

Lepto strikes the liver and also the kidneys, but this disease is caused by bacteria. Severe infections cause shock and death, but if caught early an aggressive treatment with antibiotics can fight it off. Symptoms include vomiting, excessive thirst with decreased urination and dehydration, and abdominal pain. Lepto is highly contagious, and an infected dog can also pass the bacteria through his urine for some time, even after treatment. The disease is also contagious to people.

Parainfluenza Virus

Parainfluenza is one of the germs involved in what's commonly called "kennel cough," a respiratory condition that results in a harsh, dry cough. Kennel cough is highly contagious, and is so-named because it is usually acquired where there are many dogs living together, such as in a kennel. Kennel cough can be treated with antibiotics, rest, and the proper environment. Affected dogs must be isolated from other dogs, and especially from puppies, who are more severely stricken than older dogs.

Parvovirus

This viral infection manifests itself as an inflammation of the intestinal lining, causing sudden vomiting, bloody diarrhea, a high fever, and rapid weight loss. It is transmitted through the feces and can survive outside a dog's body for three to six months. Extremely debilitating and rapidly lethal, treatment is intensive and often unsuccessful.

Vaccinations are extremely important to the long-term health of your puppy. Remember, puppy vaccinations start at approximately eight weeks and continue regularly until the puppy reaches sixteen months old. You should stick to the regimen your veterinarian recommends. Don't miss or put off these vaccinations. Your puppy's longterm health and well-being depend on it.

Rabies

The rabies virus attacks the central nervous system, causing unpredictable and often aggressive behavior. This erratic behavior is what in turn can cause the virus to spread, because it is through the bite of an infected animal that another animal is infected. Rabies can be transmitted from species to species, too, making it a health hazard of domesticated animals and people. This is why all states require that dogs and cats be vaccinated against rabies. Incidences of rabies are common in the Northeastern United States where there are large populations of skunks, raccoons, foxes, bats, and groundhogs. If you observe erratic behavior in any of these animals, call your local animal warden immediately.

Lyme Disease

Lyme disease is a tick-borne viral disease that causes often debilitating joint pain. While a vaccine exists to protect against Lyme, check with your veterinarian for his or her opinion about whether your dog would really benefit.

Spaying or Neutering

Consider spaying or neutering your dog as preventive care for a number of reasons. Health-wise, a spayed female is far less prone to diseases of the reproductive system, because she does not have a uterus, fallopian tubes, or ovaries. A neutered male, one without testicles, is immune from testicular and prostate cancers. Behavior-wise, you will be spared the mess of the female's biannual "season," and your male will be less likely to lift his leg in your home, roam in search of females in heat, or engage in aggressive behavior.

Parasites

A parasite is an organism that lives its life dependent on a host organism. In parasite-host relationships, the host organism is harmed. The most well-known parasites for dogs are worms, fleas, and ticks. While fleas and ticks are generally more of a nuisance than an immediate threat to your puppy's health, all parasites can be not only a general threat to the host animal's well being, but can spread serious illnesses as well. The bubonic plague was spread primarily through flea bites. You probably need not worry about catching the plague from your puppy, but parasites are a definite nuisance and legitimate danger to keep under control.

Fleas

Fleas have been annoying humankind and animals for centuries, and they're almost as tough to control today as they were in the days of ancient Rome. The flea's exoskeleton is amazingly resilient, and fleas can jump several feet to land on an unsuspecting host. Despite what many dog owners believe, fleas do not spend most of their lives on their pets. In fact, fleas only stay on dogs to feed and breed. They feed by biting the dog and sucking its blood. Because fleas often harbor tapeworm larvae in their systems, besides aggravating dogs with their bites, fleas can transmit tapeworm disease to the animal via the bloodstream or by being eaten by a dog trying to chew the fleas off himself. When fleas mate, the females lay hundreds of eggs. These drop off the dog and into the environment.

Larvae hatch from the eggs in two to three weeks, and these feed on environmental debris like human or animal dandruff, mold, and other protein and vegetable matter. From the larval stage, the flea develops a cocoon shell in which it matures. In the cocoon stage, the flea can live with no nutrients for almost a year. Then all it takes is the slight vibration of an animal's passing for the cocoon to release the adult, which jumps onto its host and begins the life cycle all over again.

FACTS

Your puppy can pick up fleas almost anywhere—outdoors, in a neighbor's house, even from another dog. Chances are, by the time you spot adult fleas on your puppy, you can be sure you have a potential infestation in your home and/or yard.

You'll know you and your puppy are in trouble when you see him scratching or licking himself suddenly and with real purpose. To confirm your suspicions, part your puppy's hair to the skin or brush it backwards and see if you notice any black specks. The specks can be dense around the dog's groin area, in the hair at the base of the tail, and around the ears and neck. With a moist paper towel, wipe the specks. If they turn red, it is flea dirt—particles of digested blood the flea has excreted.

If you know your puppy has fleas, you will have to be diligent about removing them from the pup and the environment. If you only remove the fleas from your dog without eliminating the flea eggs, larvae, and cocoons from the environment, you are guaranteed a continuing problem.

Puppy owners are fortunate to have a whole slew of flea-fighting products to choose from, ones that are safer than ever for dogs and the environment. You should consult with your veterinarian before waging a war on the fleas that have infiltrated your happy home; you'll want to be sure that the products you select for use on your puppy and your home are appropriate for your dog's age, weight, and skin type, and that the ingredients don't clash with a product you choose for your home and yard.

The active ingredient in many of the topical flea products on the market these days is pyrethrum, a natural compound toxic to fleas but not harmful to pets or people. There are also formulations that stop flea eggs from developing, interrupt the reproductive cycle, and break down the tough skeleton of fleas.

Once you've selected the flea-fighters you'll need, plan a systematic approach to ridding your dog, home, and yard of all stages of the flea life cycle. Take every step seriously if you want to completely eliminate the problem. You'll need to vacuum thoroughly, using several vacuum cleaner bags and disposing of them all in air-tight plastic bags. You'll need to wash all the dog's bedding in very hot water. This may include your family's bedding, too, if the dog shares anyone's bed. Any place that your dog passes through or sleeps in can be considered a flea "hot spot," and potentially infested. Concentrate your efforts here.

To remove fleas on your puppy, wash with a flea-killing shampoo, then comb thoroughly with a fine-toothed flea comb. Dip the comb in a large glass of soapy water to drown any fleas that survived the bath. Dry your puppy thoroughly, and don't let him roll in his favorite hole in the yard or lie down in his usual spot on the porch—these are possible hot spots, too, and need to be treated with an outdoor insecticide.

Once you've treated the puppy, house, and yard, you'll never want to repeat the process, so you'll need to step up your preventive measures.

Figuring your puppy can get fleas any time he steps out of your home and into a well-populated area, you should check him regularly before coming inside. Run a flea comb through his fur. This will snag any freeloaders before they start breeding. Kill them on the comb by crushing them with your fingernail or immersing the comb in a glass of soapy water. During the warm months, when fleas are at their worst, bathe your puppy regularly with a flea-preventive shampoo, and ask your veterinarian about other products designed to keep fleas from settling on your pet. Vacuum your home frequently, and make sure to keep your pet's bedding fresh and clean.

Many puppies and adult dogs are allergic to the saliva that fleas inject into their skin when they bite them, or are particularly sensitive to fleas living on them. These dogs can develop serious skin ailments from their allergies and sensitivities, which often linger even after the flea problem has been eradicated. The excessive scratching, licking, and fur-biting they indulge in to get at the fleas leaves their skin damaged, causing further itching and, often, infection. The infection can leave the skin swollen or patchy, and can lead to permanent hair loss. Besides being unsightly, a flea allergy or sensitivity is extremely irritating to your dog. Your veterinarian will advise you on how best to treat this many-symptomed problem.

Ticks

There are many types of ticks throughout the United States, the most common being the brown tick, the wood tick, and the deer tick. All adult ticks seek out dogs and other animals as hosts for feeding and breeding. The brown tick is typically the size of a match head or small pea when engorged. The wood tick is a larger tick that, when full, swells to the size of a kernel of corn. The deer tick is a tiny tick that even when engorged is no larger than a speck. The brown tick is known to transmit Rocky Mountain spotted fever, while the deer tick is the carrier of Lyme disease, both of which can be deadly.

The sooner you spot a tick or ticks on your puppy, the better. You need to remove the tick(s) immediately, then monitor the spot from which you removed the tick. To take a tick off your puppy, first wet a cotton ball with alcohol or a dab of petroleum jelly. Apply this to the tick to suffocate or numb it, then, with tweezers or with gloves on your hands, pull the tick gently off the pup. Deposit the tick in a jar filled with alcohol or nail polish remover. If your puppy comes out of a trip to the woods loaded with ticks, you may want to get a tick dip from your veterinarian to help remove them all at once.

Tick bites rarely become infected, but you'll want to keep an eye on your puppy's skin in the area from which the tick was pulled off, especially if it was a deer tick. Often a red, circular rash will develop around the bite—an early indicator of Lyme disease. If you notice any redness or swelling in the area of a tick bite, make an appointment to have it checked by the veterinarian.

Unfortunately, it's almost impossible to keep ticks off your puppy if you spend any time outdoors with him. Your best bet, yet again, is preventive care: bathing your puppy with a flea and tick shampoo formulated for his needs; taking your veterinarian's advice about what products work best to keep ticks off your dog; and always checking your dog thoroughly when you return from an outdoors adventure.

What to Do about Worms

Like the infectious diseases that are easily avoided by proper vaccinations, worms (intestinal parasites) are another potentially deadly enemy of your puppy's health that are easily avoided by proper care, hygiene, and attention.

There are several types of worms that infect dogs: tapeworms, whipworms, roundworms, hookworms, and heartworms are the most common.

Puppies and adult dogs become infected by worms by contact with contaminated soil; raw, contaminated meat (like a dead animal in the woods); or ingestion of an infected host (like a flea). That's why it's so important to clean up after your dog in the yard and around the house, and to have fecal exams performed by the veterinarian regularly (microscopic examination is often the only way to detect the presence of internal parasites).

You might suspect your puppy or dog has worms if his appetite decreases, he has an upset stomach, he loses weight, and you see blood or mucus in his stools. These symptoms are characteristic of an advanced state of parasitic infection; a dog can have a slight infection and appear normal until your veterinarian detects worms in his feces. For common infestations, there are safe, effective, and fast-acting worming medications available.

Heartworm

The heartworm is a particularly deadly parasite because it infests and grows in the canine heart. Left untreated, heartworms literally strangle the heart, causing it to fail and the dog to die.

Heartworm is transmitted by infected mosquitoes. When they land on a dog to bite, heartworm larvae are deposited on the skin. The larvae burrow their way through the dog's skin, growing into small worms as they go. When they finally reach a blood vein, the worms travel to the heart, where they mature. Heartworms can grow four to twelve inches long, and a dog can be infected for years before symptoms are noticeable. A dog diagnosed with heartworm is in trouble either way. Treatment is intense and can even cause the inevitable death it seeks to avoid.

Shetland Sheepdog

Photo by Mary Bloom©

Today's dog owners are extremely fortunate to have preventive medication readily available. In some parts of the country veterinarians suggest giving dogs the preventive daily or monthly (depending on the type) only in seasons in which the mosquito is most active; in other parts of the country, veterinarians keep dogs on the preventive all year round as a safety precaution. Ask your veterinarian what's best for your dog and stick with the program. If you take your dog off preventive medicine for more than several months, he must be tested for the presence of heartworm before being allowed to go back on it.

Emergencies

First things first: call your veterinary emergency clinic! Hopefully you'll have this number by the phone already and you'll know how to get to the center if it's not where you normally take your dog. The last thing you want to worry about is finding an emergency clinic when every minute counts.

What qualifies as an emergency? Basically, any condition that you perceive as being serious or life-threatening, including:

- Being hit by a car
- Being bitten in a dog fight
- A broken limb
- An extreme allergic reaction—whether to an insect bite, a medication, or a food

- Ingesting poison
- A burn
- Any profuse, unexplained bleeding
- Shock or coma
- Heatstroke or frostbite
- Choking
- Sudden, severe vomiting or diarrhea
- A seizure
- Erratic behavior
- Being stuck with porcupine quills

ALERT

Always approach a wounded dog carefully. They are in great pain and don't always understand that you are trying to help. Many an owner has been bitten by approaching an injured dog too soon after they've been injured. Let them calm down before you approach. Approach slowly and carefully and calmly. If you are not calm, the dog will pick up on your anxiety and it will heighten his or her own.

Emergencies elicit two states that don't help matters any—shock and/or fear in the dog, and panic in the owner. When dealing with an emergency, keep reminding yourself to stay calm and stay focused on what you can do for your dog. Ideally, you should have someone drive you to the clinic while you handle the dog.

ESSENTIALS

The most important thing to do in any emergency is to stay calm. Staying calm in these situations can mean the difference between life and death in extreme cases.

After you've called the veterinary clinic as well as someone to come help you if you're alone with the dog, follow these steps:

Evaluate the dog's condition and deliver any first-aid procedures, such as reducing bleeding, putting on a muzzle so the dog doesn't bite you or someone else, and applying any ointment or wrapping a wound.

Keep your dog still and warm by reassuring him while down and keeping a blanket on him. Make preparations to transport him so he experiences as little turbulence and commotion as possible.

Environment

When was the last time you washed your puppy's bed? How about picking up after your puppy in the yard—do you do it regularly? If you don't keep your puppy's environment clean, it will affect not only him, but your whole family. You don't want your dog tracking feces in on his paws when he comes in from the yard, and you don't want a smelly, dirty dog bed in the middle of your family room. So keep your puppy's environment clean and you'll all feel better for it.

CHAPTER 16

Ailments to Be on the Lookout For

I t is recommended that you thoroughly examine your puppy at least once a week. This doesn't have to be like a visit to the vet for your dog. Just spending an hour or so lovingly petting and checking out each of your puppy's major trouble zones will give you the opportunity to look your puppy over, and give your puppy some of that undivided attention it thrives on. Remember that this is a personal checkup and in no way does it replace regular visits to the vet.

Skin

The puppy's skin is a dynamic and vital organ. No matter if your puppy is short- or long-haired, his skin is always shedding dead cells and replacing them with new ones. The skin is made of two layers: the epidermis, or outer layer of skin cells, and the dermis, or second layer. A puppy's skin is prone to many problems that can affect either or both layers of skin, most notably itching, hair loss, swelling and inflammation, and flaking. Because skin problems are often the most visible and pronounced of ailments afflicting dogs, it's not surprising that they represent a large percentage of the overall cases referred to veterinarians.

Scratching and Itching

While all animals occasionally scratch themselves (including us humans!), excessive or constant scratching or itching is the sign of a problem. The most common causes are fleas, hypersensitivity (an immunologic or allergic reaction), and pyoderma (a bacterial infection). If the underlying cause isn't determined, the condition can grow increasingly worse.

At the first signs of itching, check your puppy for fleas. As described in the last chapter, you can do this by moving the fur backwards and looking for fleas themselves, or "flea dirt"—the digested blood fleas excrete that indicate their presence. If your dog has fleas, you will need to remove them from his body and from the environment.

Some puppies and dogs are so sensitive to flea bites that they develop flea allergy dermatitis. The dog develops an immunologic hypersensitive reaction to the saliva injected by the flea when it feeds on the dog. By constantly licking, scratching, and chewing at his skin, the dog develops areas of hair loss, which can further progress to open sores that lead to infection. The areas most affected seem to be the base of the tail and lower back.

Flea allergy dermatitis typically develops when a dog is three to five years old, and it can be extremely tough to reverse, even if your dog is flea-free! The sooner your veterinarian can diagnose the condition, the sooner you can begin treatment and hope to alleviate the symptoms.

Treatment will involve being vigilant about keeping your dog and home flea-free, the use of special shampoos, dips, or ointments to prevent itching, and possibly prescribing anti-inflammatory drugs.

Dogs can also develop immunologic hypersensitivities to foods—anything from beef to wheat to dairy. This is why so many premium diets feature ingredients like lamb, rice, or turkey.

Remember, you are the difference between a happy and healthy puppy and an ill one. Your being observant of their everyday habits and health can mean the difference when it comes time for veterinary visits.

FACTS

Allergies

A hypersensitivity reaction to things in the environment like certain fabrics, detergents, molds, or fungi, usually means the dog is allergic to that thing. Symptoms usually develop when the dog is one to three years old and begin to show in the spring or fall. Areas of the body most affected include the face, stomach, paws and, oddly enough, the creases of the elbows. If your dog is constantly rubbing his face, licking and scratching his paws, or scratching his tummy or elbows, you should suspect an allergic hypersensitivity. Left untreated, the itching will lead to areas of broken, exposed skin that are ripe for infections. Often paw licking will develop into a behavioral habit, perpetuating the condition.

Because of the enormity of potential allergens in the dog's environment, your veterinarian will need to evaluate your dog's symptoms carefully and perform blood and skin tests to try to determine the allergen. Once pinpointed, elimination of the source is necessary, and you will probably need to use special shampoos and ointments to alleviate itching.

Infections

Bacterial infection is the result of skin that's under attack and losing the battle. The skin of a healthy puppy has certain bacteria that live on its surface and within the hair's follicles. This "good" bacteria wards off infection by "bad" bacteria. But when something happens to disrupt the balance, harmful bacteria invade and proliferate, causing serious infection and some severe and very painful problems.

Hot Spots

These are quarter-sized areas of red, moist, swollen sores, typically found on longhaired puppies during warm, humid weather. They can be caused by the puppy's licking itself in response to some other problem like a parasitic infection, or general hypersensitivity. Often the cause goes undiscovered. Treatment involves applying antibiotic ointment to the wound and using an Elizabethan collar on the puppy so he cannot reach the spot to continue licking or chewing at it.

Skin-Fold Pyoderma

Dogs with areas of thick folded skin on their bodies, like Chinese Shar-Pei, Bloodhounds, Mastiffs, Pugs and others, can develop infections in between the folds. That's because the fold creates a warm, moist spot—prime breeding grounds for bacteria. Regular inspection of the folds can help prevent infection, and antibiotic ointment can help treat it.

Another spot bacteria may breed rapidly is between the toes, and this is only exacerbated by the dog's licking. Scratches or cuts to the skin between the toes often go unnoticed, which can also lead to infection. Again, good grooming habits can go a long way to preventing this condition.

Seborrhea

When there is an imbalance of new cell growth to replace dying cells, the result is a thickening of the skin with noticeable shedding of the dead cells. This is called seborrhea. Symptoms include extreme flakiness; an overall greasiness to the skin and coat; an unpleasant and persistent odor to the coat; itchiness and bald patches of thick skin. The causes of seborrhea include hormonal imbalance, parasitic infection, excessive bathing or grooming, and nutritional disorders—all factors that contribute to the skin's not being able to properly regulate itself. Diagnosis is fairly simple, but treatment can be quite involved and may necessitate antibiotics, special shampoos, and anti-inflammatories.

Eyes

Eyes and their surrounding tissues are susceptible to a number of problems. Dogs have three eyelids: top and bottom, and a third eyelid called the nictitating membrane, an extra layer of protection against the elements. The eyelids and the nictitating membrane all produce tears to lubricate the eye.

German Shorthaired Pointer

Photo by Mary Bloom©

If one or both of your puppy's eyes is tearing excessively, suspect a problem. It could be that a speck of dust or dirt or a grass seed has lodged between the eyelid and the eyeball. If you can see the particle, you can try to remove it with blunt tweezers or a moistened paper towel or cotton ball. To help the eye heal, apply some antibiotic ophthalmic ointment such as Neosporin just inside the lower lid.

Likewise, if an eye appears red or swollen, the dog may have an infection caused by a foreign body. It is best to consult your veterinarian if such a condition exists.

Entropion and Ectropion

Sometimes eye irritation in puppies or dogs is caused by the eyelashes rubbing against the eye. If the eyelid rolls inward, causing the eyelashes to aggravate the eye, the condition is called entropion. When the eyelid rolls outward the condition is known as ectropion. Dogs with ectropion have exposed eyelid tissue that's particularly prone to damage and infection. Entropion and ectropion are both common congenital defects that require surgical repair.

Conjunctivitis

The membrane that lines the inner sides of the eyeball up to the cornea is called the conjunctiva. If it becomes infected, you'll notice a discharge from the corner of the dog's eye. The discharge may be clear and watery or opaque and thick. Typically this is the result of a bacterial infection. Your veterinarian can give you the best diagnosis.

Ears

Puppies' ears come in all shapes and sizes, from small and erect to long and pendulous. The most common problems they're susceptible to are cuts, hematomas, and infections. Many breeds' ears are cropped to both enhance appearance and to reduce the incidence of ear infection.

The Inner Ear

The skin of a healthy inner ear should be pink with some waxy light-brown secretion in the ear canal. If you notice your puppy scratching at his ears, excessively rubbing the side of his face against the floor or other surfaces, or whining with discomfort when you stroke around his ears, suspect an infection or other problem. The skin that lines the ear canal is the perfect host to bacteria, which thrive in warm, moist environments. Puppies who swim regularly, who live in humid environments, who have long, hairy ears, or whose ears are not regularly inspected for excessive dirty wax buildup can easily develop an infection. Your veterinarian will diagnose it and give you instructions for treatment.

Ear mites can be another source of itchy, inflamed inner ears. These microscopic parasites also like warm, moist environments, where they feed on skin flakes. A scraping at the vet's office will confirm this diagnosis.

The Outer Ear

Ear flaps are most prone to cuts, bites, and hematomas. As long as a cut is not deep, it is simple to treat by cleaning it thoroughly and applying antibiotic ointment. Often dogs involved in a fight will get their ears bitten. If the bite is deep, take the dog to the veterinarian; otherwise, wash it thoroughly, apply antibiotic ointment, and monitor it for infection.

Hematomas are the result of a pooling of blood in the ear flap. This can happen after a dog shakes his ears violently, scratches them excessively, or knocks them against a sharp object. Consult your veterinarian about the best way to deal with a hematoma.

Deafness

Some breeds of dogs have genetic defects that cause them to either be born deaf or develop deafness at an early age. Conscientious breeders will test their dogs if they suspect a problem and remove affected dogs from their breeding programs. This is most common in Dalmatians and some terriers. Older dogs often lose some or all of their hearing. They still manage to get around in familiar, safe environments, but special care should be paid to them.

FACTS

Your puppy's body temperature should range no greater than from 101 to 102.5 degrees Fahrenheit. Any temperature above or below those is time to call your veterinarian.

Nose

First of all, forget the folk remedy that says a puppy with a warm, dry nose is sick. Yes, a puppy's nose should typically be cool and moist, and if it's not the puppy may have a fever. But some sick puppies will have cool, runny noses. Regardless, the nose is an all-important organ to the puppy. Smell is his most acute sense; through it he learns the most about his environment and the other creatures in it.

Runny Nose

Because the nose itself doesn't have any sweat glands, when a puppy is excited or sick, the nasal mucous membrane will secrete water. Only secretions that persist for several hours indicate a problem.

Sneezing

This indicates an irritation to the front of the nasal cavity (coughing or gagging means the irritation is further back). It could be the inhalation of dust or dirt, which would cause the dog to sneeze several times and then stop, or it could indicate a fever or infection if it persists. If the sneezing is accompanied by discharge from the nose and/or eyes, see your veterinarian.

Mouth

The dog's mouth is made up of the lips, teeth, gums, and tongue, and is the passageway to the esophagus. While the lips and tongue can be injured by cuts or burns, injury and disease most commonly affect the teeth and gums, and it is on these that we will concentrate.

QUESTIONS?

How do I take my puppy's temperature?
Shake a rectal thermometer until it reads approximately 95 degrees Fahrenheit. Dab petroleum jelly on the end and coat the tip so that insertion will be smooth. While the puppy is standing, hold the tail up with one hand, while with the other you insert the thermometer by gently twisting as your press in. Hold the puppy in place for approximately three minutes or so. This should be sufficient for taking the puppy's temperature. Do not let the puppy sit at any time during this period or before extracting the thermometer.

Teeth

The average adult dog has forty-two teeth in his mouth (this can vary by breed, with shorter-faced breeds having less teeth). With improper oral hygiene, the teeth can become encrusted with plaque and tartar, leading to smelly (dog) breath, inflamed or infected gums, tooth loss, and general deterioration of the mouth.

Because of the high incidence of dogs suffering from periodontal disease, veterinarians and others in the pet industry have gone out of their way to educate owners and provide them with materials that make taking care of their dog's teeth easy.

Healthy puppies and young dogs have bright white teeth and pink gums. It is possible to keep your dog's teeth looking almost as good as they did when he was a pup. This requires regular brushing, proper feeding and chew toys, and inspection for problems.

Collie

Photo by Mary Bloom©

Get your puppy used to having his mouth handled by regularly lifting his lips and gently opening his mouth. Look at his teeth and gums. Is the gum line red or swollen? Are the teeth white all the way to the gums? Do you see any chipped teeth?

You should brush your puppy's teeth several times a week. To do this, you can purchase one of several types of doggy toothbrushes on the market. Some even come with their own doggy toothpaste that's specially flavored so dogs like the taste. Remember, never use human toothpaste on your puppy or adult dog. He won't like it, and it's bad for him. If you don't want to try the special toothbrushes and paste, you can wrap a small strip of gauze or cheesecloth around your finger to use as a scrubber. Use a paste of baking soda and water as the dentifrice. To brush, lift your puppy's lip and brush or rub against the teeth with your finger. Try to get the brush or your finger all the way to the back of the mouth to reach the molars. Open the mouth and move the brush or your finger along the inside of the teeth along the gum line. Work quickly, gently, and thoroughly. The whole process should only take a few minutes. When you're finished, reward your puppy with a crunchy snack—dogs love those miniature carrots!

During your annual checkups at the veterinarian's office, the doctor can advise you whether your puppy's teeth need to be surgically scraped to have any lingering or stubborn tartar removed. Since this procedure requires anesthesia, discuss it with your vet at length before subjecting your puppy to it.

Gums

As previously stated, healthy gums are pink and should be firm. Red, swollen, painful gums are a sign of gingivitis and require immediate attention. Your veterinarian will probably need to scrape your dog's teeth to remove offending tartar, after which you'll need to aggressively brush and inspect your dog's teeth. Severe gingivitis can lead to infection and tooth decay.

Choking and Gagging

If your puppy starts to choke or gag, there may be something caught in the back of his mouth. If possible, try to remove the object yourself. If it's lodged too firmly and your puppy is struggling and choking, take him to the veterinarian immediately. Try to calm and reassure the dog.

The Digestive System

This system is made up of the esophagus, stomach, small intestine, liver, gall bladder, spleen, colon, rectum, and anus. The problems most typically associated with this system are:

- Vomiting
- Bloat
- Diarrhea
- Constipation
- Flatulence
- Anal sac disorders

Every dog will experience upsets of the digestive system in the course of his life; most problems are easily treated and symptoms resolve within hours or days.

Vomiting

If your puppy is vomiting, there is definitely something wrong with him. Determining what that something is, however, is trickier than you might think. You'll need to take special note of what he vomits and how he vomits to figure out what's wrong.

The most common cause of vomiting is simply overeating or eating so quickly the food is gulped down and then comes back up again. Puppies and adult dogs will also commonly vomit after eating grass, and some dogs get car sick and vomit in the car. If your dog vomits what's obviously partly digested food or chewed grass and only vomits once or twice, or is distressed by the car, don't worry about it. If you notice blood in the vomit, or if the vomiting is severe and frequent, make an appointment to see the veterinarian. These are signs that your puppy is truly not well. Make an appointment with your veterinarian immediately.

Bloat

This condition is also called gastric dilatation, which is exactly what it is: a swelling up of the stomach due to gas, fluid, or a combination. When the stomach fills up this way, it is prone to twisting, which quickly leads to shock and death. Puppies and adult dogs can develop bloat by eating too much dry kibble; exercising vigorously after eating; or gulping their food or their water. Some breeds seem prone to it, and it appears to run in some breed lines. Dogs experiencing bloat become restless, drool heavily, try to vomit or defecate unsuccessfully, and cry in pain when their stomachs are palpated. It is imperative to get your puppy to the veterinarian as soon as possible if you suspect bloat.

Diarrhea

Like vomiting, the type and consistency of diarrhea vary depending on what's really wrong with the puppy. When all is normal, the puppy eats and drinks and his digestive system absorbs nutrients from the food and water and passes along undigested materials in the stool, which should be firm and consistent in color. Any irritation to the intestines or the bowel will trigger diarrhea. These irritations can vary from a change in food or water; overexcitement; eating something that can't be digested or is toxic; or something that produces an allergic response. The color, consistency, odor, and frequency of the diarrhea can help you and your veterinarian determine the underlying cause and set about providing the proper treatment.

Constipation

If you notice your puppy straining to defecate, or even whimpering or whining while doing so, with the result being no passing of stool, your puppy is constipated. Most cases of constipation are caused by inappropriate diet, which causes stools to form improperly and either block the colon or become painful to pass. Try giving your puppy one-half to two tablespoons of a gentle laxative like Milk of Magnesia. Take the puppy out often so you don't risk an accident in the house. If you don't get results in twelve to twenty-four hours, consult your veterinarian.

Flatulence (Passing Gas)

Having an overly flatulent dog is no fun! Through no fault of his own, a dog who passes gas can clear an entire room in no time. Chalk your dog's flatulence up to inappropriate diet yet again. A diet high in meats, fermentable foods like onions, beans, or even some grains, or dairy products can lead to excess gas. Review your dog's diet carefully, including the ingredient list of his dog food, and slowly integrate a diet change. If this doesn't yield results, your veterinarian can help.

Anal Sac Disorders

Dogs have two anal sacs, one on each side of the rectum at about five and seven o'clock, commonly called "scent sacs." They secrete a distinctive odor that leaves the dog's scent when he defecates. If the sacs become blocked, they can become sore and infected and will need to be expressed. If your dog frequently scoots across the floor dragging his bottom or wants to lick the area often, suspect an anal sac problem and ask the vet to show you how to handle expressing them to relieve the buildup.

Respiratory System

Dogs breathe through their respiratory system, a series of airways that comprise the nasal passages, throat, windpipe, and bronchial tubes that lead to the lungs. Any of the following symptoms indicate a problem in the system:

- Rapid breathing
- Noisy breathing
- Coughing

Rapid Breathing

Dogs will breathe heavily and rapidly in a number of circumstances, such as after strenuous exercise, in excessive heat, or if they're excited or stressed. If your puppy is breathing rapidly while at rest and you can't attribute any of these other factors to his condition, consult your veterinarian.

Noisy Breathing

This includes wheezing, sneezing, labored breathing, hoarseness, and any odd sound the dog makes while trying to breathe. Owners of some short-faced breeds live with this problem. Their dogs have shorter airways and will regularly snort, snore, or breathe heavily. For other dogs, noisy breathing is generally due to an obstruction, though it can also indicate a lung disease or heart failure. It's best to have your veterinarian listen and look.

Coughing

Coughing results from the effort to extricate an obstruction in the airways, whether it's a bone chip, a collapsed windpipe, or a fluid buildup in the lungs caused by a respiratory disease like kennel cough. Kennel cough is highly contagious between dogs and can spread rapidly at a dog show or in a kennel. There is a vaccine to help prevent kennel cough, and if caught early treatment is successful.

FACTS

Aspirin has always been a bit of a wonder cure for humans. It can also be a cure all for dogs as well. Many veterinarians have suggested aspirin for arthritis in older dogs. When puppies have hurt themselves, have a fever, or are not feeling well, you can give them an aspirin. For puppies up to eighteen months of age, you will want to give them children's aspirin. Give them half of a tablet (small to medium dog) to one whole tablet (medium to large). For dogs older than eighteen months, you can give them half to one whole regular aspirin, using the same guide.

Urinary and Reproductive Systems

The components of the urinary system are the bladder, prostate, and urethra, as well as the kidneys and uterus. The system works together. The two kidneys' jobs are to siphon excess waste created by ordinary metabolism, yet regulate water and minerals. Wastes are deposited into the ureter, which empties into the bladder. Urine passes from the bladder to outside the body via the urethra (in the male, the urethra also transports semen).

If all is functioning well, your puppy will urinate regularly (not frequently), and his urine will be clear and yellow in color. A problem of the kidneys, bladder, urethra, or prostate will be evident as straining to urinate, blood-tinged or cloudy urine, excessive drinking accompanied by excessive urination, or pain upon urination. The problem could be something as minor as dehydration or as complicated as renal failure. You must consult your veterinarian for a diagnosis.

Reproductive System

The reproductive system of the female (bitch) includes two ovaries, a uterus, and fallopian tubes. A spayed female will have all of these removed. Intact females will experience regular heats and are prone to false pregnancies and infection of the uterus called pyometra. As advised previously, you and your female dog will be happier and healthier if she is spayed. Some believe that a spayed bitch is prone to obesity. While it is true that she will not be under the same hormonal influence that keeps an intact bitch in form, with regular exercise and the proper diet, a spayed bitch can be kept in top shape.

The male dog's reproductive system includes the testicles, penis, and prostate gland. Intact males are prone to damage or injury of the penis or scrotum, cancer of the testes, and inflammation, enlargement, or cancer of the prostate. Once again, you and your dog will live happier, healthier lives if the dog is neutered. Neutering is the surgical removal of the testicles. The empty scrotum eventually shrinks and leaves no scar. Neutering not only guarantees the male won't develop testicular cancer or prostate problems, it also lessens a male's territoriality, making him (with proper care and training) a friendlier pet. Neutering does not significantly change a dog's temperament, however; if you have an aggressive male, neutering will not solve the problem, but combined with training, it can certainly help.

Other

Following are a few other things you should be aware of for your puppy's health. When you get your puppy you should ask the breeder if there are any other particular problems common to that breed that you should be on the lookout for.

The Circulatory System

At the center of the circulatory system is the all-important heart, a muscle that pumps blood to the rest of the body. Diseases that affect the canine heart include birth defects, aging, infectious disease, and heartworm. Heartworm is a condition that can be deadly but is easily avoided by giving regular preventive heartworm medication, as discussed previously.

FACTS

One of the things puppies love is snow! However, as the streets and sidewalks are treated with salt to keep the snow at bay, it also works against your puppy. Too much salt wears on their pads, and eventually splits may form. This makes life very painful for your puppy. Bag Balm is the solution. This is the same balm that dairy farmers put on cows to keep their milking skin from chafing in the winter. It will work wonders for your puppy as well. Keep your puppy off his feet for a few days until his pads heal.

The Nervous System

All activity in the nervous system generates from the brain, the spinal cord, and the peripheral nerves. Spinal cord diseases, seizures, head injuries, and paralysis are some of the problems that can result from injury or disease of this system.

Seizures and Epilepsy

A seizure is caused by a sudden burst of electrical activity in the brain, affecting the entire body by causing uncontrolled convulsions: foaming at the mouth, jerking of the limbs, snapping of the jaws, or rolling of the eyes. Depending on the severity, the dog may collapse and slip into unconsciousness. Seizures can be caused by trauma to the brain or the healing associated with it, or by a hereditary condition.

Epilepsy is a state of recurrent and similar seizures that typically happen in three phases: sudden restlessness accompanied by champing or foaming at the mouth; falling to the ground with head thrown back and pupils dilated, slobbering and drooling; and a recovery phase in which the dog is disoriented. The more violent phases, one and two, happen in just a few minutes; the recovery phase may last hours. You must consult with your veterinarian and your puppy's breeder if your puppy has epilepsy.

Paralysis

Complete paralysis is the result of permanent damage to the spinal cord. But a dog can experience partial paralysis due to a spinal cord disease or infection. Lyme disease is a form of tick paralysis in which the effects of the tick bite come on slowly, impairing movement to the point of paralysis. A speedy diagnosis is key to recovery. Normally the paralysis resolves with treatment by antibiotics.

Musculoskeletal System

Bones and muscles support the body and protect the internal organs. All dogs, regardless of size, have an average of 319 different bones in their bodies. The bones are connected by ligaments and surrounded by muscles.

If your puppy is limping or is favoring a particular leg (lame), chances are he's got a bone or joint disease, a strained muscle or tendon, or possibly a broken bone. The causes range from something as severe as a congenital disorder like hip or elbow dysphasia, to something as ordinary as a strained muscle or age-related as arthritis. Your veterinarian should give you a professional diagnosis.

Hip Dysphasia

Canine hip dysphasia (often referred to as CHD or just HD) is a disorder of the hip socket. In a healthy hip, the head of the thigh bone (femur) should fit snugly in the hip socket (acetabulum). If the ligaments around the socket are loose, the head of the femur will start to slip from the socket. This causes gradual hind end lameness and pain. Treatment varies depending on the age of the dog, the severity of the condition, and the options available to dog and owner.

While a specific cause of CHD has not been identified, it is suspected to be an inherited disorder. It has happened, however, that CHD-free parents have produced pups that develop hip dysphasia. Weight, nutrition, and environment have all been implicated in the possible exaggeration or development of CHD, which normally manifests at an age of rapid growth.

CHAPTER 17

Stuff You Can Do with Your Puppy

O kay, so you're an active person and you want to take your dog with you into the great outdoors. Certainly one of the most fun things to do is to go out into nature with man's best friend, and tread both well-worn paths and blaze new ones as well, all with your trusty companion right there beside you. Or, maybe you're not quite the outdoorsperson, but still want to partake in a few activities with your pooch, other than lounging around the house and walking through the park.

Preparing for the Great Outdoors

There are lots of things people take for granted with their dogs when they're going hiking or camping that they shouldn't. One of those things is their dog's health. Make sure you take your dog for a complete and thorough examination. The one thing that Cheryl S. Smith advises in her classic book *On the Trail with Your Canine Companion* is to make sure your dog is healthy. She ought to know, hers is the best book on the subject. She insists that not only should you get a check up, but get a certificate of health from your vet. Many campgrounds require such paperwork before they will let a dog in.

It's also important to have papers proving that your dog has been vaccinated for rabies. While few, if any, campgrounds require Canine Good Citizen certificates, if they are on the fence, Ms. Smith argues, they may be swayed by producing this document.

Another important thing is identification. It's very important. If you're really out there, and Rex decides he's going to chase some deer, or some other wild quarry, and suddenly becomes separated from you, you're going to want to make sure that his tags with identification and information are on him. Make sure the tags are not temporary ones, but strong ones made of very hard impact tested plastic, or better yet, metal. Make sure they are very firmly fastened to the collar and that the collar is secure.

More than anything, you need to get your dog in shape. Don't assume just because he can outrun you that he's in shape. Make sure to take him for some long walks in the weeks leading up to the trip. That's all you need in the middle of your trip—your dog-turned-weekend-warrior to come up lame in the middle of a hiking expedition. Or worse, to have been sick before the trip started, and for the illness to blossom while you're somewhere deep in the heart of the woods. Make sure to exercise your dog several weeks prior to leaving.

You will find that especially in the woods, like in the city, training is invaluable. Because the dog has descended from the wild, we assume that he knows how to act, and what certain things are. However, may I remind you, we too are descended from wild animals and we don't have a clue either. A well-trained dog comes when called. If your dog sees some wildlife, he may start to give chase or track it. You need to be able to recall him on a moment's notice. It's in these situations when you realize how important good training is. Work on the basics: come, sit, stay, down—and the long down.

As you might have for yourself, make sure you bring a first-aid kit, with enough of the right supplies for both you and your dog. Many a dog has cut his foot or hurt himself racing through the forest like a roller coaster in summer. A first-aid kit will help you keep your dog healthy and infection-free, and may save your dog's life as well as your trip.

ESSENTIALS

Many new dog owners are afraid of seeing their puppies getting run over by larger or older dogs at the dog run. People with puppies, especially in urban areas, will form puppy play groups. Sometimes dog runs have puppy hours. Ask your local parks service or veterinarian if he or she knows of any such groups.

Hiking and Camping

Hiking presents all kinds of problems we'll only brush upon lightly here. First and foremost, though, you need to be wary in the woods for your puppy's safety. Don't assume he knows what he's doing. Try to keep him in sight at all times. Make sure he'll come to you if called.

There are many things you need to watch out for in the forest. First, there are other animals, especially animals like skunks, raccoons, and porcupines. While the skunk will only add a whole new dimension to your hiking and camping experience, encounters with raccoons and porcupines may be fatal. Raccoons are very powerful animals and tenacious fighters. They may also have rabies. If your puppy has an encounter with a porcupine, your trip is over. You really shouldn't attempt to remove the quills yourself. You should find the help of a veterinarian immediately. Pulling out the needles incorrectly might cause more harm and pain than when they went in.

Other animals to fear are deer and bears. The bear is a formidable foe for any animal, wild or domestic. If your puppy is game enough to take him on, you may be in for some real problems. Deer are not such easy prey either. Especially if there are females in season or competing males, your puppy may find out the hard way that Bambi is more than capable of taking care of himself. Many a dog has not survived a goring by an attacked buck. And last but not least, wild boars also present problems. They are not very big, but have razor sharp tusks. These pigs are some of the angriest wildlife we know in North America, and present a danger to man and beast. The last major animal you should be aware of is other dogs. If your dog doesn't get along with other dogs, then maybe you might want to keep Fido on a short lead. Be careful, you don't want to be sued because your dog attacked someone else's dog, or vice versa. Those are the main animals to be concerned about. Actually, there are many more than we can list here, because some are only regional. You may want to consult local wildlife management or parks authorities where you'll be traveling before you leave home.

Siberian Husky

Photo by Mary Bloom©

Certainly the other things we need to worry about are plants and other humans. More often than not, I get poison ivy once a year. I never go very deep into the woods without being fully protected. However, my dogs don't step lightly when they see it. They are completely oblivious. There are many such situations that present themselves in the forest.

Be careful to try to direct your dog away from any poisonous plants whenever possible. Also, dogs are known to chew all kinds of grasses. Try to discourage this, especially in the woods.

Make sure your dog is friendly with other humans. Should you happen upon a stranger in the woods, you don't want to see your fellow hiker with his arm halfway consumed by Spot. Make sure your dog is stranger friendly, especially in these environs, where you're never sure how or when you'll run into other human beings.

QUESTIONS?

Does tomato juice really work for a skunk-sprayed dog?
Yes, it does. I have always used it. I wash the dog twice with tomato juice and then once with dog shampoo. And remember to rinse thoroughly with clean water after each round of washings. While many claims have been made by products as well as experts, I have never had a personal experience that resulted in a dog that came clean with one wash. Usually it requires maybe two or three right in a row to expunge only 90 percent of that gross smell. The rest will wear off in a couple of days.

Camping

Once at a campsite, you may want to find a way to station your puppy while you set up camp. Many manufacturers make stakes that are created for just this kind of temporary use. Many look like giant corkscrews. This is a good way to give everyone some down time, including Rover.

One of the things I must suggest strongly is to let your puppy or dog sleep in the tent with you. While your dog, I am sure, is an impassioned protector, he is more than likely to get hurt if night predators arrive. These animals only want your food and are not interested in fighting. However, if provoked, a bloody mess may occur.

Remember to keep your puppy far away from the fire. Puppies sometimes get too close because their fur insulates them from the heat of the flames. There is nothing more disgusting than the smell of burnt fur. Remember, you're supposed to cook the weenies, not the dogs!

Do I have to keep my puppy on his leash while we're hiking?
In most state parks the answer is an unequivocal yes! You should call ahead to understand the rules and regulations, as they vary from state to state and park to park. Also, depending on the location, you might need to worry about the foot traffic.

Vacations and Travel

I have to be honest, when my wife and I travel with the dogs in our station wagon, we don't use crates. However, I do believe that crates are the best possible way to go. They are not always practical, however, given your specific destination. If it's at all possible, you should bring the puppy's crate and use it.

Now, if you have a station wagon, and you want to put the dog(s) in the back, that's perfectly fine. A space separator or gate is a good idea. It prevents the dogs from trying to hop over the seat and lessens the room they have to move around. They will tend to lie down more often, knowing that there's nowhere else to go. This is also good, because if you're in an accident, the dogs should be safe all the way back there.

ALERT

The United States has no set quarantine restrictions on pet dogs coming into this country, but does require a valid health certificate showing that the dog is free of rabies and any other infectious diseases. Other countries are far more restrictive; England and Australia, for example, have stiff six-month quarantines on all pets coming into their countries. As the owner, you must pay for the cost of this.

If you don't have a station wagon, SUV, or truck with a cargo area, then   short lead, which we attached to a spot in the center of the car. The dogs were not tied down uncomfortably. There was enough slack so that they could sit up, but not enough for them to pace. This is also good in case of an accident. Your pets are safer back there.

Lastly, let's talk about windows. Yeah, dogs love to stick their heads out of windows and let their tongues hang out. But if everybody's dog jumped off the Brooklyn Bridge, would you let yours? It's not good for Fido, so nix that stuff fast. The windows in back should be rolled down enough so as to let a good amount of air in, but not wide enough so that the dog can stick his or her head out the window.

Swimming

It has always seemed to me that there is no dog on earth that is so crazy about swimming as our German Shorthaired Pointer, Exley. Once, while in Connecticut, he swam across the Mianus River. By the time we drove to the other side to retrieve him, he had swum back to the other bank. This is not a story you want to repeat.

Make sure to keep an eye on your dog. Don't let him swim out too far. Don't let him swim in waters that don't look clean or are overrun with algae. And be careful of rough waters. While some dogs are good swimmers, others are not. Try to exercise some common sense and know your dog's limits.

Fetch

Obviously, fetch is really big with most dogs and puppies, but it can be a little repetitive (not that they mind). However, there are a number of organized activities that you and Spot can become a party to, should you decide that Spot needs to fulfill some higher destiny. But seriously, if you want to have some fun with your dog, there are countless activities you can engage in. In this chapter we'll look at fun things you can do and even some that are organized by rules set forth by the AKC. Many of these require lots of training on your part. The activities are not particularly hard, but all require time—and all are fun.

Shows

So, you're a consummate stage mother? Maybe you bought Fido because he came from championship lines, and you wanted to try your hand at showing? Maybe you've been to a dog show and it looks like fun. Or maybe it's just something you want to try once. Believe me, you're not alone. There are somewhere around 20,000 dog shows per year, twelve to thirteen of which conform to AKC recognized standards. Millions of people compete in these events and an even larger number attend these events as spectators. This is called the sport of dogs by show people.

FACTS

There are many different people involved with showing:

- Breeder—The person or people who bred the dog
- Owner—Not necessarily the breeder
- Handler—Person in the ring with the dog

In most cases, each dog has all three people helping him to win at these very competitive events.

Now, first, let me caution you. Dog showing is very competitive. You are not the first yahoo who went out and bought a pet, and thought, "Gee, wouldn't it be fun to show Rover?" Dog show people can be snotty. Many are very dedicated to their "sport," and don't take dabblers very seriously. In some cases, they actually loathe them. You will have to attend many shows in your breed before some of them talk to you without looking down their noses. Many will first ask you if you bred the dog yourself, or from whom you bought it. You have to understand, many people who "compete" are breeders whose livelihood, or at least some part of it, comes from dogs. You're just one more obstacle for them to overcome.

FACTS

The AKC sponsors a level of training and competition for younger people called junior showmanship. This is a fun and exciting way to introduce children into the world of dog showing. Many of the handlers in the ring during puppy sweepstakes are junior showmanship handlers.

That said, there are also many lovely people in the sport, and the camaraderie and competition are lots of fun indeed. It's also fun because you'll be talking to many people who have dogs just like yours, and you'll trade all kinds of information and learn that much more. And the spectators are right there and fun to talk to. They will all want to pet your dog and talk to you. And Rover will have fun too!

The Five Major Classes of Dog Shows

- Puppies (six to nine months and nine to twelve months)
- Novice
- Bred by Exhibitor
- American Bred
- Open

The dogs are judged on general appearance, which includes things like head, neck, forequarters, hindquarters, coat, color, gait, and temperament. The dogs are not judged one against another: "This dog is prettier than that dog." NO! The dogs are each judged by a person well versed in the breed, who decides if the dog is the best possible representation of what the ideal dog of the breed should look like.

In the next level, the winners are all brought in, and the judge picks out the best dog from all the winners. This is called the "winners' dog." Several dogs are picked as "reserve winners." The bitch group is also judged in the same way. The reserve winners are placed in order of finish, as in horse racing—second, third, and fourth. These selections are made in case the "winners' dog" is disqualified for any reason later on. The winners' dog and bitch both receive points toward their championships.

In the next level, you start all over again. You're winners' dog. You've won the group who showed, but now at this next section, any dog that has finished his or her championship at any other show, is welcomed to compete. The competition is mixed now. Now, you go through the same exercise all over again. The judge looks over the field, where the competition is much tougher, and he or she will judge them in some kind of order like we just went through. At this point the judge picks a Best of Breed award. This can be either male or female. Then he picks a Best of Opposite Sex (in other words, he picks a male as Best of Breed, then he picks a female as Best of Opposite Sex, or vice versa).

Now, sometimes, if this is a breed-only event, that's it. The day is over. They showed German Shorthaired Pointers all day, and when the smoke cleared, you walked away with some big-time championship points, and Spot is thrilled. You're exhausted. However, today we are not at a breed-only show, so there's more to do.

German Shorthaired Pointer

Photo by Mary Bloom©

At a full show, other breeds will be showing at the same time as you. All 144 recognized breeds are competing. You get a small breather here, and then you go back on stage. The next competition is the group competition. You remember when we were looking at the various dogs in Part 1? All the dogs were separated out by group—Herding, Sporting, Working, Non-Sporting, Toy, Terrier, and Hound. Since you own a German Shorthair Pointer, you will be judged in the Sporting Group. The Best of Breed of each breed, that one dog only (and that's you!), will compete against all the other Best of Breeds who won in this group. In other words, you'll be competing against the Best of Breed of the Golden Retrievers, Labrador Retrievers, etc. Again, do they pick these dogs because a German Shorthaired Pointer is prettier than a Labrador? NO! An experienced Sporting Group judge will judge each animal against the ideal of what that breed should be. Each dog is rated against its breed's standard. Is this Lab a better representation of a Lab than this Pointer is as an example of a Pointer? Get it?

Now, you are lucky to get out of the Sporting Group alive. So, here we are, and it's the final run around the ring. You are with the six other dogs who have won their groups. Yet another judge looks you all over, and in the same way the groups were judged, he or she chooses a winner, which will be crowned Best in Show.

For sure, you're really thrilled. What an exciting experience. And it only took a couple of days to pull off! You see, especially something as big as an all-breed show takes several days to complete. These shows are usually held outside, at a large fairground. The competitions, depending on the breed, can take all day. But if you like dogs (and apparently you do), then you just had more fun than you ever imagined.

Handlers

There are people in the dog show industry called handlers. These people make a living showing other people's dogs in competitions. Many breeders use handlers because they cannot be all around the country, showing their many dogs. Some breeders will have more than one dog on the road. In situations like these, some breeders don't see their dogs for months and months at a time. They will sometimes fly into a city just to visit their dog and handler and watch the show, and then leave the dog with the handler and fly back home. This is the life of a championship dog for people who are serious about dog shows.

Now, it is a lot of fun showing your dog yourself. You drive to strange cities, stay in motels that allow dogs, and hang out with dog people for several days. It's this time spent with your dog that makes it the most fun. But, if you are serious about winning, you may want to consider a handler. These people are traveling from show to show, and know the many ins and outs of the ring. They know tricks of the trade, and are very astute to the politics of the show ring. They are not cheap and have many expenses to cover. The recommended books in Appendix I will give you much more in-depth coverage of what you need to compete and win if you are serious about showing.

Obedience and Agility Competitions

The idea of obedience is to help meld you and your dog into a working team. This should be fun for both you and your dog, and will make him a better pet and you a better owner in the process. Agility stresses team work, expert training, and athleticism. And the third requires not just a good nose, but an understanding of what is required in what might become a very serious profession.

Obedience

The idea is to be able to train your dog so that he can eventually be trained to comprehend and act on commands, regardless of distance or interference. This is the most popular of all trials among non-breeders, as these are things that will make life easier for most owners. There are actually puppy Kindergarten classes, which will take dogs as young as three months. And there are pre-novice groups as well. Both these classes work with you and your dog on lead. In Obedience, there are three levels that increase with difficulty. They include Novice, Open, and Utility. In any trial, the dog must score 170 or more of the possible 200 points to earn his or her title.

QUESTIONS?

What about the rest of us?
There are other organizations that sponsor Obedience and Agility Trials that are very much the same. They are sponsored by the UKC. For years, many Pit Bulls, Jack Russell Terriers, and other dogs have competed for the UKC's titles. The good news is that you don't have to be a purebred. Mixed breeds are encouraged to compete and complete as well.

Novice is the first group where you can earn a title. The title one earns is called a CD, which stands for Companion Dog. There are six simple tasks your dog needs to complete before he can have this title conferred upon him: stand for confirmation, heel on lead, free heel, long sit, recall, and long down. These are all off lead.

Open is a little more difficult. The exercises required are: retrieve (usually a dumbbell) over flat route; retrieve over high jump, free heel, drop on recall, broad jump, long sit, and long down. For completing this course, your dog will earn a CDX, which stands for Companion Dog Excellent.

Utility work is definitely ranked as the hardest, with good reason. These are some of the most advanced trials there are. There are five events: ability to distinguish between two scents, a signal event, group examination, directed retrieve, and directed jumping. If your dog finishes this course with a passing grade, he receives a UD, or Utility Dog certificate. Of course, there are those overachievers who have qualified for UDX (yes, you've guessed it—Utility Dog Excellent) and even the OTCh (Overall Obedience Champion).

Agility Trials

This is slightly more fun than obedience, but obviously not quite as useful. Agility teams you and your dog together as a pair who needs to perform a certain number of tasks or exercises. It's a lot of fun to train and is very much like playing with your dog. The idea is that not only does Spot have to complete the exercise correctly (a feat in and of itself) but he also has to race against the clock. It can get exhausting. But it's very rewarding and often hilarious. The dogs seem to have more fun at these trials than in any other.

The dogs are broken up by size. No one expects a toy dog to make the same jumps a Doberman Pinscher can. As in Obedience, there are levels. In Agility, there are four: Novice Agility (the title you earn is NA); Open Agility (the title you earn is OA); Agility Excellent (the title you earn is AX); and the final class is Master Agility Excellent (title you earn is MX).

Basically your dog needs to complete an obstacle course. In order to gain the title, he must complete the course three times (at least one must be completed under a different judge). In these exercises, the dogs are required to run through and around poles, make a series of jumps, climb, balance, and race through tunnels.

It's very much scored like the Obedience Trials. Top score is 200 points. Infractions are deducted. This is fast becoming one of the most popular of all trials because first, anyone can enter, and second, it is tremendous fun. You'll laugh and be astounded. It's always an exceptional show.

Cairn Terrier

Photo by Mary Bloom©

Herding Trials and Tests

Herding is one of the oldest relationships we have with dogs. These exercises are used to gauge the development of what is still a very important job for many herding dogs. It's also lots of fun! The AKC separates herding dogs into four distinct groups. These are: Shepherd (usually used with sheep and usually lead a flock); Drover (works livestock from behind, usually sheep or cattle); Livestock Guarding (they do not move livestock, but guard it from other predators); and All-Round

Farm Dogs (these usually can respond quickly to different situations and can perform a number of different jobs).

The first few exercises are called tests. These test the general, inborn instincts of your animal and his ability to be trained. After that, you're off to the pasture. There are six different levels to achieve.

The first two tests are Herding Tested (HT) and Pre-Trial Tested (PT). In these, your dog's abilities are judged, again, based on inborn reaction as well as certain trained functions. The next levels are progressively harder. The idea is that a dog must keep ducks, sheep, or cattle together, sometimes under very difficult circumstances. The four remaining certificates to be achieved are: Herding Started (HS); Herding Intermediate (HI); Herding Excellent (HX); and Herding Champion (HCh).

Lure Coursing

This is probably one of the best spectator sports in all of dogdom. These are the sight hounds. Over an open but rigged course, sight hounds (used by man to hunt over open plains since the time of the Pharaohs), chase a flag at speeds that seem unimaginable. Yes, sight hounds hunt by sight. The dogs included are Afghan Hounds, Basenjis, Borzoi, Greyhounds, Ibiza Hounds, Rhodesian Ridgebacks, Salukis, Scottish Deerhounds, and Whippets. A lure, or prey (which in most cases is a fluttering plastic bag) is pulled along a series of wires very quickly. The dogs give chase.

The dogs are judged on overall ability, quickness, endurance, follow, and agility. There are three titles to be earned, which include Junior Courser (JC), Senior Courser (SC), and Field Champion (FC).

CHAPTER 18

Creating a Super-Dog: Beyond Basic Obedience

O bedience training is a rewarding endeavor that doesn't require extensive travel or financial resources. Anyone can participate—top competitors include people of all ages and physical condition. Dogs of all breeds and backgrounds (rescued and formally abused dogs, too) appear in the winner's circle. Most handlers participate for the reward of a better-trained dog, the camaraderie with peers, and the thrill of earning an occasional title.

Choosing a Dog Trainer or School

Whether you are looking for professional, in-person guidance, socialization for you or your puppy, or all of the above, dog training programs are popular nationwide.

Gather names by looking in the phone book and newspaper, and by asking your veterinarian, humane society, groomer, kennel, friends, neighbors, coworkers, or relatives for recommendations.

Call and ask questions about class curriculum, training philosophy, location, years in business, class size, instructor qualifications, and cost. If you are satisfied with your phone conversation, go watch a class in session. If you are unsure whether you'd like to join this organization, visit other dog training classes.

Many competitors hire private instructors either as their sole means of coaching or to supplement the group. In either case, most trainers gather informally with other trainers to practice working their dogs around distractions. Your canine social circle will quickly expand as you go to training classes, seminars, and practice matches.

When selecting a private instructor, inquire about techniques, his personal obedience trial experience, and titles earned. Ask, too, about his experience with your breed, and for client referrals. Finally, good rapport with a private instructor is a must. It will help you stay inspired and motivated to work your dog when the going gets tough.

Whichever route you choose expect to occasionally be frustrated or mildly skeptical. Give training a chance to work. Periodic confusion is a normal part of the learning process and not a reason to quit.

Advanced Training Exercises

Perhaps you're not sure if you are interested in obedience competition, but you definitely want to continue training your dog beyond the basics. The following exercises are fun to train and improve control, and will be helpful should you decide to compete. Congratulations for your interest. Let's get started!

Hand Signals, Whistles, and Snap Commands

It's imperative to use clear, concise, and consistent commands. But don't feel obligated to use a customary or standard command like "Heel" if you'd prefer to use a word like "Side" or a foreign word like "Fuss." In fact, perhaps you don't want to use words at all. A snap of your fingers followed by a point to the ground could mean lie down; in fact that will come in handy when you are brushing your teeth and you want your dog to stop misbehaving. Whistles are commonly used in the field because the sound travels so well. Initially, though, the dog must be trained close to the handler to understand the association between behaviors and whistles. Generally one toot of the whistle means sit and stay and multiple toots mean come into "Heel" position.

Australian Shepherd

Photo by Mary Bloom©

Teaching hand signals is easy. Always give your hand signal in a distinct way so the puppy doesn't assume you are just scratching your nose. Obedience trial regulations allow the handler to use a single motion of the entire arm and hand but penalize any body motion. I suggest beginning with the down, sit, stay, heel, and come hand signals. Teaching watchfulness so he doesn't miss your signal may be difficult. Any time your puppy's attention wonders, use sneakaways to bring back his focus.

Teaching your dog any task is the same whether you use a standard command or something else: Give the cue (the specific hand signal, whistle, verbal command, etc.) as you show him what you want and give praise.

Rapid-Fire Commands

Teach your puppy to obey the commands you practiced in the Basic Training Chapter in fast motion. If you've gotten into the bad habit of waiting for your puppy's attention before giving commands, he may be in the habit of not giving you his attention as quickly as he should.

GOAL: To improve your puppy's reliability and enable him to obey commands given in quick succession.

HOW TO PRACTICE: Command "Sit," release with "Chin-touch okay," command "Come" and run twenty feet, release, command "Down," release, "Heel" your puppy at various speeds and include halts and turns, release and command "Down." That sequence should take fifteen to twenty-five seconds. Once you've mastered that, work up to sequences of three to five minutes.

Play During Training

Is your puppy still difficult to control when his adrenaline rises and he gets really excited? Develop an on/off switch so he can have a grand old time acting like a dog but instantly obey commands you give. Not only does this allow you to gain control of an energetic dog, it also teaches him to respond to your commands without a warm-up.

HOW TO PRACTICE: Use toys, vigorous movement, and intense verbal praise to encourage rambunctious behavior; use sneakaway any time puppy is uninterested in your play. Start giving commands when your dog has become focused on playing or has gone out of control. Tell him "Sit" or "Down," and then move around, praise him, and toss a toy or drop food as a distraction: Use quick, concise, strong corrections whenever necessary. Return, praise, release, and play. Command "Heel" and walk toward the food or toys, around them, over them, back toward them and then halt in front of these distractions, ready to enforce an automatic sit. Pick up a toy and play with good-natured teasing. Tap it on the ground, hide it behind your back, run away with it, then toss it for him. If he shows a lack of interest, scramble to get it and act like you won a prize. Play keep-away and hard-to-get. When he shows interest and resumes playing, give a command, then release him quickly and play with him some more. Then, holding the leash, toss a toy or throw food and call, "Come."

SSENTIALS Puppies quickly learn that the more promptly they obey, the sooner they get to play and thus, play becomes a reward for obedience—not a bribe. While better obedience is a great benefit of practicing Play During Training, you'll also be discovering how to elicit nice play, which is the hallmark of a truly well bonded relationship.

Retrieving

Many puppies and dogs have natural aptitude for retrieving. Others though—even many of the retrieving breeds—consider this task boring, repulsive, or simply a game in which they grab something and teach you to chase them. Obedience and field trial trainers have comprehensive programs to teach this exercise to future competitors. But if you simply want to have some fun with your well-trained pet, bringing out the natural retriever in your dog is fairly simple.

First, get something your puppy wants to play with—a squeaky toy, a soft or stuffed item, a bone, or a ball. Encourage his interest by tapping it on the ground, rubbing it on his body, and hiding it behind your back. When he is interested in the item, toss it out a few feet. If he hesitates to chase or grab it, snatch it up yourself and tease him by tapping it in front of him, hiding it, then tossing it again. You will retrieve more than he will the first few sessions, but your interest in the toy will bring out his competitive spirit and desire to capture it before you do.

Maybe your puppy needs no encouragement to chase but he won't bring it back or drop it. Keep a leash or line on him and as soon as he picks up the item, praise as you run away from him, holding the line in your hand. Since a jerk of the line may cause him to drop the item, adjust the speed of your run so he is pulled toward you.

ESSENTIALS

If your puppy locks his jaws and refuses to relinquish his prize, give rapid-fire commands. Deliver your commands and reinforcement so quickly that your dog stops focusing on his vice-grip hold on the toy and starts concentrating on your commands. When your puppy drops the toy as soon as you begin rapid-fire commands, it's time to start teaching the "Drop it" command. Tell him to "Sit," then command "Drop it" and enforce by jerking the leash sideways or blowing in his nose.

Speak

Teaching your puppy to speak on command is an excellent way to develop watchdog intuition. Many dogs don't naturally bark at the door but can be taught to do so. If you practice knocking on the door and asking your dog to speak, most dogs automatically learn to bark when someone's at the door. Also, many clever tricks can be built around the puppy's ability to bark on command.

To teach "Speak" you must find an object, activity, or situation that causes your dog to bark and praise him lavishly. When it becomes easy to initiate barking, begin giving a command and/or signal, and praise. After a few sessions, your command or signal is likely to trigger barking.

Canine Good Citizen R

This is one event that the AKC sponsors that applies to all dogs, purebred and mixed-breed. The idea is that the dogs who complete these ten tests are certified to be good canine citizens who can behave themselves whether they are alone with their owner, with other people, or with other dogs. These events are usually sponsored by local clubs or community-minded organizations.

The Ten Tests

1. Acceptance of a friendly stranger.
2. Acceptance of being petted by a friendly stranger.
3. The dog accepts inspection and grooming.
4. The dog demonstrates heeling while on a loose lead.
5. The dog displays that he can move through a crowd properly.
6. Dog completes long sit or down.
7. Dog shows that he can immediately calm down after play.
8. The dog shows he can accept other dogs politely, with no show of dominance.
9. The dog must react calmly to sudden distractions.
10. The dog displays that it can be left alone and still exhibit good manners.

If you intend to make your dog a significant part of your life (especially if you live in an urban or suburban area), then taking advantage of Canine Good Citizen R testing is a very good idea. It's not only fun to learn and do, but it's valuable to be able to trust your dog and how he interacts with others. To find out more information about Canine Good Citizen R, call the AKC at (919) 233-9767.

Labrador Retriever

Photo by Mary Bloom©

Therapy Dogs

These dogs aren't in need of therapy, they help give it. They are the therapy. It's well known in the medical community that visits to long-term care facilities (nursing homes; mental illness facilities, etc.) often create tremendous reactions from the patients. They usually get patients who are socially closed off to interact and help them to create personal relationships. In other words, therapy dogs are therapeutic. The dogs that make the grades for these types of assignments must be well behaved and love affection. You need to have a dog that could pass the Canine Good Citizen R test (though that is not a prerequisite).

If you enjoy doing nice things for others, many different therapy dog programs are run throughout the country. This is a great way to train your dog and help others at the same time. You both will feel that much better for doing it.

ESSENTIALS

Most puppies aren't ready for therapy use. The restrictions are mostly obedience. Basically, they don't want your puppy jumping up on people or acting wild. They need calm dogs who just want to be petted. Obviously, this is a simplification, but it's the basic understanding. You have to remember, you're going to be spending time in hospitals, adult care facilities, and other managed living situations. Your dog has to be able to manage in those environments without causing problems. On the other hand, nothing brightens someone's day like a puppy.

CHAPTER **19**

The Terrible Twos

Yes, we're talking about dogs. Like humans, dogs go through a similar stage, often referred to in the dog world as the Terrible Twos. This period usually occurs somewhere between eight and twenty-four months. As it is with humans, the Terrible Twos are not a pleasant period in a dog's life. Neither will they be pleasant in yours. However, with understanding and with proper recognition, you can survive this ordeal and use it to strengthen your relationship with your puppy.

The Warning Signs

Here's an example. Exley was a wonderful puppy with lots of energy. He loved to play, exercise, and go through his obedience training. He could do a medium stay, he could perform a long distance stay outside with many distractions, he would come when called, he would sit at a long distance, etc. Exley was highly socialized. He could be very playful with other dogs. Actually in the end, he didn't care as much for other dogs as he preferred scouring the brush along the park's borders, trying to scare up small, local game, i.e., squirrels, birds, etc. Of course, he was perfectly housebroken and didn't chew on shoes or anything that wasn't appropriate.

And then one day he started to behave badly. He didn't respond when summoned. This happened several times. In fact, the more I called him, the more he ran off in the opposite direction. He began being more aggressive with other dogs, sometimes getting in fights. He wouldn't perform medium or long downs. He would resist direction. He urinated in the house, barked incessantly, and he became destructive. What was I doing wrong?

I called up the rescue person who sold him to me, and asked what I had done wrong. The person from rescue just snickered, and said, "Uh, oh, didn't you know about the Terrible Twos?" I asked her if she had been drinking this early in the morning. "Since when did dogs have the Terrible Twos?"

"Forever," she replied. But it is only recently that this stage has really been recognized and identified by obedience trainers and dog behaviorists.

This story is not unusual. Many owners find their once well-trained puppy's education is immediately wiped out by the invasion of these hormones that send them off into fits. Many of the warning signs may be problems that you haven't been able to solve from your earlier training sessions. However, many a well-trained puppy has wandered afoul of his or her owner once puberty has struck.

What are some of the warning signs? Many of the warning signs are small in the beginning. However, when you stop and think about them, they add up. Many different symptoms are manifestations of other worries. For example, many dog behaviorists have opined that aggression toward people or other dogs is a sign of insecurity on the dog's part.

Chihuahua

Photo by Mary Bloom©

Dominance is the theme that is used over and over again in describing one of the main problems with the Terrible Twos. As the dog matures, he tries to ensure his place in the pack and the world. He wants to secure his status within the home, as he would in a pack. If he has grown substantially, maybe larger than several children in the house, he may be aggressive or pushy with small children. He might snap at someone either in the family or someone who is just visiting.

FACTS

Some behaviorists and other dog experts feel that there is no such thing as the Terrible Twos. Many claim it is a fabricated excuse for those dogs that have not been trained enough early on. They can cite many dogs they have worked with that have not exhibited this type of regression in their training. However, there is as large a group of dog experts that believe that the Terrible Twos are in fact a reality of dog maturation. The simple truth is that some dogs seem to suffer more than others during this period. Some exhibit no effects, while others rampage off.

Position with other dogs is also very important, which is why the aggression towards other dogs often manifests itself at this age. While your puppy will enjoy play, he or she will also use play to establish dominance. Sometimes these displays of dominance can get out of hand, and then a fight breaks out. And certainly there's the competition for females. I have actually seen a Bichon Frise attack a full-grown male German Shepherd in an attempt to establish himself in the pecking order of one available young female dog.

Common Problems

- Doesn't come when called
- Refuses to obey commands
- Staring
- Inappropriate urinating
- Growling
- Aggression
- Inappropriate in-house behavior
- Needier

How Long Does It Last?

The Terrible Twos normally last for about three to five months. Some dogs go through this period more quickly than others. Some dogs go through it earlier than others. Some dogs go through it later than others. Some dogs seem to skip it entirely.

How bad will it be? It's never easy to tell. However, one good rule of thumb is that the more active your dog, the higher the probability that it will go through some version of puppy adolescence.

FACTS

Active dogs, or dogs that require more exercise, seem to have a more pronounced bout of Terrible Twos than some less active breeds. This probably comes from the fact that they require more activity from the beginning. Their needs during this sensitive period are heightened.

The real problem lies in the fact that your dog will continue to test you through this time period. You will tire of the countless corrections and training exercises. It seems, in short, like a battle of wills between you and your puppy. And to him it is. He is trying to move up in the pecking order of the pack. It will take countless episodes and lots patience to get through this very regressive period.

Dominance

Let's talk about dominance. Many behaviorists believe that the Terrible Twos are based on the dog trying to find his place in the world—the pack. Again, the pack can be your family unit, or his standing with other dogs. When a dog questions his place in the pack, he is not only wondering about himself. He's thinking about your place in the pack. Actually, he's challenging you. As all dogs do in their canine world, he wants to take a shot at being the leader. Male dogs are especially well-known for this. I have seen many male dogs attempt to establish dominance in the household of a single female friend. For better or for worse, this is when this kind of behavior begins and is established.

ESSENTIALS

Don't get on the same level with the dog, i.e., don't get down on your knees when playing with the dog. Make the dog sleep on the floor during this period (premium bed space is the right of the dominant dog). Practice long downs once or twice a day. Reinforce all training strenuously.

Now, there are many different ways to handle this kind of behavior. And there are many different theories on what each action means, and a variety of ways you can react. Two things are very much agreed upon. First, you are the leader of the pack. There can be no other leader. Secondly, regardless of how bad it gets, and it will get horrendous, you cannot take your anger out on your dog.

How do you establish dominance? In many ways. Certainly repeating basic training is boring but it is one of the best ways to re-establish your position in the family pack. It is also a great way to prevent obedience training from coming undone at this time. Repeating things like heel, sit, stay, long stay, and down are excellent ways to continue the training you began earlier in your puppy's life.

As the rescue person who put me together with my dog told me at the time, "Your dog will assume leadership in absence of a real leader. In this time period especially, you cannot be a friend. You must be a leader. If your dog sees you as a friend or buddy, he will attempt to assume the dominant role in the relationship."

Common Problems and Solutions

The following section explains what recent works have explained about these behavior patterns in relation to the Terrible Twos. Some of the answers to these problems may seem simplistic, and others may seem repetitive, but in the end, dealing with these problems, some of which were covered in previous chapters, will help you to cope with this stage of growth in your puppy's life.

Doesn't Come When Called

Certainly, this is one of the first signs. And if you never established a good routine with this command, this is certainly one of the first places your dog will push the envelope. Again, this is a dominance issue. Many dogs use this as a means to exhibit their ability to lead. In pack life, the leader decides where the pack is going. Your puppy wants to lead. When I used to walk my dog in our park, where dogs did not have to be on lead before 9 A.M., I spent many a morning chasing my young dog, calling out his name (and maybe a few expletives).

This is of course the wrong thing to do. Never chase a dog when what you want him to do is return to you. By following him I was reinforcing his desire to lead. I was validating his leadership role. This is wrong. Follow the steps in Chapter 14 to regain the upper hand in this aspect of your relationship with your puppy.

Refuses to Obey Commands

Sit. Stay. Down. These are the types of behaviors that define leader and pack member roles. If your puppy refuses to acknowledge your commands, or feigns following and then slinks off, he is telling you that he is challenging your authority. No self-respecting pack leader would accept that type of behavior.

Press forward by reinforcing your position as pack leader. Introduce or reintroduce standard obedience commands. In times like these, your dog needs a job to help him understand what his role in the household is. Your dog is happiest when he has a job. Your dog wants you to be strong. He will only challenge your authority as long as you remain lax. Strong trainers and owners find that many dogs they work with suffer less anxiety during this phase of puppyhood. By being strong in this department during this time period in your puppy's life, you will make both your lives a lot easier.

Staring

You should avoid trying to stare down an adult dog. It's a great way to spook them. However, a dominant dog stares down less dominant dogs. Getting into staring contests with your dog is a bad idea. But should you find yourself in one, don't be the first to look away. In a stare-down with your puppy, make sure he breaks eye contact first. While this might sound childish, you cannot afford the loss in prestige by losing a stare-down. Losing a stare-down while trying to enforce other obedience measures is like laughing when you're trying to give someone serious advice. It ruins everything. Don't get caught up in stare-downs. But if you find yourself in one, make sure you win.

ESSENTIALS   Several experts have stated that one of the best things you can do for your dog during this period is provide lots of exercise. Obedience and exercise will give your dog something to do, a job, keeping them occupied and lively. It will give your puppy an outlet for all the anxiety or insecurity he or she may be feeling—and make him or her less stressed out about their place in your household.

Inappropriate Urinating

Now, this is a tricky one. Don't assume your dog is going through the Terrible Twos if you've just introduced another dog, a cat, or some other animal into the house. Urine is the written language of the animal world. It is the international, interspecies code, identifying you and your status in the world.

Boston Terrier

Photo by Mary Bloom©

Now, if it is Terrible Twos, he's marking his territory. Your dog is sending you a message that these are his lands, and that everyone within those lands belongs or answers to him. Obviously, this cannot stand. You need to deal with this swiftly and absolutely. Refer to the problem section for how to handle this problem. Swift action will head this one off at the pass, and keep you and your friend in good stead of each other.

There were also many cases of dogs urinating either on one another or on humans. Again, among dogs, this is a sign of dominance. Acceptance of this sign signals your submission. The appropriate dog response is a fight. You don't want to do that. However, should your dog try to mark you or another person, immediate correction is absolutely necessary. By allowing or tolerating such behavior you will be sending mixed signals.

Allowing this to happen might encourage further aggressive behavior, which you really can't have.

ESSENTIALS

During the Terrible Twos, it's very important to make sure you keep your place in the household as the lead dog. Sometimes you will have to implement some tactics with your little furry friend that you really don't want to. Fido may whine or howl or bark. Don't intercede. It's a sign of weakness. Don't be cruel, but keep in mind Shakespeare—be cruel to be kind.

Growling

Growling is a warning. It is used as an aggressive means of communication between animals. Its meaning is unmistakable. Its implication is also. An animal that growls at you is letting you know that it is either afraid of you or has no fear of you. Regardless, it is a warning of attack. The idea is to make you back down. Whether guarding food or property, the dog has the wrong message. And he is sending the wrong message.

With any type of aggressive behavior your puppy might be exhibiting, make sure you do everything you can to curb it. Whether against another dog or another human being, aggression unchecked will only lead to a life full of challenges and misunderstandings. A dog growls because it is unsure of the situation, or it doesn't like someone or something. Growling at other dogs or at humans is completely unacceptable behavior in our social society. Again, you'll want to use the problem-solving section to see how to do this.

Aggression

Any type of aggression, especially during this period, is usually attributable to the Terrible Twos and the canine maturation process. There are many places aggression can rear its ugly head: towards other dogs, towards children, towards strangers, towards you. Corrections must take place immediately or else this type of menacing action will continue to grow and entrench itself in the dog's adult personality.

First, when your puppy starts acting aggressive with other dogs, your dog is trying to rise in the ranks. I have seen puppies who played together very well one day become mortal enemies the next. I have seen puppies who were submissive to their elders last month try to fit their mouths around those same dogs not thirty days later. This is your dog sending out the message that he has arrived. However, you cannot condone this. It must be corrected immediately. Your dog cannot be allowed to act out in such a manner. Condoning it or passing it off is only going to encourage further outbreaks. The canine good citizen does not act out like that towards other dogs. Should action like this continue, you will risk several unpleasant scenarios. Mainly, other dog owners will shun you, which is a social death in the dog world, since dogs are social animals. Secondly, should something serious result, you could end up with someone else's veterinarian's bills and a citation from local law enforcement. Or, in extreme cases, your dog might be seized by your local animal control department.

SSENTIALS

Sometimes the best answer for overcoming the Terrible Twos is to take your puppy back to school. Obedience training is the best weapon against the Terrible Twos. It's a great way for you to exercise dominance, and the repetition of the training will help your dog know its place in the pack.

Aggression towards humans is very much the same story, and if the behavior goes unchecked, then surely you will end up in some very dire situations. First, a puppy experiencing the Terrible Twos might get aggressive with the children. This isn't always the case. Some dogs seem to sense, regardless of their situation, that the children are pups. If your dog is well adjusted, this should be the case. However, it's been known to happen that some dogs see the children as competitors. This usually happens in a situation where training has not been strong enough, where the dog is extremely insecure, and the dog is acting out on those insecurities. By putting those children in their place, some dogs think wrongly, they can move up the food chain in a couple of quick hops. Basically your dog is saying to you that he or she is more important than the children. He or she deserves more consideration. Immediate correction is the only possible reaction.

Aggression towards strangers is sometimes wrongly encouraged by pet owners. Many people think to themselves that it's good to have the dog for protection. However, dogs cannot discern between good and bad people, intruders or friends, much as you might think they can. These nuances, or shades of difference, are not easily detected by your dog. If this kind of behavior is left alone or encouraged, you will eventually have an antisocial dog. He or she will have to be separated from people, especially during gatherings of friends or family, which is sheer torture for a dog, since again, they are social animals. Again, immediate correction is imperative.

SSENTIALS Consulting a local obedience trainer during this period is one of the best options you have in this situation. A well-known, respected trainer will have lots of experience and stories to help you overcome this period in your puppy's growing process.

Aggression towards you is the ultimate challenge a dog can make. This must be dealt with swiftly and can never be tolerated. Any kind of allowance or tolerance in a situation like this can eventually lead to a dog that can't be controlled. A dog that cannot be controlled, even by his or her owner, is a dog that is destined for a horrible life or a tragic end.

Dogs are social animals, and especially when going through this phase in their maturation, they don't understand the larger implications of their actions. What you want is a happy, healthy, secure, confident dog who will help you greet friends and family members, and be a good member of your family and a good neighbor. Curbing his or her aggression quickly and effectively is the best thing you can do for your dog in the long haul.

Inappropriate In-house Behavior

Ransacking the garbage. Tearing up the furniture, rugs, etc. Defecating indoors. These are all signs of insecurity on the dog's part. While they may seem to a human as destructive acts meant to upset you, the dog is acting out his or her anxieties. This is their way of communicating, since they can't talk. What your dog is trying to tell you is that he or she doesn't know his or her place in the house. They desire rigidity and stability. They are looking to get some kind of direction from you.

Bulldog

Photo by Mary Bloom©

Simply put, immediate correction is also the first priority. However, a scolding is the most you should manage should you not catch them in the act. The way to combat some of these situations is by preventive measures. Maybe you'll want to limit access to only a few rooms until this inappropriate behavior ceases. Make sure not to leave valuable items within reach of Rover. Keep the garbage under the sink or in a closet. Maybe your puppy should be quarantined to the kitchen while you're not home for a while, or until these manifestations clear up. Usually many of these types of problems will occur while you are not home. But I have seen and heard about dogs who have perpetrated these things while someone was actually in the room or in the next room. So don't be surprised when it happens to you. It's a sign that someone wants to move upward on the ladder to top dog.

Acting Needy

It has happened that many people's puppies have become more needy during this stage in their lives. They crave more attention. Sometimes they will do things, even things they know are wrong, just so that you will spend time with them. I know that seems odd, but that's what seems to be the case. Again, as with humans, the interaction is the need, whether it's good or bad is secondary. Make sure you give your puppy plenty of attention, but don't spoil them too much. A needy dog can become an annoyance. Establishing a routine is an excellent antidote for this kind of problem. Remember to praise your puppy whenever possible, but do not lavish too much attention on your pup, or else they will expect it as part of their everyday lifestyle. They need to be a member of the household, not the center of attention.

Conclusion

As stated previously, some dogs seem to exhibit one, if not many, of these signs during this period in their lives. However, many also seem never to display any of these traits. Be prepared. The best weapons against the Terrible Twos are extra obedience training and extra exercise. These two things seem to alleviate the anxiety and stress of the age group, and give a valve with which to release the extra nervous energy that puppies seem to have at this time in their lives. Dogs crave a job responsibility. They crave direction. In absence of any activity or direction, they will provide it themselves. If this goes unchecked, you can find yourself in too many difficult spots. A preventive game plan is the best course of action to minimize this odd period in your puppy's life.

APPENDIX I

Resources

Following are addresses and/or telephone numbers for a number of different resources. Included are magazines, books, and Web sites. These resources merely scratch the surface of all the information out there. Be sure to always check with your veterinarian before following any health advice you might read, no matter how credible the source.

Print Guides

Magazines

✉ AKC Gazette
American Kennel Club
51 Madison Avenue
New York, NY 10010

✉ Bloodlines Journal
United Kennel Club
100 East Kilgore Road
Kalamazoo, MI 29001

✉ Dogs in Canada
Canadian Kennel Club
89 Skyway Avenue, Suite 200
Etobicoke, ON M9Q 6R4

✉ Dog Fancy
Fancy Publications
3 Burroughs
Irvine, CA 92718

✉ Dog World
MacLean Hunter Publishing Corporation
29 North Wacker Drive
Chicago, IL 60606

Books

Puppies

✐ *Puppy Care and Training: A Guide to a Happy Healthy Pet* by Bardi McLennan (Howell Book House)

✐ *Dog Behavior: A Guide to a Happy Healthy Pet* by Ian Dunbar (Howell Book House)

✐ *The Art of Raising a Puppy* by the Monks of New Skete (Little, Brown)

✐ *The Perfect Puppy: How to Raise a Well-Behaved Dog* by Gwen Bailey (Reader's Digest)

✐ *How to Raise a Puppy You Can Live With* by Clarice Rutherford, David H. Neil (Alpine Publications)

✐ *Your Purebred Puppy: A Buyer's Guide* by Michele Welton (Owl Books)

✐ *Civilizing Your Puppy* by Barbara J. Wrede, Michele Earle-Bridges (Barrons)

✐ *I Just Got a Puppy: What Do I Do?* by Mordecai Siegal, Matthew Margolis (Fireside)

✐ *SuperPuppy Goes to Puppy Class: How to Train the Best Dog You'll Ever Have!* by Peter J. Vollmer (SuperPuppy Press)

✐ *101 Essential Tips: Puppy Care* by Bruce Fogle (Dorling Kindersley)

Dogs

✐ *The Complete Dog Book* by the American Kennel Club (Howell Book House)

✐ *The Complete Dog Book for Kids* by the American Kennel Club (Howell Book House)

✐ *The Intelligence of Dogs* by Stanley Coren (Free Press)

✐ *The Lost History of the Canine Race* by Mary Elizabeth Thurston (Avon)

✐ *Pack of Two* by Caroline Knapp (The Dial Press)

✐ *Selecting the Best Dog for You* by Chris Nelson (TFH)

✐ *Through Otis's Eyes* by Patricia Burlin Kennedy, Robert Christie (Howell Book House)

Adoption and Rescue

- *The Adoption Option* by Eliza Rubenstein, Shari Kalina (Howell Book House)
- *Save That Dog!* by Liz Palika (Howell Book House)
- *Second-Hand Dog* by Carol Lea Benjamin (Howell Book House)

Health

- *The Consumer's Guide to Dog Food* by Liz Palika (Howell Book House)
- *Dog Doctor* by Mark Evans (Howell Book House)
- *Dog Owner's Home Veterinary Handbook* by Delbert G. Carlson, D.V.M., James M. Giffin, M.D. (Howell Book House)
- *The Doctors Book of Home Remedies for Dogs and Cats* by editors of *Prevention* magazine (Rodale)

Training & Behavior:

- *Back to Basics: Dog Training by Fabian* by Andrea Arden (Howell Book House)

- *Dog Perfect* by Sarah Hodgson (Howell Book House)
- *Dr. Dunbar's Good Little Dog Book* by Ian Dunbar (James & Kenneth Publishers)
- *Dual Ring Dogs* by Amy Ammen, Jacqueline Frasier (Howell Book House)
- *How to Be Your Dog's Best Friend (The Monks of New Skete)* by Job Michael Evans (Little, Brown)
- *People, Pooches & Problems* by Job Michael Evans (Howell Book House)
- *Surviving Your Dog's Adolescence* by Carol Lea Benjamin (Howell Book House)
- *When Good Dogs Do Bad Things* by Modercai Siegel (Little, Brown)

Pet Loss

- *The Loss of a Pet* by Dr. Wallace Sife (Howell Book House)
- *When Your Pet Dies* by Jamie Quakenbush (Simon & Schuster)

Organizations and Associations

Animal Advocacy

- American Humane Association
  63 Inverness Drive East
  Englewood, CO 80112
  (303)792-9900
  www.americanhumane.org

- American Society for the Prevention of Cruelty to Animals
  424 East 92nd Street
  New York, NY 10128-6804
  (212) 876-7700
  www.aspca.org

- Delta Society (for Therapy Dogs)
  P.O. Box 1080
  Renton, WA 98057
  (206) 226-7357
  www.deltasociety.org

- Doris Day Animal League
  900 2nd Street NE, Suite 303
  Washington, DC 20002
  (202) 842-3325
  www.ddal.org

Friends of Animals, Inc.
P.O. Box 1244
Norwalk, CT 06856
(203) 866-5223
www.friendsofanimals.org

The Humane Society of the United States
2100 L Street, NW
Washington, DC 20037
(202) 452-1100
www.hsus.org

Pets Are Wonderful Council (P.A.W.)
500 North Michigan Avenue
Suite 200
Chicago, IL 60611
(312) 836-7145

Project BREED
18707 Curry Powder Lane
Germantown, MD 20874-2014
(301) 428-3675
www.projectbreed.org

Therapy Dogs International
6 Hilltop Road
Mendham, NJ 07945
(201) 548-0888
www.tdi-dog.org

Breed Registeries

American Kennel Club
51 Madison Avenue
New York, NY 10010
www.akc.org
(212) 696-8200

American Rare Breed Association
100 Nicholas Street NW
Washington, DC 20011
www.arba.org

Canadian Kennel Club
Commerce Park
88 Skyway Avenue, Suite 100
Etobicoke, ON M9W 6R4
www.ckc.ca

Mixed Breed Dog Club of America
1937 Seven Pines Drive
St. Louis, MO 63146-3717

United Kennel Club
100 East Kilgore Road
Kalamazoo, MI 49001-5598
(616) 343-9020
www.ukcdogs.com

World Kennel Club
P.O. Box 60771
Oklahoma City, OK 73146
(405) 570-7929
www.worldkennelclub.com

Federation Cynologique Internationale
31 Place Albert I
B6530 Thin
Belgium
www.bestdogs.com/FCI/Default.htm

AKC-affiliated Breed Clubs

American Brittany Club, Inc.
Joy Searcy
800 Hillmont Ranch Road
Aldeo, TX 76008

American Pointer Club, Inc.
Lauri Shroyer
7208 Sugar Maple Court
Rockville, MD 20855
(301) 926-1599

German Shorthaired Pointer Club of America
Patte Titus
4103 Walnut Street
Shaw AFB, SC 29152-1429
checksix@cpis.net

German Wirehaired Pointer Club of America, Inc.
Karen Nelsen
25821 Lucille Avenue
Lomita, CA 90717

American Chesapeake Club, Inc.
Dyane Baldwin
RD2 Box 287A
Newport, PA 17074
pondholo@igateway.com

Curly-Coated Retriever Club of America
Marilyn Smith
251 NW 151 Avenue
Pembroke Pines, FL 33028
tootsye@aol.com

Flat-Coated Retriever Society of America, Inc.
Kurt Anderson
42 Drazen Drive
North Haven, CT 06473
73210.136@compuserve.com

Golden Retriever Club of America
Linda Willard
P.O. Box 20434
Oklahoma City, OK 73114

Labrador Retriever Club, Inc.
Christopher Wincek
12471 Pond Road
Burton, Ohio 44021
Rodarbal@aol.com

English Setter Association of America, Inc.
Mrs. Dawn S. Ronyak
114 South Burlington Oval Drive
Chardon, OH 44024

Gordon Setter Club of America, Inc.
Nikki Maounis
P.O. Box 54
Washougal, WA 98671

Irish Setter Club of America, Inc.
Mrs. Marion Pahy
16717 Ledge Falls
San Antonio, TX 78232-1808

American Water Spaniel Club
Ann Potter
HR 3 Box 224
Johnson City, TX 78636

Clumber Spaniel Club of America, Inc.
Ms. Barbara Stebbins
2271 SW Almansa Avenue
Port St. Lucie, FL 34953

American Spaniel Club, Inc.
Ellen Passage
35 Academy Road
Hohokus, NJ 07423-1301

English Cocker Spaniel Club of America, Inc.
Kate D. Romanksi
P.O. Box 252
Hales Corners, WI 53130

English Springer Spaniel
Field Trial Association, Inc.
Cheryl Sligar
5180 North Dapple Gray Road
Las Vegas, NV 89129
CSligarESS@aol.com

Field Spaniel Society of America
Lynn Finney
Box 247
Lyndell, PA 19354
bttrblu@worldaxes.com

Irish Water Spaniel Club of America
Evelyn Van Uden
3061 Moore Road
Ransomville, NY 14131

Welsh Springer Spaniel Club of America, Inc.
Karen Lyle
W254 N4989 McKerrow Drive
Pewaukee, WI 53072-1300

Vizsla Club of America, Inc.
Mrs. Florence Duggan
451 Longfellow Avenue
Westfield, NJ 07090

Weimaraner Club of America
Dorothy Derr
P.O. Box 2907
Muskogee, OK 74402-2907

American Wirehaired
Pointing Griffon Association
Patricia Loomis
7920 Peters Road
Jacksonville, AR 72076
patloomis@aol.com

Afghan Hound Club of America
Norma Cozzoni
43 West 612 Tall Oaks Trail
Elburn, IL 60119

Basenji Club of America
Anne L. Graves
5102 Darnell
Houston, TX 77096-1404

Basset Hound Club of America, Inc.
Melody Fair
P.O. Box 339
Noti, OR 97461-0339
HEIRLINE@aol.com

National Beagle Club
Susan Mills Stone
2555 Pennsylvania NW
Washington, DC 20037

American Black & Tan Coonhound
Stan Bielowicz
222 Pate Rogers Road
Fleming, GA 31309

American Bloodhound Club
Ed Kilby
1914 Berry Lane
Daytona Beach, FL 32124

Dachshund Club of America, Inc.
Carl Holder
1130 Redoak Drive
Lumberton, TX 77657

Greyhound Club of America
Margaret Bryson
15079 Meeting House Lane
Montpelier, VA 23192

American Foxhound Club
James M. Rea
P.O. Box 588
Clarkesville, GA 30523

Harrier Club of America
Kimberly Mitchell
301 Jefferson Lane
Ukiah, CA 95482

Ibizan Hound Club of the United States
Stephanie Bonner
3098 Elm Road
Duluth, MN 55804
sbonner@duluth.infi.net

Irish Wolfhound Club of America
Mrs. William S. Pfarrer
8855 U.S. Route 40
New Carlisle, OH 45344
(937) 845-9135

Norwegian Elkhound Association
of America, Inc.
Debra Walker
3650 Bay Creek Road
Loganville, GA 30249
(770) 466-9967

Otterhound Club of America
Dian Quist-Sulek
Rt.#1, Box 247
Palmyra, NE 68418
(402) 441-7900

Petit Basset Griffon Vendeen
Club of America
Ms. Shirley Knipe
426 Laguna Way
Simi Valley, CA 93065
(805) 527-6327

Pharaoh Hound Club of America
Rita L. Sacks
P.O. Box 895454
Leesburg, FL 34789-5454
(352) 357-8723

Rhodesian Ridgeback Club
of the United States, Inc.
Dawn Sajadea
P O Box 5215
River Forest, IL 60305-5215
dsajadea@tezcat.com

Saluki Club of America
Judy Tantillo
208 Forked Neck Road
Shamong, NJ 08088
Fax: (609) 268-3455
asuwish@cyberEnet.net

Scottish Deerhound Club of America, Inc.
Mr. Tom Gentner
3477 Flanders Drive
Yorktown Heights, NY 10598
tgentner@aol.com

American Whippet Club, Inc.
Mrs. Harriet Nash Lee
14 Oak Circle
Charlottesville, VA 22901
(804) 295-4525

Akita Club of America
Sandi Soto
5602 North Church Street
Tampa, FL 33614
Fax: (813) 889-0668
akitainu@cyberspy.com

Alaskan Malamute Club of America, Inc.
Stephen Piper
3528 Pin Hook Road
Antioch, TN 37013-1510
spiper@nashville.net

Bernese Mountain Dog Club of America, Inc.
Ms. Roxanne Bortnick
P.O. Box 270692
Fort Collins, CO 80527

American Boxer Club, Inc.
Mrs. Barbara E. Wagner
6310 Edward Drive
Clinton, MD 20735-4135

American Bullmastiff Association, Inc.
Linda Silva
15 Woodland Lane
Smithtown, NY 11787

Doberman Pinscher Club of America
Nancy Jewell
13451 North Winchester Way
Parker, CO 80134

Giant Schnauzer Club of America, Inc.
Kathy DeShong
7855 Whistling Winds Lane
Brighton, IL 62012
(618) 466-6768
gscamerica@aol.com

Great Dane Club of America, Inc.
Kathy Jurin
1825 Oaklyn Drive
Green Lane, PA 18054

Great Pyrenees Club of America, Inc.
Maureen Maxwell-Simon
7430 Jonestown
Harrisburg, PA 17112

Greater Swiss Mountain Dog
Club of America, Inc.
Dori Likevich
11713 Duncan Plains Road
Johnstown, OH 43031
twinpine01@aol.com

Mastiff Club of America, Inc.
Karen McBee
Rt. #7, Box 520
Fairmont, WV 26554
mmcbee@access.mountain.net

Newfoundland Club of America, Inc.
Steve McAdams
PO Box 370
Green Valley, IL 61534

Portuguese Water Dog Club
of America, Inc.
Ms. Joan-Ellis Van Loan
99 Maple Avenue
Greenwich, CT 06830

American Rottweiler Club
Doreen LePage
960 South Main Stree
Pascoag, RI 02859
doreen@ids.net

St. Bernard Club of America, Inc.
Penny Janz
33400 Red Fox Way
No. Prairie, WI 53153

Samoyed Club of America, Inc.
Lori Elvera
3017 Oak Meadow Drive
Flower Mound, TX 75028
kenoshasam@aol.com

Siberian Husky Club of America, Inc.
Fain Zimmerman
210 Madera Drive
Victoria, TX 77905
sledog@tisd.net

Standard Schnauzer Club of America
Joan Sitton
160 Carmel Riviera Drive
Carmel, CA 93923

Airedale Terrier Club of America
Mrs. April Stevens
4078 Hickory Hill Road
Murrysville, PA 15668

Staffordshire Terrier Club of America
Dr. H. Richard Pascoe
785 Valley View Road
Forney, TX 75126

Australian Terrier Club of America, Inc.
Ms. Marilyn Harban
1515 Davon Lane
Nassau Bay, TX 77058

Border Terrier Club of America, Inc.
Pattie Pfeffer
801 Los Luceros Drive
Eagle, ID 83616

Bull Terrier Club of America
Mrs. Becky Poole
2630 Gold Point Circle
Hixson, TN 37343
(423) 842-2611
rockytp@voyageronline.net

Cairn Terrier Club of America
Christine M. Bowlus
6152 Golf Club Road
Howell, MI 48843
(517) 545-4816

Dandie Dinmont Terrier Club
of America, Inc.
Mrs. Gail Isner
151 Junaluska Drive
Woodstock, GA 30188

American Fox Terrier Club
Mr. Martin Goldstein
P.O. Box 1448
Edison, NJ 08818

Irish Terrier Club of America
Cory Rivera
22720 Perry Street
Perris, CA 92570

United States Lakeland Terrier Club
Mrs. Edna Lawicki
8207 East Cholla Street
Scottsdale, AZ 85260
(602) 998-8409

American Manchester Terrier Club
Ms. Sandra Kipp
Box 231
Gilbertsville, IA 50634

Miniature Bull Terrier Club of America
Kathy Schoeler
8111 NW 46th Street
Ocala, Florida 34482

American Miniature Schnauzer Club, Inc.
Jane Gilbert
5 Salt Meadow Way
Marshfield, MA 02050
JMJRGlbrt@aol.com

Norwich and Norfolk Terrier Club
Heidi H. Evans
158 Delaware Avenue
Laurel, DE 19956

Scottish Terrier Club of America
Polly O'Neal
4058 Stratford
Abilene, TX 79605
(915) 672-4229
pbo@camalott.com

American Sealyham Terrier Club
Judy E. Thill
13948 North Cascade Road
Dubuque, IA 52003

Skye Terrier Club of America
Karen J'Anthony
1667 East Lebanon Road
Dover, DE 19901

Soft Coated Wheaten Terrier Club of America
Genie Kline
585 Timberlane Road
Wetumpka, AL 36093

Staffordshire Bull Terrier Club, Inc.
Catherine Swain
P.O. Box 5382
Montecito, CA 93150

Welsh Terrier Club of America, Inc.
Secretary: Derry Coe
26841 Canyon Crest Road
San Juan Capistrano, CA 92675

West Highland White Terrier
Club of America
Judith White
8124 Apple Church Road
Thurmont, MD 21788

Affenpinscher Club of America
Sharon I. Strempski
2 Tucktaway Lane
Danbury, CT 06810

American Brussels Griffon Association
Denise Brusseau
5921 159th Lane NW
Anoka, MN 55303

American Cavalier King Charles Spaniel Club
Martha Guimond
1905 Upper Ridge Road
Green Lane, PA 18054

Chihuahua Club of America, Inc.
Diana Garren
16 Hillgirt Road
Hendersonville, NC 28792

American Chinese Crested Club, Inc.
Kathleen Forth
Rt. 3 Box 157
Decatur, TX 76234

English Toy Spaniel Club of America
Ms. Susan Jackson
18451 Sheffield Lane
Bristol, IN 46507-9455

Italian Greyhound Club of America, Inc.
Teri Dickinson
4 Hillcrest Drive
Allen, TX 75002
Fax: (972) 396-8993
tdickinson@compuserve.com

American Maltese Association, Inc.
Pamela G. Rightmyer
2211 South Tioga Way
Las Vegas, NV 89117

American Manchester Terrier Club
Sandra Kipp
Box 231
Gilbertsville, IA 50634

Miniature Pinscher Club of America, Inc.
Mrs. Janice Horne
3724 88th SE
Mercer Island, WA 98040

Papillon Club of America, Inc.
Mrs. Janice Dougherty
551 Birch Hill Road
Shoemakersville, PA 19555
(610) 926-5581

Pekingese Club of America, Inc.
Mrs. Leonie Marie Schultz
Route 1, Box 321
Bergton, VA 22811

American Pomeranian Club, Inc.
Brenda Turner
3910 Concord Place
Texarkana, TX 75501-2212

Poodle Club of America, Inc.
Mr. Charles R. Thomasson II
503 Martineau Drive
Chester, VA, 23831-5753

Pug Dog Club of America, Inc.
Mr. James P. Cavallaro
1820 Shadowlawn Street
Jacksonville, FL 32205

American Shih Tzu Club, Inc.
Bonnie Prato
5252 Shafter Avenue
Oakland, CA 94618

Silky Terrier Club of America, Inc.
Ms. Louise Rosewell
2783 South Saulsbury Street
Denver, CO 80227

Yorkshire Terrier Club of America, Inc.
Mrs. Shirley A. Patterson
2 Chestnut Ct., Star Rt.
Pottstown, PA 19464

American Eskimo Dog Club of America
Vivian Toepfer
2206 Idaho Avenue
Stockton, CA 95204

Bichon Frisé Club of America, Inc.
Mrs. Bernice D. Richardson
Secretary, 186 Ash Street
North Twin Falls, ID 83301

Boston Terrier Club of America
Marian Sheehan, Secretary
8130 East Theresa Drive
Scottsdale, AZ 85255
(317) 356-1140

Bulldog Club of America
Toni Stevens, Secretary
P.O. Box 248
Nobleton, FL 34661

Chinese Shar-Pei Club of America, Inc.
Georgette Schaefer, Secretary
210 White Chapel Court
Southlake, TX 76092-8500

Chow Chow Club, Inc.
Irene Cartabio, Secretary
3580 Plover Place
Seaford, NY 11783

Dalmatian Club of America, Inc.
Mrs. Sharon Boyd
2316 McCrary Road
Richmond, TX 77469

Finnish Spitz Club of America
Bill Storz
34 Sunrise Drive
Baltic, CT 06330

French Bulldog Club of America
Gail Pehlke
20756 South River Road
Shorewood, IL 60431
regails@aol.com

Keeshond Club of America, Inc.
Tawn Sinclair
11782 Pacific Coast Hwy
Malibu, CA 90265

American Lhasa Apso Club, Inc.
Esther DeFalcis
3691 Tuggle Road
Buford, GA 30519

Schipperke Club of America, Inc.
Dawn Hribar
70480 Morency
Romeo, MI 48065

National Shiba Club of America
Liz Kinoshita
2417 Ramke Place
Santa Clara, CA 95050
lyzk@concentric.net

Tibetan Spaniel Club of America
Valerie Robinson
103 Old Colony Drive
Mashpee, MA 02649
(508) 477-7637
deetree@capecod.net

Tibetan Terrier Club of America
Sharon Harrison
P.O. Box 528
Pleasanton, TX 78064

Australian Cattle Dog Club of America
Katherine Buetow
2003B Melrose Drive
Champaign, IL 61820
acdca@cattledog.com

United States Australian
Shepherd Association
Andrea Blizard
34 Deckertown Tpke.
Sussex, NJ 07461

Bearded Collie Club of America, Inc.
Amber L Carpenter
541 Crestwood
Camden, AR 71701

American Belgian Malinois Club
Marcia Herson
209 Harrison Avenue
Harrison, NY 10528
mhcil@aol.com

Belgian Sheepdog Club of America, Inc.
Carilee Cole
11071 East Stanley
Davison, MI 48423
cecole@juno.com

American Belgian Tervuren Club, Inc.
Diane Schultz
Rt. 1 Box 759
Pomona Park, FL 32181

The Border Collie Society of America
April Quist
2854 Kennedy Street
Livermore, CA 94550-8003

Briard Club of America, Inc.
Dianne Schoenberg
3215 NE 89th
Seattle, WA 98115
diannes@u.washington.edu

Canaan Dog Club of America, Inc.
Sally Armstrong-Barnhardt
2300 Crossover Road
Reno, NV 89510-9354
k9teacher@aol.com

Collie Club of America, Inc.
Mrs. Carmen Louise Leonard
1119 South Fleming Rd
Woodstock, IL 60098
(815) 337-0323
seccca@aol.com

German Shepherd Dog Club of America, Inc.
Blanche Beisswenger
17 West Ivy Lane
Englewood, NJ 07631

Old English Sheepdog Club of America, Inc.
Allene Black
220 Elm Street
Enfield, CT 06082
gwynedd@tiac.net

Web Sites

General

- The Puppy Place
  www.thepuppyplace.org

- Dog Scouts of America
  www.dogscouts.com

- Dog Owner's Guide
  www.canismajor.com/dog/tpuppy.html

- BreederLink Homepage
  www.breederlink.com

- Dog Breeders Online Directory
  www.breeders.net

- Canine Connections Breed Rescue Information
  www.cheta.net/connect/canine/Rescue

- Canine.Net
  www.canine.net

- Dogs On-Line
  www.dogsonline.com

- Pro Dog Breed Rescue Network
  www.prodogs.com

Training and Behavior

- American Dog Trainers Network
  www.inch.com/~dogs

- Campbell's Pet Behavior Resources
  www.webtrail.com/petbehavior/index.html

- Dog Obedience and Training Page
  www.dogpatch.org/obed.html

- Raising Your Dog with the Monks of New Skete
  www.dogsbestfriend.com

Health

- AVMA (American Veterinary Medical Association)
  www.avma.org

- FDA Center for Veterinary Medicine
  www.fda.gov/cvm

- Iams Company Homepage
  www.iamsco.com

- National Animal Control Poison Center
  www.prodogs.com/chn/napcc/index.htm

- Waltham World of Pet Care
  www.waltham.com

Catalog/Resource

- Flying Dog Press
  www.flyingdogpress.com

- Dog Lover's Bookshop
  www.dogbooks.com

APPENDIX II

The Complete AKC Pedigree List

The following is a complete list of AKC-registerable breeds. The maximum height is measured to the shoulders. Both the height and weight are for male dogs, who tend to be slightly larger than females. The maximum heights and weights indicated are the normal upper levels for each dog; it is quite possible for an individual dog to be much larger or smaller. Also provided are some of the points owners should consider before getting a particular breed.

The Sporting Group

Breed	Max Height	Max Weight	Possible Downfalls
American Water Spaniel	18 inches	45 pounds	Can develop chewing and digging habits
Brittany	20 inches	40 pounds	Will become nervous and hyperactive if not given lots of exercise
Chesapeake Bay Retriever	26 inches	80 pounds	Sheds a lot; never lets a puddle go to waste
Clumber Spaniel	19 inches	85 pounds	Can develop joint problems
Cocker Spaniel	15 inches	30 pounds	Needs gentle care; should not sleep outside
Curly-Coated Retriever	27 inches	40 pounds	Can be a bit stubborn
English Cocker Spaniel	16 inches	30 pounds	Has a tendency to bark if not properly trained
English Setter	26 inches	70 pounds	
English Springer Spaniel	20 inches	50 pounds	Needs exercise or will become overweight
Field Spaniel	19 inches	55 pounds	Needs extra care on ears and coat
Flat-Coated Retriever	25 inches	70 pounds	Very energetic and strong, needs lots of exercise
German Shorthaired Pointer	23 inches	70 pounds	Needs to be outside a lot to be truly happy
German Wirehaired Pointer	26 inches	80 pounds	Will demand long walks
Golden Retriever	24 inches	75 pounds	Needs lots of exercise
Gordon Setter	27 inches	80 pounds	Big, hairy dog—needs lots of brushing
Irish Setter	27 inches	75 pounds	Needs extra grooming, exercise, and training
Irish Water Spaniel	24 inches	65 pounds	Can be very hyper
Spinone Italiano	28 inches	85 pounds	Too laid back for active sorts, needs too much exercise for others

The Sporting Group *(continued)*

Breed	Max Height	Max Weight	Possible Downfalls
Labrador Retriever	25 inches	80 pounds	Possibly the most hyper puppies in the universe, adults usually settle down
Pointer	28 inches	75 pounds	Needs and loves the active life
Sussex Spaniel	15 inches	45 pounds	Needs a fair amount of grooming and exercise
Vizsla	24 inches	60 pounds	Requires gentle handling
Weimaraner	27 inches	85 pounds	Will try to become the alpha member of the household
Welsh Springer Spaniel	20 inches	50 pounds	Craves lots of attention
Wirehaired Pointing Griffon	24 inches	70 pounds	Needs lots of grooming

The Hound Group

Breed	Max Height	Max Weight	Possible Downfalls
Afghan Hound	27 inches	60 pounds	Requires extensive grooming; can be destructive if too bored
Basenji	17 inches	25 pounds	Requires lots of patience when training
Basset Hound	14 inches	55 pounds	When these usually laidback dogs catch a scent, just try and stop them from following it
Beagle	15 inches	30 pounds	Very spunky, very curious, and likes to bark
Black and Tan Coonhound	27 inches	100 pounds	Tends to run off "on the hunt" if loose
Bloodhound	27 inches	110 pounds	Can be shy
Borzoi	28 inches	105 pounds	Needs lots of exercise; sheds a lot
Dachshund (Standard)	18 inches	20 pounds	Prone to spinal damage from jumping and falling
Foxhound, American	25 inches	70 pounds	Needs lots of exercise
Foxhound, English	24 inches	65 pounds	Happiest in rural areas

The Hound Group (continued)

Breed	Max Height	Max Weight	Possible Downfalls
Greyhound	30 inches	70 pounds	Will chew on things if not extensively exercised; somewhat fragile
Harrier	21 inches	55 pounds	Doesn't like to be alone
Ibizan Hound	28 inches	55 pounds	Can jump over most short fences
Irish Wolfhound	34 inches	135 pounds	As fast as he is big, needs space and attention
Norwegian Elkhound	21 inches	60 pounds	Needs lots of grooming and weekly baths
Otterhound	27 inches	120 pounds	Likes to howl
Petit Basset Griffon Vendéen	15 inches	35 pounds	Can be noisy
Pharaoh Hound	25 inches	60 pounds	Often wary of strange children
Rhodesian Ridgeback	27 inches	85 pounds	Requires extra training
Saluki	28 inches	65 pounds	Prone to some health problems
Scottish Deerhound	33 inches	120 pounds	A big dog that fares best living indoors
Whippet	22 inches	28 pounds	Can be shy

The Working Group

Breed	Max Height	Max Weight	Possible Downfalls
Akita	28 inches	105 pounds	Lots of shedding; can be aggressive; a fenced yard is highly recommended
Alaskan Malamute	25 inches	75 pounds	Very strong and energetic
Anatolian Shepherd	32 inches	140 pounds	Wary around strange people and dogs, but very gentle in general
Bernese Mountain Dog	28 inches	90 pounds	Needs lots of brushing and exercise
Boxer	25 inches	80 pounds	Adventurous, likes to get loose and run around

The Working Group *(continued)*

Breed	Max Height	Max Weight	Possible Downfalls
Bull Mastiff	27 inches	130 pounds	A very large and powerful dog that needs a firm master
Doberman Pinscher	28 inches	85 pounds	Although easy to train, if not trained properly, the results can be disastrous
Giant Schnauzer	28 inches	85 pounds	Requires frequent professional grooming
Great Dane	32+ inches	120 pounds	Need lots of attention, very big and strong
Great Pyrenees	32 inches	130 pounds	Requires extensive socializing (otherwise can be overly protective)
Greater Swiss Mountain Dog	29 inches	135 pounds	Has a history of joint and blood disorders
Komondor	28 inches	105 pounds	Independent minded; requires diligent and extensive grooming
Kuvaz	30 inches	115 pounds	Sheds a lot; needs lots of exercise
Mastiff	34 inches	220 pounds	Huge! Although very gentle, can be dangerous in rough play
Newfoundland	30 inches	150 pounds	Needs to be outdoors, loves water
Portuguese Water Dog	23 inches	60 pounds	Will demand attention
Rottweiler	27 inches	110 pounds	Can be dangerous without proper training
Saint Bernard	28 inches	135 pounds	Although gentle, its sheer size can make it a danger to small children
Samoyed	24 inches	65 pounds	Needs lots of grooming
Siberian Husky	24 inches	65 pounds	Sheds constantly; loves and needs to run
Standard Schnauzer	20 inches	50 pounds	Very energetic; can jump high fences

The Terrier Group

Breed	Max Height	Max Weight	Possible Downfalls
Airedale Terrier	23 inches	45 pounds	Requires frequent, often difficult, grooming
American Staffordshire Terrier	19 inches	50 pounds	Originally bred as a fighting dog; requires extensive socializing
Australian Terrier	11 inches	15 pounds	Can be aggressive or shy toward strangers
Bedlington Terrier	17 inches	23 pounds	Needs daily grooming
Border Terrier	15 inches	16 pounds	Needs more than average grooming; can be assertive
Bull Terrier	16 inches	40 pounds	Needs lots of companionship
Cairn Terrier	10 inches	15 pounds	Needs a firm, strong master
Dandie Dinmont Terrier	11 inches	24 pounds	Very independent minded
Fox Terrier (Smooth)	16 inches	19 pounds	Sheds more than average; can be hyperactive
Fox Terrier (Wirehaired)	16 inches	20 pounds	Very energetic and sometimes mischievous
Irish Terrier	18 inches	30 pounds	Has a tendency to run into things possibly causing injury or damage
Jack Russell Terrier	14 inches	17 pounds	Known to dominate households
Kerry Blue Terrier	20 inches	40 pounds	Needs a hair trimming every couple months
Lakeland Terrier	15 inches	18 pounds	
Manchester Terrier (Standard)	Varies	7–22 pounds	Can be noisy
Miniature Bull Terrier	14 inches	20 pounds	Mischievous
Miniature Schnauzer	14 inches	15 pounds	Needs lots of grooming
Norfolk Terrier	10 inches	12 pounds	Doesn't do well alone
Norwich Terrier	10 inches	12 pounds	Perhaps too brave for its own good sometimes
Scottish Terrier	10 inches	22 pounds	Often bad tempered
Sealyham Terrier	11 inches	25 pounds	Independent nature
Skye Terrier	10 inches	25 pounds	Can sometimes be aloof

The Terrier Group (continued)

Breed	Max Height	Max Weight	Possible Downfalls
Soft Coated Wheaten Terrier	19 inches	40 pounds	Acts like a puppy for its entire life
Staffordshire Bull Terrier	16 inches	38 pounds	Needs lots of exercise to stay in shape
Welsh Terrier	16 inches	23 pounds	Requires a fair amount of grooming and baths
West Highland White Terrier	12 inches	22 pounds	Can be dominating

The Non-sporting Group

Breed	Max Height	Max Weight	Possible Downfalls
American Eskimo Dog	19 inches	35 pounds	Requires regular, often difficult brushing
Bichon Frisé	12 inches	14 pounds	Requires frequent grooming
Boston Terrier	12 inches	25 pounds	Must be kept indoors; sensitive to extreme temperatures
Bulldog	16 inches	50 pounds	Will need daily face-wrinkle cleanings
Chinese Shar-Pei	20 inches	60 pounds	Often does not get along with other animals
Chow Chow	20 inches	70 pounds	Needs a more than average amount of grooming
Dalmatian	23 inches	70 pounds	Very strong and active; needs a fenced yard
Finnish Spitz	20 inches	35 pounds	Can be noisy
French Bulldog	12 inches	28 pounds	Expensive to buy and own
Keeshound	18 inches	65 pounds	Lots of fur, which won't all stay on the dog
Lhasa Apso	11 inches	16 pounds	Likes to bark at the slightest suspicious sound
Löwchen	14 inches	18 pounds	Requires lots of grooming
Poodle (Standard)	15 inches	65 pounds	Very active

The Non-sporting Group *(continued)*

Breed	Max Height	Max Weight	Possible Downfalls
Shipperke	13 inches	16 pounds	Although very fluffy, their coats are not very soft
Shiba Inu	17 inches	25 pounds	Can be a bit nervous
Tibetan Spaniel	10 inches	15 pounds	Shouldn't be left alone for any considerable period
Tibetan Terrier	16 inches	30 pounds	Requires frequent grooming; can be shy

The Herding Group

Breed	Max Height	Max Weight	Possible Downfalls
Australian Cattle Dog	20 inches	50 pounds	Absolutely tireless
Australian Shepherd	23 inches	60 pounds	Needs lots of brushing; prone to hip dysphasia
Bearded Collie	22 inches	60 pounds	Needs lots of exercise and preferably room to run
Belgian Malinois	26 inches	80 pounds	Somewhat sensitive, high strung, and prone to separation anxiety
Belgian Sheepdog	26 inches	75 pounds	Needs lots of space and exercise; needs more than average grooming
Belgian Tervuren	17 inches	23 pounds	Requires daily, albeit quick, grooming
Border Collie	22 inches	55 pounds	Fast, playful, and will never be too tired
Bouvier des Flandres	28 inches	120 pounds	A big dog that sheds a lot
Briard	27 inches	120 pounds	Will try (and usually succeed) to herd you and your children
Canaan Dog	24 inches	55 pounds	Independent minded
Collie	26 inches	75 pounds	Requires more than average grooming
German Shepherd Dog	26 inches	85 pounds	Very big and very active

The Herding Group *(continued)*

Breed	Max Height	Max Weight	Possible Downfalls
Old English Sheepdog	25 inches	70 pounds	Sheds a lot
Puli	17 inches	35 pounds	Difficult and time consuming to bathe
Shetland Sheepdog	16 inches	27 pounds	Barks more than average
Welsh Corgi, Cardigan	12 inches	38 pounds	Sheds more than average
Welsh Corgi, Pembroke	12 inches	30 pounds	Sheds a lot; needs extra brushing

The Complete AKC Toy Group

Breed	Max Height	Max Weight	Possible Downfalls
Affenpinscher	11 inches	9 pounds	Will not be ignored
Brussels Griffon	10 inches	12 pounds	Will demand lots of attention
Cavalier King Charles Spaniel	13 inches	18 pounds	Difficult to find (rare)
Chihuahua	5 inches	6 pounds	Too fragile for outdoor living
Chinese Crested	13 inches	12 pounds	Hairless—needs lotion in dry weather, or for the sun
English Toy Spaniel	10 inches	14 pounds	Requires more than average brushing
Havanese	11 inches	13 pounds	Sometimes overly friendly
Italian Greyhound	15 inches	13 pounds	Sensitive to the cold
Japanese Chin	11 inches	7 pounds	Sensitive and sometimes finicky
Maltese	10 inches	7 pounds	Requires daily brushing
Manchester Terrier (Toy)	12 inches	12 pounds	Barks more than average
Miniature Pinscher	12 inches	12 pounds	Barks a lot
Papillon	11 inches	10 pounds	Prone to eye problems
Pekingese	9 inches	14 pounds	Stubborn
Pomeranian	11 inches	7 pounds	Can be demanding and somewhat hyper
Poodle (Toy)	10 inches	15 pounds	Can be hyper
Pug	11 inches	18 pounds	Craves lots of attention
Shih Tzu	10 inches	16 pounds	Requires extensive daily grooming

The Complete AKC Toy Group (continued)

Breed	Max Height	Max Weight	Possible Downfalls
Silky Terrier	10 inches	11 pounds	Needs a brief daily brushing; somewhat fragile
Yorkshire Terrier	7 inches	7 pounds	Fragile

The Miscellaneous Class

Breed	Max Height	Max Weight	Possible Downfalls
German Pinscher	20 inches	35 pounds	Not recommended for homes with children
Polish Lowland Sheepdog	20 inches	80 pounds	Needs firm training
Plott Hound	25 inches	60 pounds	Has a very loud bark
Toy Fox Terrier	11 inches	7 pounds	Very energetic

Index

THE EVERYTHING SERIES!

BUSINESS

Everything® Business Planning Book
Everything® Coaching and Mentoring Book
Everything® Fundraising Book
Everything® Home-Based Business Book
Everything® Landlording Book
Everything® Leadership Book
Everything® Managing People Book
Everything® Negotiating Book
Everything® Network Marketing Book
Everything® Online Business Book
Everything® Project Management Book
Everything® Robert's Rules Book,
    $7.95($11.95 CAN)
Everything® Selling Book
Everything® Start Your Own Business Book
Everything® Time Management Book

COMPUTERS

Everything® Build Your Own Home Page Book
Everything® Computer Book

COOKBOOKS

Everything® Barbecue Cookbook
Everything® Bartender's Book, $9.95
    ($15.95 CAN)
Everything® Chinese Cookbook
Everything® Chocolate Cookbook
Everything® Cookbook
Everything® Dessert Cookbook
Everything® Diabetes Cookbook
Everything® Fondue Cookbook
Everything® Grilling Cookbook
Everything® Holiday Cookbook
Everything® Indian Cookbook
Everything® Low-Carb Cookbook
Everything® Low-Fat High-Flavor Cookbook
Everything® Low-Salt Cookbook
Everything® Mediterranean Cookbook
Everything® Mexican Cookbook
Everything® One-Pot Cookbook

Everything® Pasta Cookbook
Everything® Quick Meals Cookbook
Everything® Slow Cooker Cookbook
Everything® Soup Cookbook
Everything® Thai Cookbook
Everything® Vegetarian Cookbook
Everything® Wine Book

HEALTH

Everything® Alzheimer's Book
Everything® Anti-Aging Book
Everything® Diabetes Book
Everything® Dieting Book
Everything® Hypnosis Book
Everything® Low Cholesterol Book
Everything® Massage Book
Everything® Menopause Book
Everything® Nutrition Book
Everything® Reflexology Book
Everything® Reiki Book
Everything® Stress Management Book
Everything® Vitamins, Minerals, and
    Nutritional Supplements Book

HISTORY

Everything® American Government Book
Everything® American History Book
Everything® Civil War Book
Everything® Irish History & Heritage Book
Everything® Mafia Book
Everything® Middle East Book

HOBBIES & GAMES

Everything® Bridge Book
Everything® Candlemaking Book
Everything® Card Games Book
Everything® Cartooning Book
Everything® Casino Gambling Book, 2nd Ed.
Everything® Chess Basics Book
Everything® Collectibles Book
Everything® Crossword and Puzzle Book

Everything® Crossword Challenge Book
Everything® Drawing Book
Everything® Digital Photography Book
Everything® Easy Crosswords Book
Everything® Family Tree Book
Everything® Games Book
Everything® Knitting Book
Everything® Magic Book
Everything® Motorcycle Book
Everything® Online Genealogy Book
Everything® Photography Book
Everything® Poker Strategy Book
Everything® Pool & Billiards Book
Everything® Quilting Book
Everything® Scrapbooking Book
Everything® Sewing Book
Everything® Soapmaking Book

HOME IMPROVEMENT

Everything® Feng Shui Book
Everything® Feng Shui Decluttering Book,
    $9.95 ($15.95 CAN)
Everything® Fix-It Book
Everything® Homebuilding Book
Everything® Home Decorating Book
Everything® Landscaping Book
Everything® Lawn Care Book
Everything® Organize Your Home Book

EVERYTHING® KIDS' BOOKS

All titles are $6.95 ($10.95 Canada)
unless otherwise noted
Everything® Kids' Baseball Book, 3rd Ed.
Everything® Kids' Bible Trivia Book
Everything® Kids' Bugs Book
Everything® Kids' Christmas Puzzle
    & Activity Book
Everything® Kids' Cookbook
Everything® Kids' Halloween Puzzle
    & Activity Book ($9.95 CAN)

All Everything® books are priced at $12.95 or $14.95, unless otherwise stated. Prices subject to change without notice.
Canadian prices range from $11.95–$31.95, and are subject to change without notice.

Everything® Kids' Hidden Pictures Book
($9.95 CAN)
Everything® Kids' Joke Book
Everything® Kids' Knock Knock Book
($9.95 CAN)
Everything® Kids' Math Puzzles Book
Everything® Kids' Mazes Book
Everything® Kids' Money Book ($11.95 CAN)
Everything® Kids' Monsters Book
Everything® Kids' Nature Book ($11.95 CAN)
Everything® Kids' Puzzle Book
Everything® Kids' Riddles & Brain Teasers Book
Everything® Kids' Science Experiments Book
Everything® Kids' Soccer Book
Everything® Kids' Travel Activity Book

KIDS' STORY BOOKS

Everything® Bedtime Story Book
Everything® Bible Stories Book
Everything® Fairy Tales Book
Everything® Mother Goose Book

LANGUAGE

Everything® Conversational Japanese Book
(with CD), $19.95 ($31.95 CAN)
Everything® Inglés Book
Everything® French Phrase Book, $9.95
($15.95 CAN)
Everything® Learning French Book
Everything® Learning German Book
Everything® Learning Italian Book
Everything® Learning Latin Book
Everything® Learning Spanish Book
Everything® Sign Language Book
Everything® Spanish Phrase Book,
$9.95 ($15.95 CAN)
Everything® Spanish Verb Book,
$9.95 ($15.95 CAN)

MUSIC

Everything® Drums Book (with CD),
$19.95 ($31.95 CAN)
Everything® Guitar Book
Everything® Home Recording Book
Everything® Playing Piano and Keyboards Book
Everything® Rock & Blues Guitar Book
(with CD), $19.95 ($31.95 CAN)
Everything® Songwriting Book

NEW AGE

Everything® Astrology Book
Everything® Divining the Future Book
Everything® Dreams Book
Everything® Ghost Book
Everything® Love Signs Book,
$9.95 ($15.95 CAN)
Everything® Meditation Book
Everything® Numerology Book
Everything® Paganism Book
Everything® Palmistry Book
Everything® Psychic Book
Everything® Spells & Charms Book
Everything® Tarot Book
Everything® Wicca and Witchcraft Book

PARENTING

Everything® Baby Names Book
Everything® Baby Shower Book
Everything® Baby's First Food Book
Everything® Baby's First Year Book
Everything® Birthing Book
Everything® Breastfeeding Book
Everything® Father-to-Be Book
Everything® Get Ready for Baby Book
Everything® Getting Pregnant Book
Everything® Homeschooling Book
Everything® Parent's Guide to Children
with Asperger's Syndrome
Everything® Parent's Guide to Children
with Autism
Everything® Parent's Guide to Children
with Dyslexia
Everything® Parent's Guide to Positive Discipline
Everything® Parent's Guide to Raising a
Successful Child
Everything® Parenting a Teenager Book
Everything® Potty Training Book,
$9.95 ($15.95 CAN)
Everything® Pregnancy Book, 2nd Ed.
Everything® Pregnancy Fitness Book
Everything® Pregnancy Nutrition Book
Everything® Pregnancy Organizer,
$15.00 ($22.95 CAN)
Everything® Toddler Book
Everything® Tween Book

PERSONAL FINANCE

Everything® Budgeting Book
Everything® Get Out of Debt Book

Everything® Get Rich Book
Everything® Homebuying Book, 2nd Ed.
Everything® Homeselling Book
Everything® Investing Book
Everything® Money Book
Everything® Mutual Funds Book
Everything® Online Business Book
Everything® Personal Finance Book
Everything® Personal Finance in Your
20s & 30s Book
Everything® Real Estate Investing Book
Everything® Wills & Estate Planning Book

PETS

Everything® Cat Book
Everything® Dog Book
Everything® Dog Training and Tricks Book
Everything® Golden Retriever Book
Everything® Horse Book
Everything® Labrador Retriever Book
Everything® Poodle Book
Everything® Puppy Book
Everything® Rottweiler Book
Everything® Tropical Fish Book

REFERENCE

Everything® Astronomy Book
Everything® Car Care Book
Everything® Christmas Book,
$15.00 ($21.95 CAN)
Everything® Classical Mythology Book
Everything® Einstein Book
Everything® Etiquette Book
Everything® Great Thinkers Book
Everything® Philosophy Book
Everything® Psychology Book
Everything® Shakespeare Book
Everything® Tall Tales, Legends, & Other
Outrageous Lies Book
Everything® Toasts Book
Everything® Trivia Book
Everything® Weather Book

RELIGION

Everything® Angels Book
Everything® Bible Book
Everything® Buddhism Book
Everything® Catholicism Book
Everything® Christianity Book
Everything® Jewish History & Heritage Book

All Everything® books are priced at $12.95 or $14.95, unless otherwise stated. Prices subject to change without notice.
Canadian prices range from $11.95–$31.95, and are subject to change without notice.

Everything® Judaism Book
Everything® Koran Book
Everything® Prayer Book
Everything® Saints Book
Everything® Understanding Islam Book
Everything® World's Religions Book
Everything® Zen Book

SCHOOL & CAREERS

Everything® After College Book
Everything® Alternative Careers Book
Everything® College Survival Book
Everything® Cover Letter Book
Everything® Get-a-Job Book
Everything® Hot Careers Book
Everything® Job Interview Book
Everything® New Teacher Book
Everything® Online Job Search Book
Everything® Personal Finance Book
Everything® Practice Interview Book
Everything® Resume Book, 2nd Ed.
Everything® Study Book

SELF-HELP/ RELATIONSHIPS

Everything® Dating Book
Everything® Divorce Book
Everything® Great Marriage Book
Everything® Great Sex Book
Everything® Kama Sutra Book
Everything® Romance Book
Everything® Self-Esteem Book
Everything® Success Book

SPORTS & FITNESS

Everything® Body Shaping Book
Everything® Fishing Book
Everything® Fly-Fishing Book
Everything® Golf Book
Everything® Golf Instruction Book
Everything® Knots Book
Everything® Pilates Book
Everything® Running Book
Everything® Sailing Book, 2nd Ed.
Everything® T'ai Chi and QiGong Book
Everything® Total Fitness Book
Everything® Weight Training Book
Everything® Yoga Book

TRAVEL

Everything® Family Guide to Hawaii
Everything® Family Guide to New York City, 2nd Ed.
Everything® Family Guide to Washington D.C., 2nd Ed.
Everything® Family Guide to the Walt Disney World Resort®, Universal Studios®, and Greater Orlando, 4th Ed.
Everything® Guide to Las Vegas
Everything® Guide to New England
Everything® Travel Guide to the Disneyland Resort®, California Adventure®, Universal Studios®, and the Anaheim Area

WEDDINGS

Everything® Bachelorette Party Book, $9.95 ($15.95 CAN)

Everything® Bridesmaid Book, $9.95 ($15.95 CAN)
Everything® Creative Wedding Ideas Book
Everything® Elopement Book, $9.95 ($15.95 CAN)
Everything® Father of the Bride Book, $9.95 ($15.95 CAN)
Everything® Groom Book, $9.95 ($15.95 CAN)
Everything® Jewish Wedding Book
Everything® Mother of the Bride Book, $9.95 ($15.95)
Everything® Wedding Book, 3rd Ed.
Everything® Wedding Checklist, $7.95 ($12.95 CAN)
Everything® Wedding Etiquette Book, $7.95 ($12.95 CAN)
Everything® Wedding Organizer, $15.00 ($22.95 CAN)
Everything® Wedding Shower Book, $7.95 ($12.95 CAN)
Everything® Wedding Vows Book, $7.95 ($12.95 CAN)
Everything® Weddings on a Budget Book, $9.95 ($15.95 CAN)

WRITING

Everything® Creative Writing Book
Everything® Get Published Book
Everything® Grammar and Style Book
Everything® Grant Writing Book
Everything® Guide to Writing a Novel
Everything® Guide to Writing Children's Books
Everything® Screenwriting Book
Everything® Writing Well Book

··

Introducing an exceptional new line of beginner craft books from the Everything® series!

All titles are $14.95 ($22.95 CAN)

Everything® Crafts—Create Your Own Greeting Cards
1-59337-226-4
Everything® Crafts—Polymer Clay for Beginners
1-59337-230-2

Everything® Crafts—Rubberstamping Made Easy
1-59337-229-9
Everything® Crafts—Wedding Decorations and Keepsakes
1-59337-227-2

Available wherever books are sold!
To order, call 800-872-5627, or visit us at *www.everything.com*
Everything® and everything.com® are registered trademarks of F+W Publications, Inc.